Checking Out

Chekhov

A GUIDE TO THE PLAYS FOR ACTORS, DIRECTORS, AND READERS

ACADEMIC
STUDIES
PRESS

Checking out
Chekhov
A GUIDE TO THE PLAYS FOR ACTORS, DIRECTORS, AND READERS

SHARON MARIE
CARNICKE

BOSTON
2013

Library of Congress Cataloging-in-Publication Data:
The bibliographic data for this title is available from the Library of Congress.

ISBN 978-1-936235-91-9 (hardback)
ISBN 978-1-61811-320-7 (paperback)

Cover design by Ivan Grave

Published by Academic Studies Press in 2013
28 Montfern Avenue Brighton, MA 02135, USA
 press@academicstudiespress.com
www.academicstudiespress.com

TABLE OF CONTENTS

BIOGRAPHY OF THE AUTHOR

Sharon Marie Carnicke (Ph.D. in Russian and Theatre Arts, Columbia University) is Professor of Theatre and Slavic Studies and Associate Dean of the School of Dramatic Arts at the University of Southern California. She has worked professionally as an actor, director, dancer, and translator. She is one of the foremost scholars on Stanislavsky's System and author of the ground-breaking *Stanislavsky in Focus* (now in its second edition). She has spoken and taught master classes on Stanislavsky both nationally and internationally in Australia, Italy, France, Finland, Norway, Puerto Rico, and elsewhere. Her many publications also include *The Theatrical Instinct* (a study on the avant-garde director Nikolai Evreinov) and *Reframing Screen Performance* (co-authored with Cynthia Baron). Her widely-produced translations of Anton Chekhov's plays (including her Kennedy Center award-winning translation of *The Seagull*) are published as *Chekhov: 4 Plays and 3 Jokes*, which was a finalist for the 2010 National Translation Award (the American Literary Translators Association).

TO THE READER

Writing this book was a pleasure. It affords me the opportunity to share the Chekhov whom I have gotten to know by acting in, directing, and, most especially, by translating his plays. Translation forced me to confront each word and phrase so closely that I felt as if I were acting all the roles in my head. The individualized patterns of speech, the musical repetitions of phrases and images, and the tantalizing ambiguities within the dialogue became clues to the subtle ways in which Chekhov's characters think, behave, and interact with each other. As I translated, I also had to deconstruct and then rebuild the structures and rich patterns of details that make up each play. This process made Chekhov's careful craft and his rich dramatic imagination equally clear. I also realized that many of my theatrical insights into Chekhov's work would not have been possible without the wider knowledge I had also gained as a Russian scholar. In his dramaturgy, Chekhov not only reflects, but also cleverly plays with the cultural and artistic contexts which surrounded him during his lifetime.

I offer my book to actors and directors who stage Chekhov, to students of theater and Russian literature, and to anyone who seeks a greater appreciation of his unique sensibility. I blend a theater practitioner's approach to Chekhov's plays with a scholarly study of him as a Russian writer. I hope that reading this book will prove as pleasurable as did its writing.

ACKNOWLEDGEMENTS

I am grateful to many people who helped with this book. My colleague Professor Thomas Seifrid (University of Southern California) suggested that I write it; and the team at Academic Studies Press made it a reality. Mary Joan Negro (Associate Professor of Theatre Practice, University of Southern California) read and commented upon the complete book in draft form. R. Andrew White (Associate Professor, Valparaiso University) shared with me his enthusiasm for and experience with directing and teaching Chekhov. Discussions with Milton Justice (The Stella Adler Studio, Hollywood) about directing and teaching Chekhov and with Dr. William Gunn (University of Southern California) about melodrama spurred my ideas along the way.

My undergraduate students significantly shaped my thinking about how best to present Chekhov's complexity simply, especially the members of three of my seminars at the University of Southern California: "Checking out Chekhov" in fall 2008 and 2009 and "The Performing Arts" in spring 2012. My colleague, Richard Fliegel (University of Southern California), had suggested the witty title of the 2008 and 2009 seminars, which I have also borrowed as the title for this book.

Special thanks also go to a number of other individuals. Patricia Padilla serendipitously gave me a gift that kept me out of the library—a complete set of Anton Chekhov's works in Russian; she then carefully read my typescript. Nicola Carreon scanned photos, typed, and formatted footnotes. Chesed Escobedo helped proofread and finalize the typescript. Andrei Malikov and Rose Leisner (alumni of the University of Southern California) were invaluable in helping me clarify my prose, copyediting, checking transliterations, and formatting the text and illustrations.

Partial funding to assist in the book's preparation was generously provided by the University of Southern California's Undergraduate Research Grant and by Dean Madeline Puzo of the USC School of Dramatic Arts.

My thanks would be incomplete without mentioning at least some of the directors and actors who worked with me on Chekhov's plays over the course of my career. Among these are: Gene Nye of Lion Theatre Company (New York) for giving me my first opportunity to translate Chekhov for his production of *Three Sisters*; John David Lutz (University of Evansville) whose beautiful production of *The Seagull* won me a translation award from the American College Theatre Festival at the Kennedy Center (Washington, D.C.); the late John Blankenchip (University of Southern California) who supported my work with Chekhov for many years; Kate Burton, who directed my translation of *The Cherry Orchard* for the University of Southern California's MFA program in acting while I was completing this book; and most especially the several émigré directors who honored me by choosing to use my translations of plays which they knew in the original Russian—Lev Vainstein, Albert Makhtsier (Theatre in Action in New York), Eugene Lazarev (formerly of the Moscow Art Theatre), and Edward Rozinsky (Miami, Florida). The actors include Louisa Abernathy and Setrak Bronzian who taught me the power of physical humor when I directed them in the A/ACT production of Chekhov's short plays (Los Angeles).

PERMISSIONS

I am deeply grateful to those who have generously granted permissions for this book. Brian Rak and Hackett Publishing Company, Inc. have permitted me to quote passages from my translations and introduction in *Chekhov: 4 Plays and 3 Jokes* (2009); Dr. Mark Konecny and Professor John Bowlt have permitted me to reproduce Soviet postcards of the Moscow Art Theatre productions of *Uncle Vanya*, *Three Sisters*, and *The Cherry Orchard* from the collection of the Institute of Modern Russian Culture (IMRC, University of Southern California). Reproductions of Soviet postcards of *The Seagull*, *Uncle Vanya*, and Chekhov's life and works, as well as the photograph of *The Proposal*, are from my personal collection. See below for specific attributions.

ILLUSTRATIONS

Cover Photograph: A portrait in oils of A. P. Chekhov by his brother N. P. Chekhov, 1883. S. M. Carnicke's collection.

1. A. P. Chekhov, 1902. S. M. Carnicke's collection.
2. The Chekhov family at the Korneyev estate, 1890. S. M. Carnicke's collection.
3. A. P. Chekhov and O. L. Knipper, 1901. S. M. Carnicke's collection.
4. A. R. Artyom as Chebutykin, *Three Sisters*, the Moscow Art Theatre, 1901. IMRC's collection.
5. A. P. Chekhov and Maksim Gorky in Yalta, 1901. S. M. Carnicke's collection.
6. A. P. Chekhov and L. N. Tolstoy in Yalta, 1901. S. M. Carnicke's collection.
7. K. S. Stanislavsky as Astrov and O. L. Knipper as Yelena, *Uncle Vanya*, the Moscow Art Theatre, 1899. S. M. Carnicke's collection.
8. M. A. Zhdanova as Anya and O. L. Knipper as Ranyevskaya, the 1904 production of *The Cherry Orchard*, as performed at the Moscow Art Theatre in 1912. IMRC's collection.
9. I. M. Moskvin as Yepikhodov and N. G. Aleksandrov as Yasha, *The Cherry Orchard*, the Moscow Art Theatre, 1904. IMRC's collection.
10. S. M. Carnicke as Natalya Stepanovna and George Naylor as Lomov, *The Proposal*, the Potato Players (New York), 1978. S. M. Carnicke's collection.
11. K. S. Stanislavsky as Astrov, A. R. Artyom as Telegin, M. P. Lilina as Sonya, and A. L. Vishnevsky as Vanya, *Uncle Vanya*, the Moscow Art Theatre, 1899. IMRC's collection.
12. O. L. Knipper as Arkadina and K. S. Stanislavsky as Trigorin, *The Seagull*, the Moscow Art Theatre, 1898. S. M. Carnicke's collection.
13. V. A. Simov's 1898 set for Acts I and II of *The Seagull*, the Moscow Art Theatre, photographed in 1905. S. M. Carnicke's collection.
14. Cartoon Illustration by V. I. Porfiryev for Chekhov's *On the Moon* (*Na lune*) as published in *Fragments* (*Oskolki*), 1885. A. P. Chekhov, *Polnoe sobranie sochinenii i pisem v tridtsati tomakh* [The Complete Works and Letters in Thirty Volumes], Vol. 3 (Moscow: Nauka, 1975), 457.

TRANSLITERATIONS OF RUSSIAN WORDS, NAMES, AND TITLES OF WORKS

Within the text of my book I use the same informal transliteration system that is used in my published translations of Chekhov's plays (see *Annotated Bibliography*) in order to assist English-speaking readers with Russian pronunciation ("Stanislavsky," "Sergeyevich," "Maria," "Semyon," etc.). However, I use the formal Library of Congress system within the footnotes and bibliography in order that Russian readers can better access my sources ("Stanislavskii," "Sergeevich," "Mariia," "Semen," etc.). This means that two systems of transliteration coexist within my book. Thus, readers will often find names in the text spelled differently than in the footnotes and bibliography. For example, "Stanislavsky" and "Balukhaty" appear in the text, but "Stanislavskii" and "Balukhatyi" are used in formal citations.

I also use the Library of Congress System throughout my book to give Russian titles for literary and dramatic works. The transliterated titles can be found either in footnotes or in parentheses after the English translations. The only Russian titles that do not appear in my text are those of Chekhov's four major plays; the large number of references to them would make the inclusion of their Russian titles clumsy and redundant. Therefore, for reference I give them here: *The Seagull (Chaika)*; *Uncle Vanya (Diadia Vania)*; *Three Sisters (Tri sestry)*; and *The Cherry Orchard (Vishnevyi sad)*.

When I quote from English-language sources I maintain whatever transliteration systems were used within those sources. For clarity, I mark any non-standard transliterations with "[*sic*]" (for example, "Nemirovitch-Dantchenko [*sic*]" instead of "Nemirovich-Danchenko").

ELLIPSES AND DATES

Chekhov uses "…" frequently in his plays to suggest many different kinds of dramatic interruptions in a character's speech. I always retain these ellipses in my translations of his texts. As a scholar I also use ellipses to show where I have made an abridgement in a quotation. Therefore, to make my interventions clear, I enclose my ellipses in brackets ([…]). I also use brackets to enclose any words that I have added to quotations to make them flow grammatically within my text.

All biographical dates are given according to the Julian calendar, which was used in Russia during Chekhov's life; dates are therefore twelve days earlier than in the Gregorian calendar, used elsewhere.

THE USAGE OF RUSSIAN NAMES

In my translations of Chekhov's works and other Russian language sources, I use Russian names as they appear in the original texts. However, Russian names can be puzzling for English speakers and so I provide here some helpful information. Formal address in Russian consists of the first name and patronymic (a name derived from one's father's first name), for example "Anton Pavlovich" (Anton Son-of-Pavel) or "Maria Pavlovna" (Maria Daughter-of-Pavel). When used together, the name and patronymic serve as "Mr.," "Miss," and "Mrs.," signifying the speaker's respect. For example, in *Three Sisters*, the Doctor is most often respectfully called "Ivan Romanych" (Ivan Son-of-Roman). When the sisters call Vershinin "Alexander Ignatyevich" (Alexander Son-of-Ignatius), they greet him formally as a guest in their house and pay respect to his military rank. Similarly, Stanislavsky respectively refers to Chekhov as Anton Pavlovich in his memoirs.

While scholars mostly use surnames, rarely do Russians use them in conversation; these serve primarily to identify family connections (as in cast lists), to refer to famous personages (such as authors or actors), or to introduce strangers. In *The Seagull*, "Treplev" appears in Konstantin Gavrilovich's passport. The fictional writer "Trigorin" registers as famous as the actual novelist "Turgenev," because people refer to both by their last names. In *Three Sisters*, Vershinin and Andrey introduce themselves to each other with their last names because they are strangers to each other.

First names are used by one's intimate friends and family. Russian is particularly rich in nicknames, which are formed by adding diminutive endings to the first name. These diminutives can be piled onto the name almost endlessly and signify warmth, emotional closeness, and sympathy between people. A first degree diminutive is common in the family circle ("Masha" for "Maria," "Olya" for "Olga," "Andryusha" for "Andrey," etc.). Second and third degree diminutives (two or three endings) show greater and greater warmth ("Mashenka" for "Maria," "Olechka" for "Olga," etc.). Diminutives are also commonly used with children ("Bobik" and "Sofochka" in *Three Sisters*) and with servants ("Yasha" and "Dunyasha" in *The Cherry Orchard*).

Introduction

A Taste Like Olives

"Chekhov, like olives, is an acquired taste." So said my first Russian literature teacher in one of Columbia University's most popular under-graduate courses.[1] I have never forgotten his words, despite the fact that they were uttered long before I thought about translating Chekhov's plays or writing this book. Over the years, I have acquired more than a taste for Chekhov. I find him and his works endlessly fascinating. But this was not always so. At first, he seemed a bit boring. Next to Tolstoy's epics and Dostoyevsky's psychologically tormented characters, Chekhov seemed to be little more than a writer who was good at describing the undramatic events of ordinary life. His most iconic director, Konstan-tin Stanislavsky of the Moscow Art Theatre, initially shared this rather neutral view. "The plays of Chekhov do not reveal at first their poetic significance. Reading them one says to oneself: 'It's good, but... nothing special, nothing amazing.'"[2]

Only later did I realize that I had been attending to the surface tex-ture of Chekhov's works and missing the underlying comic irony, the sharp-sighted wisdom, and the artistic complexity within them. It was as if I were looking at the surface of a placid lake, completely unaware of the teeming life that lies hidden in the water's depths. Stanislavsky, too, came to understand the full impact of Chekhov's plays only after the kind of intensive reading that directing and acting entails. Such close reading reveals what his characters think but do not speak (their subtexts); how they push and pull at each other through subtle interpersonal dynamics (or inner actions); and how he communicates his themes through the rich patterns of details that he weaves from the seemingly trivial events of daily life. With these innovations Chekhov set into motion an entirely

[1] Richard A. Gregg, Russian Literature in Translation, Columbia University, 1968-9.
[2] K. S. Stanislavskii, *Sobranie sochinenii* [Collected Works], Vol. 1 (Moscow: Iskusstvo, 1988), 289.

new way of thinking about drama and acting. As Stanislavsky recalled his long history with Chekhov, he realized that, "I do not remember a single performance in which I did not discover some new feeling in my soul, and new depths and subtleties in the works."[3]

In short, in order to acquire a taste for Chekhov one needs to read him closely, thoughtfully, and even creatively. One needs to observe absolutely everything that he puts down on the page and figure out how each little thing relates to the whole. Reading him is like putting a puzzle together, bit by bit, until the complete picture emerges.

Chekhov is indeed a puzzle precisely because the surface simplicity of his works can be so easily mistaken for the whole picture. Those who take the words on the page at face value remain indifferent or become actively hostile to his works. Those who search for what's hidden within his words admire him and sometimes even idolize him. Such extremes of opinion have always characterized and continue to characterize Chekhov's reception as a dramatist. For every person who sees only the surface, there is another who has plumbed the depths. I remember visiting the drama section of a large bookstore in Los Angeles some time ago; as I browsed, I overheard two young people exclaiming happily whenever they found a play that might provide them with good material for their acting class. "Here's Chekhov. I love him," said one. "Oh no," said the other, "I hate Chekhov!" While putting the book back on the shelf, the first student added, "My friend took a class and they spent the whole term just on Chekhov." "What a nightmare!" the other responded; "I would have dropped that class immediately." These two students represent the extremes of opinion that have haunted Chekhov since his first experiments in drama.

At one extreme, Chekhov seems boring and his plots depressing. When he published "The Peasants" in 1897—a story that is now generally considered to be among his most important—the Russian state censor forbade Chekhov's conclusion because it seemed "too gloomy" for public consumption.[4] When Stanislavsky brought productions of

---

[3] Ibid., 290.

[4] "Muzhiki" (1897) in A. P. Chekhov, *Polnoe sobranie sochinenii i pisem v tridtsati tomakh* [The Complete Works and Letters in Thirty Volumes], Vol. 9 (Moscow: Nauka, 1977), 281-313; the censor is cited in Lee J. Williames, *Anton Chekhov, The Iconoclast* (Scranton: University of Scranton Press, 1989), 70.

Ivanov, Uncle Vanya, Three Sisters and *The Cherry Orchard* to the United States during the Moscow Art Theatre tours of 1923 and 1924,[5] the *New York Times'* theater critic was appalled by Chekhov's dark plots:

> The fact is patent, however incredible, however abhorrent, the Slavic temperament feeds upon self-depreciation, upon pessimism, and grows by what it feeds on. The plays of Chekhov, the very cornerstone upon which this admirable, this exemplary Moscow Art Theatre was builded, leave English-speaking peoples cold, and perhaps inclined to resentment.[6]

Recently, at the first technical rehearsal for a new production of my translation of *The Cherry Orchard*, I overheard one of the stage crew turn to another and say: "It's nice enough, but way too depressing. But then that's Chekhov!"[7]

At the other extreme, once one plumbs the depths, Chekhov seems to capture what is most universal in human experience. After viewing Michael Cacoyannis' 2002 filmed version of *The Cherry Orchard*, the *Los Angeles Times'* reviewer observed that, "we are left as always with Chekhov's effortless humanity, the sheer psychological acuity he brought to the loves, hopes and inchoate longings of his characters."[8]

---

[5] Over the course of 52 weeks the Moscow Art Theatre gave 380 performances in the United States, half of which were Chekhov's plays. Prior to these tours American audiences had seen only three professional Chekhov productions. In 1908, Vera Kommissarzhevskaya toured in a Russian language *Uncle Vanya*. In 1915 and 1916 the Washington Square Players in New York City produced *The Bear* and *The Seagull*. For more information on the Moscow Art Theatre tours see Sharon Marie Carnicke, *Stanislavsky in Focus: An Acting Master for the Twenty-First Century*, Second Edition (New York: Routledge, 2009), Chapter 2; and Carnicke, "Stanislavsky's Production of *The Cherry Orchard* in the US," in J. Douglas Clayton, ed., *Chekhov Then and Now: The Reception of Chekhov in World Culture* (New York: Peter Lang, 1997), 19-30.

[6] John Corbin, review of *Three Sisters*, *New York Times*, 31 January 1923, in Victor Emeljanow, ed., *Chekhov: The Critical Heritage* (Boston: Routledge and Kegan Paul, 1981), 241.

[7] Dir. Kate Burton, MFA Repertory Company, University of Southern California, School of Theatre, 2012.

[8] Kenneth Turan, "Translating a Masterpiece," *Los Angeles Times: Calendar Live*, 5 April 2002, http://www.calendarlive.com/movies/Reviews, accessed 29 April 2009.

One of my undergraduate students would audibly gasp whenever a scene or character struck a surprisingly familiar chord; another more soberly called Chekhov "an author capable of transcending cultures and centuries."[9]

Nowhere does the high opinion of Chekhov's worth as a dramatic writer register as loudly as it does among theater professionals, including writers, directors, and actors. Many English language playwrights not only admire, but emulate him. Writers as various as Irwin Shaw, William Inge, Paddy Chayefsky, Lillian Helman, and Arthur Miller cite Chekhov as their model. His influence is so extensive in the United States, that playwright Robert Anderson once quipped, "American playwrights have gone around, trying to be the American Chekhov."[10]

Even more surprising, however, are playwrights who translate, or more precisely adapt his plays, whether or not they can read him in the original Russian. The list reads like a who's-who of modern and contemporary drama. A few among the American playwrights are: Clifford Odets, who prepared a 1939 version of *Three Sisters* for the Group Theatre; Tennessee Williams, with his adaptation of *The Seagull* (entitled *The Notebook of Trigorin*); Jean Claude Van Itallie, who created versions of all the major plays by working though French translations; Lanford Wilson, who took a Berlitz course in Russian in order to translate *Three Sisters* in 1984 for director Mark Lamos at the Circle Repertory Company; and David Mamet, who fashioned his version of *The Cherry Orchard* in 1985 for the New Theatre at Chicago's Goodman Theatre by working from a literal translation made for him by a native Russian speaker. In 2012, two more contemporary playwrights took on Chekhov: Tracy Letts, who adapted *Three Sisters* for Chicago's Steppenwolf Company, and Annie Baker, who created an *Uncle Vanya* for the Soho Rep in New York. Among the playwrights from Great Britain who have adapted Chekhov are David Hare, Edward Bond, Pam Gems and Tom Stoppard, who baldly admits, "I've always felt very envious of Chekhov."[11]

---

[9] Jennifer Bashian and Kevin Burke, Freshman Seminar: Checking Out Chekhov, University of Southern California, Fall 2008.
[10] Laurence Senelick, *The Chekhov Theatre* (Cambridge: Cambridge University Press, 1997), 284.
[11] "Stagewrite Productions Archive," *National Theatre Education*, http://www.nt-online.org (accessed 20 August 2002).

Such acts of linguistic hubris often mean that dramatists do not so much convey Chekhov into English as turn him into mirror images of themselves, with his actual innovations in drama getting lost in the process.[12]

In turn, directors and actors venerate Chekhov by staging him in productions that sometimes reflect his time and culture and sometimes transport his characters into other eras and places. The imaginative possibilities for making his plays relevant to contemporary audiences seem as endless as reconceptualizations of Shakespeare. In fact, Chekhov is the second most frequently produced dramatist in the world today after the British bard. Theaters worldwide embrace the Russian's handful of plays with the same fervency as they do Shakespeare's more prodigious oeuvre. Moreover, in much the same way that actors and directors often envision the pinnacle of their own theatrical careers in their work with Shakespeare, so too does success in Chekhov's plays become a measure of artistic maturity. For this reason, theatrical schools and academies throughout the world often ask their students to cut their teeth on both Chekhov and Shakespeare.

One of America's most insightful theater critics, Eric Bentley, asks: "Why is it that scarcely a year passes without a major Broadway or West End production of a Chekhov play?" After all, "the Anglo-American theater finds it possible to get along without the services of most of the best playwrights," among them "Aeschylus, Lope de Vega, Racine, Molière, Schiller, Strindberg." The answer partly lies in the various reasons that theaters choose to produce Chekhov: some see his plays as part of a lucrative "commodity theater"; some are "conscious rebels" who see him as an alternative voice "against the whole system"; and "others are simply genuine artists" who stage him because he represents the best in dramatic art. But, in the last analysis, Bentley observes, staging Chekhov is bound up with a sense of artistic integrity. "It is as if the theater remembers Chekhov when it remembers its conscience."[13]

---

[12] Sharon Marie Carnicke, "Translating Chekhov's Plays Without Russian, or, The Nasty Habit of Adaptation," in Michael C. Finke and Julie de Sherbinin, eds., *Chekhov the Immigrant: Translating a Cultural Icon* (Bloomington: Slavica, 2007), 89-100.
[13] Eric Bentley, "Craftsmanship in *Uncle Vanya*," in Thomas A. Eekman, *Critical Essays on Anton Chekhov* (Boston: G. K. Hall & Co., 1989), 169-70.

While theater history seems as unimaginable without Chekhov as without Shakespeare, audiences, critics, playwrights, and theater practitioners alike often find themselves puzzled by Chekhov's dramatic writing. His plays seem all too foreign, his characters highly inscrutable, and their very names (let alone their stories) difficult to grasp. This puzzlement can turn the most enthusiastic productions "deadly," to borrow British director Peter Brook's phrase. In fact, what Brook has written about Shakespeare productions that present the bard as a hallowed monument of great theater applies all too easily to Chekhov as well:

> We see his plays done by good actors in what seems like the proper way—they look lively and colorful, there is music and everyone is dressed up, just as they are supposed to be in the best of classical theatre. Yet secretly, we find it excruciatingly boring [...]. To make matters worse there is always a deadly spectator, who for special reasons enjoys a lack of intensity and even a lack of entertainment, such as the scholar who emerges from routine performances of the classics smiling because nothing has distracted him from trying over and confirming his pet theories to himself, whilst reciting his favorite lines under his breath.[14]

Indeed, the proliferation of deadly productions that treat Chekhov's plays as untouchable, but equally unfathomable classics may well account for the fact that there are as many people today who wish to avoid him as there are those who seek him.

I believe that unanswered questions about Chekhov's plays often account for the misfiring of well-intentioned productions. Among questions that either go unanswered or insufficiently answered are the following: Was Chekhov a gloomy pessimist, reflecting upon boredom and despair? Or was he a hopeful optimist in face of the bitter realities that we all face in life—including the bitterest of all, death? Are his plays comic or tragic, ironic or sincere? Are his plays excellent examples of theatrical realism or something more poetic and symbolic, maybe even absurdist? Where can one find the action and conflict in plays where nothing much seems to happen? How can the often seemingly irrelevant dialogue and apparently static plots create dynamic and riveting performances?

---

[14] Peter Brook, *The Empty Space* (New York: Avon Books, 1968), 10.

This book is a guide to reading Chekhov's plays deeply. I do not provide a comprehensive history of all the ways in which his plays have been interpreted by directors and scholars; instead, I examine how a Chekhov play is unique and let my readers make up their own minds. I write in hopes that theater artists will work on his plays from a fully informed perspective and that students and general audiences will bring greater appreciation to their future encounters with him.

My book will take you on a journey that begins in Chapter 1 with the biographical and cultural contexts that inspired Chekhov's art. Chapters 2 and 3 take a first look at his plays through the spectacles of his fiction. Famous for his short stories long before his plays, he initially transported his innovations in narrative technique into his plays, thus creating a paradigm shift in playwriting that maintains its authority into the twenty-first century. Chapters 4 and 5 take the next important look at his dramaturgy by tracing how his own theatergoing affected his innovations, both through his avid love of the comic French vaudeville and his loathing of nineteenth-century melodrama and histrionic acting. Finally, in Chapter 6, I explore how his plays travel from page to stage, serving as blueprints for productions. Along the way, I take on issues of Chekhov's artistic style, his non-standard use of genre, his sense of irony, his comedic sensibility, and his most abiding themes.

Nearly every chapter includes a case study on Chekhov's densely simple writing. Chapter 2 provides a close study of Chekhov's own favorite story, "The Student," in order to expose how he weaves apparently trivial details into rich tapestries of associations. Chapter 3 follows this case study with multiple examples of his devilishly clever use of details in his plays. Chapter 4 takes on his comic sensibility by comparing his "joke in one act," *The Proposal*, with Eugène Scribe's one-act vaudeville, *A Peculiar Position*. Chapter 4 traces precisely how Chekhov finds his unique voice as a playwright by experimenting with melodrama from his first full-length play to his last masterpiece. Moreover, by comparing Dion Boucicault's *The Octoroon* with *The Cherry Orchard*, one can clearly see how Chekhov's experiments resulted in his turning melodrama completely inside out. Finally, Chapter 6 explores how Stanislavsky made Chekhov's innovations visible to audiences in the iconic staging of *The Seagull* at the Moscow Art Theatre.

In short, I invite you to acquire a taste for Chekhov!

Chapter One

Chekhov on His Own Terms

Anton Pavlovich Chekhov (1860-1904) created his enduring artistic legacy during a short and intense life of forty-four years. But who was he and how did his experience feed his literary and dramatic genius? These questions are far from easy to answer. He kept his distance from others. "I could not say that Anton Pavlovich was ever on very close terms with anyone. Was it even possible?" muses his great admirer, Vladimir Ivanovich Nemirovich-Danchenko[1]—a playwright and theater director who took great pains to convince Chekhov to allow the newly founded Moscow Art Theatre to produce *The Seagull*. Chekhov also kept his distance from posterity. When Moscow State University requested an autobiography for his class reunion, he replied: "An autobiography? I have a disease: autobiographophobia. To read any details about myself genuinely torments me, and to write them for publication is even worse" (to G. I. Rossolimo, 11 Oct. 1899).

In short, Chekhov was an utterly private man. He could seem as inscrutable to those who drank tea with him in his home as he seems to those of us today, who seek him by reading books, visiting his house museums, and working in his archives. Consider the words of writer Tatiana Lvovna Shchepkina-Kupernik, who was so close a friend to Chekhov that she often served as the romantic go-between for him and his mistress (the flamboyant and famous actress Lidia Borisovna Yavorskaya, on whom he modeled Arkadina in *The Seagull*).

> In Moscow, [Anton Pavlovich...] went to see the same plays we saw, visited the same circles we visited, sat up all night listening to music; yet I could not free myself from the impression that he was "not with us," that he was a spectator, and not one of the dramatis personae [of our lives].[2]

---

[1] Andrei Turkov, ed., *Anton Chekhov and His Times*, trans. Cynthia Carlile and Sharon McKee (Fayetteville: University of Arkansas Press, 1995), 64.
[2] Ibid., 27.

Chekhov faced his fame as an author and playwright with the same urgent need for privacy that had become familiar to his circle of family and friends. He initially hid behind a series of pseudonyms, publishing under his actual name only in 1883. Growing fame drove him to avoid public shows of affection and accolades for his achievements. His sister tells of an instance when she was having tea with her brother and his wife at a restaurant in the Crimea before a concert that the three of them were planning to attend. When a man at a neighboring table recognized the famous author and rose to deliver a toast in his honor, Chekhov fled outside into the garden where, despite the women's pleas, he refused not only to return to the restaurant but also to attend the concert.[3] Such private behavior transformed him into a tantalizing mystery, his very elusiveness provoking all the more interest. One cannot help but recall Trigorin's words to Treplev in *The Seagull*:

> Your fans send their regards… In Petersburg and Moscow, everyone is very interested in you. They all ask me about you. They ask, what is he like, how old is he, is he blond or brunette? For some reason they all think that you're old. And no one knows your real name, since you write under a pseudonym. You are mysterious, a real Iron Mask.[4] (trans. Carnicke, 104)

Shchepkina-Kupernik's "impression" of Chekhov as a "spectator" captures his most characteristic perspective on the world—the distanced observation of others. Once, during a dinner party he gave after his marriage to the Moscow Art Theatre actress Olga Leonardovna Knipper, his wife sent her already tipsy uncle to the kitchen where he continued to drink. When she noticed that Anton was no longer at the table, she went in search of him, only to find him peeping through the kitchen's keyhole, taking great pleasure in watching her drunken uncle.[5] This

---

[3] Mariia P. Chekhova, *Iz dalekogo proshlogo* [From the Distant Past] (Moscow: Gosudarstvennoe izdatel'stvo khudozhestvennoi literatury, 1960), 171. Cited and translated by Michael C. Finke, *Seeing Chekhov: Life and Art* (Ithaca: Cornell University Press, 2005), 27, 171. Also cited in Turkov, ed., *Anton Chekhov and His Times*, 178.

[4] A famous political agitator, imprisoned by Louis XIV, who kept his face and hence his identity hidden behind an iron mask.

[5] Harvey Pitcher, *Chekhov's Leading Lady: A Portrait of the Actress Olga Knipper* (New York: Franklin Watts, 1980), 10.

same proclivity for eavesdropping became a particularly strong characteristic in Chekhov's writing. As he explained to his eldest brother, Alexander, "If I write, then it will surely be from afar, from a crack in the wall" (13 May 1883).

In his art, Chekhov's penchant and talent for distanced observation made him into "the sharp-eyed watcher of some very silly people."[6] But in his life, this same penchant often confused friends and family alike. He could seem self-important, even vain. For example, the great actor, theater director, and co-founder of the Moscow Art Theatre, Konstantin Sergeyevich Stanislavsky, "did not find [Chekhov] particularly agreeable" at first.

> Perhaps it was [... his] habit of raising his head and looking down [through the lenses of his glasses] at the one talking to him, or his fussy manner of constantly adjusting his pince-nez, [which] made him appear to me arrogant and insincere.[7]

As time passed, Stanislavsky came to feel instead that "this was all due to [Chekhov's] touching shyness, which at the time I was unable to identify."[8] He could also seem proud and secretive, even evasive. Nemirovich-Danchenko complained to Chekhov that their conversations about the possible production of *The Seagull* at the Moscow Art Theatre were misfiring, because "there is so much devilish pride in you, or, to be exact, secretiveness, that you will just smile. (And I know your smile.)"[9]

Neither Chekhov's friends nor family were ever quite sure about which of his flirtations might be serious. Nemirovich-Danchenko explained this particular secretiveness with regard to the discretion dictated by late nineteenth-century manners. "It seems [Anton Pavlovich] was very popular with women. I say 'it seems' because neither he nor I like gos-

---

6   Robert Belknap, personal email to author, 5 May 2008, 11:12 a.m.
7   Turkov, ed., *Anton Chekhov and His Times*, 89-90. From the French for "pinched nose," the glasses that Chekhov wore to improve his eyesight were fastened to the head by clipping the lenses on the nose.
8   Ibid.
9   Vl. I. Nemirovich-Danchenko, *Tvorcheskoe nasledie: Pis'ma* [Creative Legacy: The Letters], letter to A. P. Chekhov, 22 Nov. 1896, Vol. I (Moscow: Moskovskii khudozhestvennyi teatr, 2003), 130.

sip on the subject."[10] However, discretion cannot explain the fact that the women Chekhov courted were sometimes equally unsure. A case in point was his ambivalent interaction over the course of many years with Lidia Stakhievna Mizinova—a teacher at the same high school where Anton's sister taught. "Lika" (as she was fondly called) became a frequent visitor to the Chekhov home and a virtual member of the family. (She appears in the family photograph in Illustration 2.) Anton's affection for her, however, seemed to everyone, including her, more than that of a brother.[11] While he usually expressed affection through teasing, it was soon noticed by family and friends alike that "there was only Lika that he teased more."[12] Lika responded to Anton's flirtation with love, but his persistent teasing soon confused and angered her.

Even a cursory glance at Anton's ambivalent correspondence with Lika explains her confusion. He sometimes writes as an ardent suitor, "on bended knee," insistently begging her to visit him (16 June 1892). At other times, he poses as an older brother, jokingly reprimanding her for silly or bad behavior. He even alternates between these two roles within the same letter. For example, in one letter Anton affectionately writes to "the charming, amazing Lika," telling her:

> We have an excellent orchard, dark avenues of trees, secluded little corners, moonlit nights, nightingales, turkeys.... In the river and pond there are very intelligent frogs. We often go strolling

---

[10] Turkov, ed., *Anton Chekhov and His Times*, 65. Nemirovich-Danchenko too had successfully hidden his many sexual affairs, including a possible relationship with Olga Knipper, who had been his acting student. The writer Ivan Bunin seems to imply that this relationship may have continued after Olga's marriage to Chekhov, when Bunin describes the following domestic scene. "In most cases she left for the theater, but sometimes for a charity concert. Nemirovich would call for her, wearing tails and smelling of cigars and expensive eau de cologne. She, wearing an evening dress, perfumed, beautiful, young, would go up to her husband and say 'Don't be bored without me, darling. In any case you always enjoy [your friend Bunin's] company. Good-bye, dear.' She turned to me. I kissed her hand and they left. Chekhov would not let me go until she returned" (cited in Turkov, ed., *Anton Chekhov and His Times*, 190). Of course, one must remember that Bunin did not like Knipper.

[11] Mikhail Chekhov, *Anton Chekhov: A Brother's Memoir*, trans. Eugene Alper (New York: Palgrave MacMillan, 2010), 150.

[12] Shchepkina-Kupernik in Turkov, ed., *Anton Chekhov and His Times*, 42.

and I usually close my eyes and hold my right arm in the shape
of pretzel, imagining that you are walking with me arm in arm.
(12 June 1891)

He accompanies these romantic images[13] with a sketch of a heart, shot
through with Cupid's arrow, and a pleading invitation to visit him. He
then radically shifts to the brotherly tone and reprimands Lika for using unseemly words—"like 'the devil will teach you,' 'the devil take you,'
'anathema,' 'whack on the back of the head,' 'swine,' you 'stuffed yourself,' etc."—which he teasingly assumes that she has learned from the
fictitious lover that he has invented for her, named Trofim, who works
as an ox-cart driver. "Those carters, like Trofim," Anton snidely jokes,
"are having a wonderful influence on you" (12 June 1891). Additionally,
he also signs many of his letters to Lika with whimsical pseudonyms,
among them Trofim, whose fictive letters jealously complain of her dalliance with a no-good writer and violently threaten his rival with physical harm. Anton had once told his younger brother that "his love affairs
were always a lot of fun;"[14] and his letters to Lika seem to prove that
sentiment.

However, his teasing letters only frustrated and hurt Lika, who wanted a serious relationship. By 1893 Anton's "serio-comic behavior"[15] had
left Lika without any hope of marriage. Moreover, her interpretation of
his intentions was correct. Chekhov resisted marriage until only three
short years before his death. While flirting with Lika, he had plainly
admitted to his closest male friend—the editor Aleksey Sergeyevich
Suvorin—that, "I do not intend to marry. I would like to be a small,
bald, little old man and sit behind a large desk in a handsome study"
(10 May 1891). When Lika tried to break free of Anton, she wrote to
him: "My strongest wish is to cure myself of the hopeless condition in
which I am now [...]. Please don't ask me to come to see you, and don't
try to see me."[16] Lika then fled by running off with Ignaty Nikolayevich
Potapenko, a writer and married friend of Chekhov, widely known for

---

[13]   Similar images are also used by Dr. Astrov to seduce Yelena in *Uncle Vanya*.

[14]   Mikhail Chekhov, *Anton Chekhov*, 35.

[15]   Ernest J. Simmons, *Chekhov: A Biography* (Chicago: The University of Chicago
       Press, 1962), 288.

[16]   Ibid., 288-9. Chekhov would soon give very similar words to Masha in *The
       Seagull*, who, like Lika, pines hopelessly for love from the young writer Treplev.

philandering. Potapenko took Lika to Paris, where he abandoned her when she became pregnant. Nina's spurning of Treplev for her affair with another writer, Trigorin, in *The Seagull* was clearly modeled on Lika's story. Anton and Lika later revived their friendship and remained close until his death.

Perhaps the most remarkable instance of Chekhov's need to mask his inner life involves his hiding of the physical suffering he experienced from tuberculosis—a disease that had already claimed the lives of many he knew, including his elder brother Nikolay. Chekhov took extraordinary pains to keep his illness secret from everyone including the family members who lived with him. Even after 1897, when a hemorrhage from his lungs hospitalized him, he managed to keep the full extent of his illness secret. "He never resembled a sick person," recalls his sister, with whom he lived his entire adult life. "No matter how badly he felt, he never complained, never showed it. None of his family or friends ever really knew when Anton Pavlovich felt sick. That was characteristic of Anton Pavlovich until the end of his life."[17] Only near the very end did the physical manifestations of tuberculosis finally betray him. Recalling her last meeting with Chekhov, Shchepkina-Kupernik describes him as "pale, gray faced, with sunken cheeks—he bore no resemblance to the old Anton Pavlovich. It was as if he had shrunk in size."[18] Was keeping his illness secret a way to shield his family from grief? Or, trained as a doctor, was he embarrassed to have become a patient? Was he refusing to admit the truth to himself, or had he courageously decided to live his life in spite of his untreatable disease? Like so much about Chekhov, we will never know for sure. And "this is as Chekhov wanted it."[19]

But why did Chekhov want such deep privacy? In Europe during his lifetime, as in the West today, privacy was seen as a desirable state. But this was not necessarily so in late nineteenth-century Russia, where extended families and peasant mores were prevalent. Chekhov's behavior seemed unusual to his contemporaries, who explained it in many different ways. He was seen as either arrogant and vain or shy (as by Stanislavsky above). He was called either proud and secretive or discrete

---

[17] Chekhova, *Iz dalekogo proshlogo* [From the Distant Past], 171, as cited and translated by Finke, *Seeing Chekhov*, 15.

[18] Turkov, ed., *Anton Chekhov and His Times*, 35.

[19] Finke, *Seeing Chekhov*, 1.

(as Nemirovich-Danchenko would have it above). More insightfully, perhaps, the writer Maksim Gorky furnishes an entirely different kind of explanation.

> All his life, Anton Chekhov lived on his inner wealth; he was always himself, possessed inner freedom, and never took account of what some expected from Anton Chekhov, and what others, more vulgarly demanded from him.[20]

From this point of view, Chekhov had developed such a strong sense of self, that he needed no one's approval. If Gorky is correct, then Chekhov has told us how hard won and incredibly fragile such "inner wealth" had been for him. In his frequently quoted autobiographical sketch—which he includes in a letter to his friend and editor, Suvorin, as if describing a subject for a new short story—Chekhov writes:

> What is free for writers born into the aristocracy comes at a high price for those born into the lower classes. The cost is their youth. Write a story about a young man, the son of a serf, a former shop-keeper, singer [in the church choir], schoolboy and university student, raised with respect for rank, kissing the hands of priests, bowing to others' ideas, grateful for every piece of bread, beaten many times, going to school without galoshes, picking fights, tormenting animals, loving dinners with rich relatives, playing the hypocrite with both God and people because he thought himself good for nothing. Write about how this young man presses the slave out of himself drop by drop, and how he awakens one fine morning and feels he no longer has the blood of a slave in his veins, but that of a real human being. (7 Jan. 1889)

Scholars explain Chekhov's elusive behavior in many of the same ways as had his contemporaries. Michael Finke, however, adds a unique view, when he persuasively argues that Chekhov's drive for personal privacy harbors an equally strong desire for attention. Finke sees in Chekhov "a 'phobia,' [that] simultaneously wards off and invites psychobiographical reading."[21] Finke points to odd facts in the writer's life as evidence for this view. Consider, for example, how Chekhov chose to get married.

---

[20] Turkov, ed., *Anton Chekhov and His Times*, 155.
[21] Finke, *Seeing Chekhov*, 16.

He arranged for a banquet and asked that his and Knipper's closest friends and relatives be invited, but without telling them the reason for celebration. The couple, however, never appeared among their guests. As Stanislavsky recalls, "We waited, worried and confused, till finally we received the news that Anton Pavlovich had left with Olga Leonardovna for the church to get married."[22] Chekhov had always been known for his teasing and jokes, but was this a mere practical joke? As Finke sees it, "This was no simple act of shielding one's intimate life, but an exhibitionist and theatrical staging of self-concealment."[23]

FINDING CHEKHOV

Whatever the source of Chekhov's elusiveness, it presents those who wish to stage his plays with a great challenge, because the same elusiveness underpins his drama. While planning this book, my colleague Milton Justice was preparing to direct Chekhov with his students at the Stella Adler Studio in Hollywood, and this coincidence prompted an interesting dialogue between us. Milton wondered, "Why is Chekhov so difficult to perform?" My recent research had left me trying in vain to imagine the man; and I found myself unexpectedly answering, "because he remains so hidden from us." When we stage the plays of others—Maksim Gorky, Tennessee Williams, David Mamet, for example—we tend to start with a strong sense of the authors and their core values. But there is a struggle to define the core within a Chekhov play; and the struggle seems just as necessary every time we stage him again, no matter how familiar we are with his plays.

"Yes," said Milton, "in other plays, we search for subtext, and we are confident that we can find it. But with Chekhov, we are never quite sure what lies behind his characters' words. All our guesses remain provisional. Chekhov's characters seem as hidden as he. He always forces us to speculate about them."

We ended by agreeing that the most productive way to get to Chekhov's plays is to excavate his texts through the process of rehearsal. In his stories and plays alike, Chekhov challenges his readers to diagnose

---

[22] Turkov, ed., *Anton Chekhov and His Times*, 113.
[23] Finke, *Seeing Chekhov*, 5.

Chapter One

his characters' desires, opinions, heartaches and joys in the same way that doctors diagnose illness—by attending closely to apparently trivial details. In the plays, however—where narrative voice is absent and characters speak for themselves—reading under a microscope becomes all the more necessary. Actors who must speak the words that Chekhov wrote cannot do otherwise.

Chekhov's contemporaries, even those who knew him well, had precisely the same conversation about his plays as we, leading to a very similar conclusion. In recalling his work on *The Seagull* for the Moscow Art Theatre during 1898, Stanislavsky admits:

> It was a difficult task, as, to my shame, I did not understand the play. It was only while I was working on it that I began, without realizing it, to penetrate the meaning and came to love it.[24]

Finding Chekhov in his biography seems to involve the same process of excavation. Because of his elusive personality and the many contradictory details in his life's story, his portrait seems to function much like a magic mirror, in which we see reflections of our own opinions about him. Sometimes, these reflections even become willful manipulations of the facts. As the Russian scholar Lee J. Williames has carefully detailed, critics in Russia "distorted [the image of Chekhov] repeatedly over the decades [...] for political reasons," portraying him, in turn, as a politically disengaged pessimist and a revolutionary optimist.[25]

Whenever my colleague, actor Mary Joan Negro, looks at a photograph of Chekhov, she always says the same thing. "He has such kind eyes!" (Illustration 1) She forged her professional career, in part, by playing Masha in *Three Sisters* for John Houseman's The Acting Company in 1973. Moreover, she was guided in her understanding of Chekhov by the Russian émigré director, Boris Tumarin. Whenever Mary Joan and I speak about Chekhov's plays, I feel that she sees them clearly in all their complex and rich detail. I am certain that her Masha was vividly alive on stage. But nonetheless I do sometimes wonder about her comment concerning Chekhov's "kind eyes."

---

[24] Turkov, ed., *Anton Chekhov and His Times*, 91. For more on Stanislavsky's work, see Chapter 6.

[25] Williames, *Anton Chekhov, The Iconoclast*, v.

1. Chekhov's kind eyes, 1902.

Chekhov did exude kindness in his lifetime. He had a talent for respecting people, putting them at ease and inspiring in them trust and a willingness to speak sincerely without pretense. Dozens of memoirists find his charisma in this talent. For example, once, while visiting Chekhov, Gorky was present when some aristocratic ladies came calling. They began what they considered an appropriately serious discussion for a visit with such a famous writer. But Chekhov abruptly shifted the topic from politics to marmalade. The tension in the room broke and the conversation turned "marvelous," according to Gorky. After the women left, Gorky expressed amazement at what he had just witnessed. (See Illustration 5.) "Chekhov laughed quickly and said, 'Each person needs to speak in his own language.'"[26] In 1890, Chekhov's talent for speaking with people on their own terms served him well when he interviewed the residents of Sakhalin, Russia's most notorious penal colony. There, inmates and their families spoke to him of their despair as easily as the ladies had discussed marmalade, making his 1895 exposé of prison conditions (*The Island of Sakhalin*[27]) a scathing indictment of Russia's criminal system.

Yet, "kind eyes" do not necessarily preclude unkind behavior. Take another look at Chekhov's portrait and you might see instead a man who peers out through the lenses of his pince-nez, as if through a protective glass barrier. His eyes may now seem less kind and his smile ironic and less inviting. Is this second look what Nemirovich-Danchenko had in mind when he told Chekhov, "And I know your smile"?[28] Donald Rayfield—who is considered Chekhov's most frank biographer—certainly sees Chekhov in this other way and cites his behavior just before the 1896 premiere of *The Seagull* in St. Petersburg to argue for this opinion. Chekhov mined his personal life in this play more obviously than was his wont. He exposed painful details from three of his love affairs and the tragic suicide of his best friend's son. While transmuting one's life into art is a necessary part of any creative process, Chekhov treated the friends, whom he has used as models for *The Seagull*, with less than his usual tact just prior to the play's first performance. In fact, Rayfield believes that Chekhov used the play's premiere as a vengeful "instrument for putting others at a distance."[29]

Two examples will suffice to make the point. Lika Mizinova had already frankly told Chekhov that she did not appreciate his using details

---

[26] Turkov, ed., *Anton Chekhov and His Times*, 156.

[27] *Ostrov Sakhalin* in A. P. Chekhov, *Polnoe sobranie sochinenii i pisem v tridtsati tomakh* [The Complete Works and Letters in Thirty Volumes], Vol. 14 (Moscow: Nauka, 1978).

[28] Nemirovich-Danchenko, *Tvorcheskoe nasledie* [Creative Legacy], letter to A. P. Chekhov, 22 Nov. 1896, Vol. I, 130.

[29] Donald Rayfield, *Understanding Chekhov: A Critical Study of Chekhov's Prose and Drama* (Madison: University of Wisconsin Press, 1999), 136.

about her life, following the publication of his story "The Grasshopper" in 1892.[30] Yet, as noted above, Nina's affair with Trigorin in *The Seagull* boldly mirrors Mizinova's disastrous affair with Potapenko. In advance of the first performance Chekhov warned Mizinova to expect to see her life on stage; but despite the warning she was deeply shaken at the theater.[31] With the writer Lidia Avilova—a married woman obsessively in love with him—Chekhov behaved quite differently.[32] A year earlier, Avilova had sent Chekhov a silver medallion inscribed with the page and line numbers from one of his stories. Shortly before his play's premiere, Avilova encountered Chekhov at a masked ball in St. Petersburg, where she asked him for his answer to her medallion. He told her that she would get her answer from the stage. His words, however, did not prepare her for seeing her own gift to Chekhov used as a prop by the actress playing the fictional Nina, who, like Avilova, gives a seductively inscribed medallion to the famous writer she loves. Chekhov had lent the actress Avilova's medallion, but had changed the reference numbers in the text of his play. After the performance, Avilova realized that the new citation referenced one of her own stories. When she looked it up, she found: "Young ladies should not go to balls."[33] Was this a mere practical joke or a rebuff? Rayfield believes that Chekhov's behavior with both Mizinova and Avilova was the latter:

> All the hostility and cruelty repressed by a kind and consider-
> ate man was released in one drama. It is as if to avoid the fate
> of Trigorin and Treplev, ruined by their attachments to women,
> Chekhov had to cut the links by staging the play.[34]

Given Chekhov's famous elusiveness and his self-professed "autobi-ographobia," attempts to find the historical man who lived in Russia from 1860 to 1904 are themselves acts of fiction. Ironically, these acts

---

[30] Donald Rayfield, *Anton Chekhov: A Life* (New York: Henry Holt and Company, 1997), 269.

[31] Simmons, *Chekhov*, 369; Carolina de Maegd-Soëp, *Chekhov and Women: Women in the Life of Work and Chekhov* (Bloomington, IN: Slavica, 1987), 129.

[32] Most scholars believe that Chekhov spurned Avilova's love, despite the fact she describes their love as mutually passionate in her memoirs.

[33] Rayfield, *Anton Chekhov*, 369, 398.

[34] Rayfield, *Understanding Chekhov*, 137.

are also buttressed by Chekhov's enormous number of letters that meticulously record his daily life and register his opinions. Yet, despite the amount of information that Chekhov left behind, he still manages to elude us, as he did those who knew him during his short forty-four years of life. Some biographers make sense of him by romanticizing the facts of his life and creating novelistic stories about his rags-to-riches career, his love for the actress Olga Knipper, and the tragedy of his early death. Other biographers tackle, instead, the naked facts, assembling his complicated comings and goings, disentangling his friends from his acquaintances, and reconstructing his diverse activities and interests. Both types of biographies can easily lose sight of the forest for the trees.

In my brief account of Chekhov's life below, I map out only those particular trees that I have found to be most helpful in understanding his plays. I focus on his especially close relationship with his family, his stepping in as the family's head, his two competing professions of medicine and literature, and his crucial relationship (both professional and personal) with the Moscow Art Theatre.

FAMILY

All his life, Chekhov's birth family was central to him; and, conversely, as he matured he became all the more central to them. Friends, colleagues, lovers, and wife stood at the margins, often influential and welcome visitors, but never fully accepted familial members. Thus, to find Chekhov one must begin with the family who raised him in a provincial city on Russia's vast Southern steppe. (Illustration 2)

Anton Pavlovich Chekhov was born on 16 January 1860, the third oldest son in a family of five boys and two girls. For the next forty-four years he celebrated his birthday on his saint's name day, the 17th of January, the day dedicated to St. Anthony, for whom he was named.[35] The rhythm of family life was marked by an alternation of birthday

---

[35] Celebrating one's birthday in this way was an important part of Russian culture, with name day parties being high points in the year. Act I of *Three Sisters* depicts a name day party.

2. Anton Chekhov (in a white jacket) and his youngest brother, Mikhail, are seated in the front. Immediately behind Anton to the right is his mother, Yevgenia Yakovlevna, and to the left is his sister, Masha. Left of Masha sits Lika Mizinova (the model for Nina in *The Seagull*). The tall man in the right rear of the group is Anton's father, Pavel Yegorovich. Anton's brother Ivan is left of Pavel Yegorovich. This photograph was taken while visiting with friends in 1890, a year after Nikolay's death from tuberculosis and shortly before Anton's scientific study of conditions at the penal colony of Sakhalin.

celebrations and funerals. Name day parties for his parents, siblings, and other relatives provided celebratory moments of cheer, with Anton always ready to joke, tease, and mimic the people who amused him. Frequent family deaths underlined the brevity of life. At eleven, Anton saw his mother's life-changing grief over the death of his two year old infant sister; at twenty-nine, he faced his own transformative grief when his elder brother Nikolay died at the age of thirty-seven. If the collision of joy and humor with sorrow and tears marked Chekhov's family life, so too does the same collision of contradictory emotions mark his writings, and most especially his major plays, which are hard to call either comic or tragic in the established sense of these words.

Anton's native city was Taganrog, a provincial capital near the Ukraine at the edge of the Azov Sea on one side and the Don Steppe on the other. With its military base and port (where Greek merchants traded) Taganrog had an unusually cosmopolitan population, much like the town where Chekhov's *Three Sisters* befriend the passing military men and pine away for the more thriving metropolis of Moscow. Anton also calls to mind Taganrog's sailors in his early, comic story, "At Sea" (1883),[36] which depicts the odd morality of seamen who take prurient pleasure in observing newlyweds on their wedding night through a hole in the wall, but who readily turn away in moral disgust when they realize that the groom has sold his first night privileges to a rich man for money.

Taganrog's setting inspired in Chekhov a deep and abiding love of nature. In 1871 at age eleven, he and his eldest brother had convinced their father to allow them a visit to their grandfather by hitching a ride in an ox cart that was traveling through town. In two days, the brothers traveled forty-five miles over the steppe, were caught in rainstorms without protection, got lost in the reeds of a lake, and took respite at a Jewish inn. Chekhov later transformed these experiences into his first true masterpiece of fiction, "The Steppe" (1888).[37] Throughout his life,

---

[36] "V more" in A. P. Chekhov, *Polnoe sobranie sochinenii i pisem v tridtsati tomakh* [The Complete Works and Letters in Thirty Volumes], Vol. 2 (Moscow: Nauka, 1975), 268-71.

[37] "Step'" in A. P. Chekhov, *Polnoe sobranie sochinenii i pisem v tridtsati tomakh* [The Complete Works and Letters in Thirty Volumes], Vol. 7 (Moscow: Nauka, 1977), 13-109.

his greatest pleasures—fishing and gardening—involved interactions with nature. These same activities often express the passions of his characters as well. Trigorin (*The Seagull*) prefers the leisures of fishing to the agonies of writing. Dr. Astrov (*Uncle Vanya*) seems more passionate about trees than medicine. Gayev and his sister Ranyevskaya (*The Cherry Orchard*) so love their parents' beautiful, but no longer fruiting, orchard, that they find themselves mired in the past and unable to move forward into the future.

Willy-nilly, the provincial Taganrog had entered Chekhov's blood. The last home he built for himself stood outside Yalta in the Crimea, far from his native city. Yet, he placed his house on a hill that overlooked the town and the Black Sea, mirroring in some sense the geography of Taganrog. He designed his study with a large window looking out toward the distant Black Sea. He needed only a small bookshelf, because he had already donated the majority of his books to Taganrog's library. In his Yalta retreat, Chekhov would often stand at the window and look out to the town and the sea through binoculars—a living image of the distant observer of life and nature that he had become.[38] Perhaps Chekhov understood that Taganrog, with its natural setting and its melting pot of people, had formed him as surely as did his upbringing.

However, if you begin to think of Taganrog as the setting for a childhood idyll, Chekhov's upbringing would soon put the lie to any such notion. As Chekhov once said, "There was no childhood in my childhood."[39] His parents' backgrounds embodied the history of serfdom, Russia's system of slavery, which was abolished in 1861 (one year after Anton's birth), but still left a pall over the country as the nineteenth century ceded to the twentieth. Like Lopakhin's father in *The Cherry Orchard*, Anton's father, Pavel Yegorovich Chekhov (1825-98), had been born a serf. When Pavel reached age nineteen, his father Yegor (Anton's grandfather) had somehow amassed enough money to buy his and his family's freedom from their owner Count Chertkov. Yegor had accumulated only enough to buy his sons' freedom, however; Chertkov took pity on Yegor and included his daughter (Anton's aunt) for free.

Anton's mother, Yevgenia Yakovlevna Morozova (1835-1919), was also of peasant stock. Her childhood involved disaster after disaster. Her

---

[38] Finke, *Seeing Chekhov*, 172-7.
[39] Cited and translated by Simmons, *Chekhov*, 6.

father (like her father-in-law) had bought his freedom from serfdom. But a free life proved difficult, and Yevgenia's father went bankrupt in a few years (anticipating her husband's later bankruptcy). When Yevgenia's father realized that he could find employment only on an estate three hundred miles away, husband and wife separated. Yevgenia and her sister stayed with their mother. But soon, her childhood went up in flames as their native town burned to the ground. Perhaps the fire that rages in Act III of *Three Sisters* recalls this family history. Left with nothing, Yevgenia's mother took her two daughters to join their father, only to learn, when they arrived, that he had died of cholera. They could not even find his grave. Their only salvation was the mercy shown them by his employer.[40]

This heritage of slavery and financial hardship left deep traces on the Chekhov family. Pavel, like his father before him, was a strict disciplinarian, never hesitating to impose his will on his wife and children through beatings. The slightest deviation from routine or any infraction of Pavel's many house rules triggered a physical beating. Indeed, Pavel's punishing behavior was so persistent and excessive that he was once brought to court for his violence. In 1898, when Pavel died after suffering for four days from a fatal accident in which he ruptured a hernia, Yevgenia told her family that he had died too quickly. "The longer a man takes to die, the closer he is to the kingdom of Heaven, [because] he has time to repent his sins."[41] Perhaps she was thinking of all the beatings he had inflicted on his family and determined that he had more than four days' worth of sins for which to repent. When in 1871 Anton and his brother Alexander traveled across the steppe in an ox cart to visit their grandfather, who was working as a steward[42] on an estate in the region, the two boys realized that their father's childhood had been worse than their own. While their grandfather barely tolerated their presence, their grandmother told them about the privations, beatings, and resentments caused her by her husband. After a week, the boys fled, walking six miles to a village where they could make arrangements to return home.[43]

---

[40]   Rayfield, *Anton Chekhov*, 5-7.
[41]   Ibid., 467.
[42]   Among the stewards in Chekhov's plays are the schemer Borkin (*Ivanov*) and the penny-pinching Shamrayev (*The Seagull*).
[43]   Rayfield, *Anton Chekhov*, 25.

In stark contrast to his father, the adult Anton became a model of restraint, gentleness, and courtesy. "I am short-tempered, etc., etc.," he later told his wife, "but I have become accustomed to holding back, for it ill behooves a decent person to let himself go."[44] His father's beatings had taught him the cost of doing violence to others.

Yevgenia's past turned her into a loving mother, but a self-pitying woman, accustomed to deferring to authority, especially that of her husband. But her sufferings had also taught her to pity others, a lesson that she passed on to her children. Whenever a public execution would take place in the Taganrog marketplace (which the Chekhovs could see from their windows), Yevgenia reacted by "sighing deeply and crossing herself," Anton's younger brother Mikhail recalls. "She believed that even criminals were worthy of compassion and that they were oppressed by the powerful, and she instilled in us this attitude."[45]

While Anton looked to his father for negative examples of behavior, he made his mother's compassion his own. In all his writings, he strictly refrains from criticizing his characters or commenting upon their behavior. He just describes.

> An artist must not judge his characters or what they say, but only serve as an impartial witness. I overhear the muddled, inconclusive conversation of two Russians about pessimism, and I must transmit this conversation in the same way that I hear it. Evaluating it is for the jury—that is, the reader. (to A. S. Suvorin, 30 May 1888)

At the time of Anton's birth, Pavel Chekhov owned a small shop that sold groceries, sundries, even medicines, many of them quack preparations. Alongside gourmet coffee and tea, olives and homemade mustard, one could also find the "bird's nest," a preparation made from mercury and strychnine, commonly used by peasant women to abort unwanted pregnancies.[46] When Anton later practiced medicine, as if in defiance of the "bird's nest," he became known as a caring gynecologist, much like his character Dr. Dorn (*The Seagull*).

---

[44] Ibid., 4-5.
[45] Mikhail Chekhov, *Anton Chekhov*, 19.
[46] Rayfield, *Anton Chekhov*, 21-2.

Pavel was especially proud of having joined the merchant guild, because it raised his class status, as measured by the Russian government, by two ranks above the free peasants. He was also ambitious for his sons, and thus ensured that they learn to respect authority, pay strict attention to church doctrine, and get a solid education (grounded in foreign languages, including Latin and Greek). No doubt the teachers in Chekhov's stories and plays—like the fussy Kulygin in *Three Sisters*—were modeled on those with whom he had studied in Taganrog. Similarly, the young Anton's inability to master foreign languages influenced him in the creation of those characters who reveal their pretentions through the fractured use of different languages, as does Natasha, whose French is atrocious, in *Three Sisters*.

Pavel was also proud of his literacy, both in scripture and liturgical music. As family head, he created a structure of religious readings and ritual in his home. As choir director for the local churches, he demanded that his children sing in church every morning at daybreak. No wonder Anton's stories are filled with religious knowledge and imagery! Among his most powerful stories is "Easter Night" (1886) in which the talent for writing *akathists*—holy canticles sung in the Eastern Orthodox Church—embodies the transcendent and communicative power of art.[47] No wonder Chekhov would also later create uniquely musical plays, in which the rhythms of commonly spoken words mingle with the sound effects of daily life to produce a soundscape of human experience!

Pavel's religion, however, seemed to his children mere form. Anton's younger brother Mikhail speculates that their father "enjoyed the ritual of religion more than its substance," standing "reverently" through services at the church and "play[ing] the role of priest" at home. Yet, "in everyday life, our Father had as little faith as all the rest of us sinners."[48] Thus, Pavel again taught through negative example. His apparently hypocritical ardor left Anton with great antipathy toward all forms of hypocrisy and with a healthy skepticism toward organized religion. While he embraced liturgical music as art, he found spiritual consolation in nature more often than in a church.

---

[47] "Sviatoiu noch'iu," in A. P. Chekhov, *Polnoe sobranie sochinenii i pisem v tridtsati tomakh* [The Complete Works and Letters in Thirty Volumes], Vol. 5 (Moscow: Nauka, 1976), 92-103.

[48] Mikhail Chekhov, *Anton Chekhov*, 7.

One need only look at Chekhov's story, "The Lady with the Little Dog" (1899),[49] to see how nature can console his characters, and may well have also consoled the author. The story's protagonist Gurov sat "on a bench not far from the church" (366) on a hill overlooking the sea near the resort town of Oreanda. Sitting beside him is the married woman who will soon become more than a casual lover to him. Together they "looked down on the sea, and were silent" (366). Does their position suggest that the church has excluded them because of their adulterous relationship? Or rather, does their position suggest that they have spurned the church and taken their silent prayer out into the open air? Gurov's thoughts suggest the latter idea. "The leaves of the trees did not stir, cicadas called, and the monotonous, dull noise of the sea, coming from below, spoke of the peace, of the eternal sleep that awaits us" (366). The sounds of nature seem to have replaced the church choir.

> So [the sea] had sounded below when neither Yalta nor Oreanda were there, so it sounded now and would go on sounding with the same dull indifference when we are no longer here. And in this constancy, in this utter indifference to the life and death of each of us, there perhaps lies hidden the pledge of our eternal salvation, the unceasing movement of life on earth, of unceasing perfection. (366-7)

The demands of religious ritual—which can prompt hypocrisy—have been replaced by the "constancy" and "indifference" of nature—which cannot be other than sincere. The Church may lie; but nature never does.

Gurov's thoughts continue: "Everything was beautiful in this world, everything except for what we ourselves think and do when we forget the higher goals of being and our human dignity" (367). His concluding thought strikes a spiritual chord, and one that is frequently sounded in Chekhov's plays as well.

---

[49] "Dama s sobachkoi," in A. P. Chekhov, *Polnoe sobranie sochinenii i pisem v tridtsati tomakh* [The Complete Works and Letters in Thirty Volumes], Vol. 10 (Moscow: Nauka, 1977), 128-43. All citations of this story are from Anton Chekhov, *Stories*, trans. Richard Pevear and Larissa Volokhonsky (New York: Bantam Books, 2000), 361-76. Specific page references are given in parentheses within the text.

For example, in Act I of *Three Sisters*, the sight of flowers prompts the windbag Colonel Vershinin to rethink his life. When he speaks, he, like Gurov, stands on the precipice of an adulterous love:

> Yes. But how many flowers you have here! (*Looks around.*) And what wonderful quarters. I envy you! All my life I moved from one small apartment to the next, with two chairs, one sofa, and a stove that always smoked. What my life lacks are flowers just like these... (*Wipes his hands.*) Eh! Well, now how about that! [...] I often wonder, what if a person could live life over again, consciously? What if one life, which has already been lived, were, so to speak, a rough draft, and the next the clean copy! Then I think each of us would try not to repeat ourselves, or at least, would try to arrange our circumstances differently, would get quarters with flowers and with a lot of light... (trans. Carnicke, 182-3)

Later in Act II, Masha—in hopeless love with Vershinin—also appeals to nature in her search for meaning:

> I think that one must be a believer, or must search for beliefs, otherwise life is empty, empty... To live and not to know why the cranes fly, why children are born, why there are stars in the sky... Either you know why you live, or it's all nonsense, just tinsel... (trans. Carnicke, 198)

Her words remind us that human beings—like cranes and stars—are part of nature. Just such a thought consoles Baron Tuzenbach, as he exits in Act IV to his death in a duel. "Look there," he tells his fiancée, "that tree has dried up, but it's still waving in the breeze with the others. So I think that if I die, I too will still participate in life in some way or other" (trans. Carnicke, 233).

Anton's daily life in Taganrog involved tending his father's store whenever he was not in school or singing with the choir. His day began at five o'clock in the morning in church and ended at midnight in the store. Pavel also sometimes sent the ten-year-old Anton to the railway station to sell goods from a rented stand. It was a routine of disciplined, hard work with little leisure.

Yet, despite this difficult childhood, Anton always loved to joke and tease; and his brothers often served as the butt of his wit. For example, Mikhail recalls a long family trip to visit relatives, during which Anton spent the entire time in "good-natured mocking." This time he had singled out his elder brother for special treatment, because Nikolay had chosen to wear an opera hat in the open cart. As they approached their destination, Anton finally knocked off the hat, which fell under the cart's wheels.

> Nikolay wasn't bothered; he picked it up and put it on again. [During their visit,] Nikolay could not be parted from his treasure, even to go swimming. So, naked but still wearing the hat, Nikolay was wading in the river when Anton sneaked up behind him and knocked the hat off. It fell into the river, took in some water, and disappeared.[50]

Such anecdotes readily recall the slapstick humor in Anton's early stories and one-act plays (which he appropriately called "jokes").

In 1876, Pavel Chekhov went bankrupt; he lost his store and his membership in the merchant guild. He dropped in status to one rung above the peasants, the same lowly rank as Treplev's father in *The Seagull*. With no income, Pavel escaped from debtors' prison by leaving town in the dead of night. As Mikhail recalls, when their former tenant, a civil servant with a penchant for gambling offered "to pay father's debt and save the house from auction for us," the family thought their tenant a godsend. In fact, their apparently trustworthy friend had instead paid the mortgage on the house in order to avoid a public auction and thus "secure the house for himself, as owner. [...] Our mother was left with nothing."[51] It was now Yevgenia's turn to leave Taganrog with her family in tow. While most of the family resettled in the slums of Moscow, the sixteen-year-old Anton was left behind to finish school and finalize the selling of his family's house and furniture. Echoes of this period find their way into his plays. The title of his first, unfinished full-length play, *Fatherlessness*,[52] labels his personal situation; *The Cherry Orchard* depicts

---

[50] Mikhail Chekhov, *Anton Chekhov*, 25-7.

[51] Ibid., 32.

[52] *Bezottsovshchina* was thought to be lost until a draft was discovered in 1923 among Chekhov's papers; it is now generally known by the name of its central character, *Platonov*. The text is included in A. P. Chekhov, *Polnoe sobranie sochinenii i pisem v tridtsati tomakh* [The Complete Works and Letters in Thirty Volumes], Vol. 11 (Moscow: Nauka, 1978), 5-180.

the loss of a family's home to their former serf;[53] and in *Three Sisters*, Andrey (like the Chekhovs' former tenant) becomes a civil servant addicted to gambling, who desperately mortgages the family home (like Pavel) to cope with the growing debt.

Chekhov's adult relationships with his parents say a lot about his sense of duty and familial loyalty. At age seventeen, he told a cousin that his parents "are wonderful people, whose unconditional love of their children is enough to place them above praise and excuse all their faults" (to M. M. Chekhov, 29 July 1877). This early belief proved life-long. Chekhov remained with his parents and supported them financially until his death. Such family loyalty was not uncommon among the peasantry of Russia and marks Chekhov as part of that peasant culture.[54]

Despite the beatings he endured during childhood, Anton Pavlovich never betrayed his father publicly. In one rare and private instance, he confessed to his friend and colleague Nemirovich-Danchenko, "I have never been able to forgive my father for beating me when I was a child."[55] Perhaps the best evidence for the toll that childhood took from Chekhov is the fact that he was never known to address his father affectionately as "papa."[56] After Pavel's death in 1898, Anton placed his father's walking sticks next to the fireplace in his study in Yalta. Scholar Michael Finke believes that these sticks were likely instruments used to beat Anton as a child, and thus they stood in his study as tangible reminders of what he had overcome during his life.[57]

Anton and his mother were unequivocally devoted to each other; and he hung a large portrait of her in his study. Even so, her sentimentality stood in stark contrast to the dispassionate objectivity that he developed in his life and art. Stanislavsky recalls a moment in Yalta when her behavior had more than "upset" Chekhov; he was "furious," even "fierce." She was planning to see a performance of *Uncle Vanya* and was getting dressed up for the occasion. "[Anton's] imagination presented

---

53 Lopakhin in *The Cherry Orchard*, is clearly more trustworthy a friend and more honorable a person than his real-life counterpart. Unlike the Chekhov family's tenant, Lopakhin buys his former landowners' estate in honest competition at a public auction.

54 Williames, *Anton Chekhov, The Iconoclast*, 77-9.

55 Turkov, ed., *Anton Chekhov and His Times*, 65.

56 Rayfield, *Anton Chekhov*, 33.

57 Finke, *Seeing Chekhov*, 180.

him with the following scene: the son had written a play, his mother was sitting in a box in the theater wearing a silk dress. The picture was so sentimental that he was prepared to leave for Moscow in order to avoid being a part of it."[58]

His father's tyranny, coupled with his mother's respect for others, left Anton with a strong distaste of authoritarian behavior. As Rayfield elegantly puts it, "Quiet resistance to all authority [became] the core of Anton's adult personality."[59] In short, his parental heritage induced in him a life-long dedication to freedom in all its forms and to human dignity at all costs. As he explains in a letter:

> I am not a liberal, not a conservative, not an evolutionist, not a monk, but neither am I indifferent. I would like to be a free artist, and I only fear that God has not given me the strength to become one. I hate lies and coercion in any form. [...] My holy of holies is the human body, health, the mind, talent, inspiration, love, and the most absolute freedom, freedom from coercion and lies, in whatever ways these might be expressed. (to A. N. Pleshcheev, 4 Oct. 1888)

HEAD OF HOUSEHOLD

Without doubt, family grounded Chekhov. At seventeen, he had explicitly stated his debt to his parents: "Father and mother are for me the only people on the whole earth to whom I will never grudge anything. If I make something of myself, then it is the work of their hands" (to M. M. Chekhov, 29 July 1877). He paid this debt by becoming the head of his birth family at age nineteen. Moreover, as Michael Finke puts it, his entire professional life as doctor and writer was "a struggle for something beyond personal station: he sought to 'make good' for his family."[60] Upon his father's death, Chekhov told a friend: "I shall now have to make a new nest for [my mother and sister]."[61] He was referring to the planned house in Yalta, where he was moving because of his

---

58 Turkov, ed., *Anton Chekhov and His Times*, 107.
59 Rayfield, *Anton Chekhov*, 16.
60 Finke, *Seeing Chekhov*, 179.
61 Rayfield, *Anton Chekhov*, 468.

deteriorating health. Yet, he does not speak of himself to his friend, only of his dependents, once again testifying to the primary place that family held in his thoughts.

When Anton graduated from high school in 1879, he had earned grades that allowed him a scholarship to Moscow State University, where he enrolled in medical school. But, in moving to Moscow, Anton also became the de facto head of his large, woefully dependent, and largely dysfunctional family. His father had at last found menial work as a clerk, but his two older brothers were in trouble. Alexander (an intelligent writer) had become an alcoholic; Nikolay (a gifted visual artist and illustrator) was suffering from tuberculosis and addicted to morphine treatments. (For Nikolay's portrait of Anton, see the cover illustration.) In effect, Anton stepped into his father's role as breadwinner and decision-maker. Remarkably, Pavel not only ceded his position to his son, but also respected Anton's new authority within the family. Mikhail recalls a change in Anton's manner as well. "He spoke in a new way, using phrases that were decisive and even curt: 'It's not true'; 'One must be fair'; 'We can't lie.'"[62]

It was now up to Anton to pay the rent, buy the food, and make sure his younger siblings finished school; and his new role proved salubrious for the family. "Working together, we slowly began to improve the family's financial situation. Everyone worked hard."[63] Within seven years, Anton moved the Chekhovs out of Moscow's slums and red-light district into an airy, comfortable, middle-class two-story house.

When Anton's level-headed sister—Maria Pavlovna Chekhova (1863-1957), called "Masha" by the family—graduated as a school teacher, she became his right hand, hosting his guests, protecting his privacy, working as his secretary, and managing the household for him whenever medicine and literature called him away. He came to rely upon her absolutely, and she willingly protected his legacy during his life and after his untimely death. Indeed, their strong devotion to each other is worth a second look.

Anton and Masha were always close. In their first Moscow apartment, Anton "often knocked on the [thin] partition [between his and his sister's rooms] at night in order to tell her about an idea he had had, or

---

[62] Mikhail Chekhov, *Anton Chekhov*, 49.
[63] Ibid., 49.

even a complete story that had suddenly occurred to him."[64] Later, when their living circumstances improved, Masha placed "a huge portrait of her brother" in her room.[65] There were, however, costs on both sides to their close friendship. Marriage for either, it seemed, threatened their comfortable status quo.

Like Olga in *Three Sisters*, Masha never married despite her longings. Had her brother taken "aside every one of Masha's suitors and dissuaded them," as Rayfield asserts?[66] According to Masha, Chekhov twice prompted her to reject marriage proposals. In the first instance, a friend had unexpectedly turned into her suitor. When she asked Anton's advice, he told her that he would answer for her.[67] In the second instance, Masha was attracted to her brother's friend Alexander Ivanovich Smagin, a handsome Ukrainian farmer; and he was a persistent suitor, proposing three times over the course of a number of years. He last proposed in 1892 when Masha was twenty-nine. In that era, when women married young, Masha would already have been considered unmarriageable. This may well have been her last chance for marriage. "I thought hard about getting married," Masha recalls. "I went to the study and said, 'You know, Anton, I've decided to get married....' [but he ...] made no reply." From this silence, "I sensed that he found this announcement unpleasant."[68] Masha turned Smagin down.

In her turn, Masha also found Anton's desire to marry Olga Knipper unpleasant. (See Illustration 3.) In the past, Masha's friends had often become Anton's own, and, at times, also the objects of his affection (as had Lika). Masha now befriended Olga for Anton's sake, and, unlike their mother who did not appreciate Olga creeping into Anton's bedroom at night, Masha was happy to accept this informal arrangement. Marriage, however, was an entirely different matter. "Now let me express my opinion about your marriage," writes Masha to her brother. "You don't need these extra worries. If you are loved [by Olga], you won't be abandoned [by her], and there is no sacrifice involved."[69] When Anton married Olga

---

[64] Vladimir Galaktianovich Korolenko in Turkov, ed., *Anton Chekhov and His Times*, 15.

[65] Shchepkina-Kupernik in Ibid., 30.

[66] Rayfield, *Anton Chekhov*, 260.

[67] Simmons, *Chekhov*, 58.

[68] Translated and cited by Rayfield, *Anton Chekhov*, 267.

[69] Ibid., 534.

in 1901, he wrote to his mother to reassure his family, that, despite the marriage, "all will be the same" (25 May 1901). Had Masha's opinion of marriage prompted this reassurance? Or was the status quo what Chekhov himself wanted? He had said as much in 1895 to his best friend, Suvorin, who was pressuring Chekhov to get married.

> Please, I will marry if you want that. But on this condition: everything must be as it was, meaning that she will live in Moscow, I in the country, and I will travel to her. [...] I promise to be an excellent husband, but give me the kind of wife, who, like the moon, does not appear in my sky every day. (23 Mar. 1895)

Effectively, he and Olga conducted their marriage in just the way he had described, she in Moscow and he in Yalta. Sometimes he traveled to her and sometimes she to him. "Again came separations and meetings," Olga recalls, "only parting became even more painful, and after a few months I began to think seriously of whether I ought to leave the stage."[70] After she fell seriously ill in 1902, she wanted all the more strongly to leave the stage and join her husband. Yet, Chekhov always insisted that she continue her career. She could only understand his resistance in terms of his own needs. On the one hand, her career provided him a window on Moscow's theatrical scene. "Did Anton Pavlovich need simply a wife cut off from the outside world?" Olga asks, and then concludes, "He greatly valued the link through me with the theater."[71] On the other hand, Olga realized that their unusual living arrangement protected the quietude of his and Masha's lives. Olga observes, "I sensed in him a solitary man, who, perhaps would find [the] upheaval [of a marriage] in his and another's life burdensome."[72] Only after Chekhov's death, when his private letters were published, did Olga read her husband's 1895 description of his vision of an ideal marriage, something she had "understood, but we never expressed it in words, never spoke of that which prevented us from uniting our lives completely."[73]

On another front, Masha's correspondence with Olga after her marriage exhibits shifting tones of voice that strangely recall Chekhov's am-

---

[70] Turkov, ed., *Anton Chekhov and His Times*, 209.
[71] Ibid.
[72] Ibid.
[73] Ibid., 210.

bivalent correspondence with Lika. For example, in one letter from June 1901 Masha harshly tells her sister-in-law: "You managed to trap my brother!" Then, referencing *Three Sisters*, in which a crude, uneducated woman first seduces a young man and next marginalizes his sisters in their own house, Masha accuses Olga of just such behavior: "I suppose you're like Natasha in *Three Sisters*! I'll strangle you with my own hands." Masha then abruptly shifts tone. "You know I love you and must have gotten strongly attached to you in the last two years." Finally, Masha ends her letter with a concession. "How odd that you're a Chekhov."[74]

By the end of Chekhov's life, his immediate household may have shrunk to three—he, his mother, and Masha—but, once having become the hub of his birth family, Chekhov retained his role as the family head until his death.

MEDICINE, CIVIC WORK, AND LIFE OUTSIDE MOSCOW

Upon graduation from Moscow State University in 1884, Dr. Chekhov opened his practice in Moscow. Perhaps he chose to study medicine because he had seen desperately ill peasants buying quack preparations at his father's store. Perhaps he hoped to cure the many members of his own family who were ill with tuberculosis. In reflecting on two family deaths from this widespread disease, Chekhov wrote, "The trouble is that both these deaths (A. and N.) are not an accident, and not an event in human life, but an ordinary thing."[75] His family seemed to think that he chose medicine because a local doctor had treated him kindly during "his first brush with a serious illness."[76] Whatever the motivation, Chekhov devoted himself to medicine his whole life, often calling it "my lawful wife." Literature took second place as "my mistress."[77]

The new doctor was already showing early symptoms of the family's disease, however. When his brother Nikolay died of tuberculosis

---

[74] Rayfield, *Anton Chekhov*, 541.
[75] An 1891 notebook entry cited and translated by Rayfield, Ibid., 239.
[76] Mikhail Chekhov, *Anton Chekhov*, 29-30.
[77] See letters by A. P. Chekhov from 11 Oct. 1888, 17 Jan. 1887, 11 Feb. 1893, and 15 Mar. 1896.

on Anton's name day, 17 January 1889, he fell into a deep depression. He handled his grief in an extraordinary way. In April 1890 he undertook a massive scientific study of Russia's most notorious penal colony, Sakhalin, in the Far East. He traveled eighty-one days by horse, rail, and steamship, through storms and the cold of Siberia to get to the remote island prison; the grueling journey affected his health and may have accelerated his death. Once in Sakhalin, he spent eight months processing questionnaires for 10,000 convicts and their families, all exiled for life. He conducted as many as one hundred and sixty interviews daily, amassing information and statistics previously unknown to Russia's government. In letter after letter, Chekhov described the nightmarish life in the colony as "hell." When he returned home, he exposed the reality of Russia's penal system in his book, *The Island of Sakhalin* (1891), and began a fundraising campaign to send books to the convicts' children.

Chekhov's decisions to expose and improve conditions in Sakhalin suggest a deeply held assumption on his part about the need for taking action. In many of his writings, lack of action registers as a symptom of the kind of emotional heartache that his characters sometimes experience but are unable to name. Words like "boredom" (*skuka*) and "misery" (*toska*) are inadequate descriptions of what they feel. The title characters in his plays *Ivanov* (1887) and *Uncle Vanya* (1899) experience just such a state of mind. Ivanov has lost all drive to succeed in managing his estate and fallen sadly out of love with his wife; Vanya feels that all potential joy in life has passed him by. Chekhov's prescription for such maladies is work. In *Uncle Vanya*, Sonya simply and practically advises her restless and unhappy stepmother to take up some sort of occupation: "Is there really so little to do? If only you wanted, there'd be something to do! [...] There's farming to do, teaching, nursing the sick. Is that so little?" (trans. Carnicke, 142) Similarly, Vanya deals with his "burden" by getting on with his work at the very end of the play. "I have to get busy with something as soon as possible," he tells his niece. "To work, to work!" (trans. Carnicke, 163)

By setting out for Sakhalin Chekhov seems to have been taking his own advice. Significantly, he chose to engage in scientific, not literary work, and thus contribute to what he saw as his primary profession. He told his friend, Suvorin, "I want to write at least one or two hundred pages, and in this way pay off some of my debts to medicine" (9 Mar. 1890). Chekhov envisioned using his research from Sakhalin to complete the long delayed medical dissertation, which would allow him to teach in the university. Alas, *The Island of Sakhalin* was rejected by Moscow State University, because it proved of more sociological, than medical, importance.[78] Nonetheless, as the Russian literary historian Dmitry Mirsky observes, "This journey was Chekhov's greatest practical contribution to the humanitarianism that was so near to his heart."[79] Chekhov's exposé of prison conditions had far-ranging impact on liberal efforts to reform the Tsarist penal system.

Over the years, Chekhov's civic work included fundraising for the victims of Russia's famine in 1891, volunteering as a doctor during the cholera epidemic in 1892, and building three schools for peasants in the villages outside Moscow and a sanatorium for tuberculosis near the city of Yalta. These endeavors earned him a national award, the Stanislaus medal (third class) in 1899.[80]

By 1892 Chekhov had earned enough money to buy a tumble-down country estate, called Melikhovo, for him and his family. It was located forty-five miles by train outside Moscow and six more miles by horse on muddy roads from the railroad station. In *Three Sisters*, Vershinin might well be speaking of Melikhovo when he says, "It's good to live here. Only it's strange that the railroad is twenty-five miles away... And no one knows why that is." Chekhov lived at his estate from 1892 until 1899 when his ill health necessitated a move to warmer climates.

In buying Melikhovo, Chekhov may have wanted to escape the cruelties of human behavior (which he had so starkly confronted at Sakhalin) and find peace in nature. The estate consisted of six hundred acres of birch forests, pastures, and farmland. The dilapidated house was large but had no bathroom or insulation. Chekhov planted a cherry orchard and flowers. He and Masha (like Vanya and Sonya in *Uncle Vanya*) tended the forests and tried to make the farm productive.

Chekhov also worked as the area's country doctor, becoming solely responsible for the health of twenty-six surrounding peasant villages and seven factories, with duties and difficulties that mirror those of Dr. Astrov in *Uncle Vanya*. Chekhov's commitment to medicine was deep

---

[78] See Williames, *Anton Chekhov, The Iconoclast*, 29-54.
[79] D. S. Mirsky, *A History of Russian Literature from its Beginnings to 1900* (New York: Vintage Books, 1958), 370.
[80] Rayfield, *Anton Chekhov*, 507.

and generous. He treated thousands of peasants for free, often spending his own money on needed medicines. He also became active in the regional government and was elected to the local council, which addressed health, environmental, and educational affairs in the same surrounding villages. Work for the good of his community grounded him as fully as did his family.

His knowledge as a doctor must have made facing his own illness especially difficult. He used a lot of ink in letters to explain away the periodic bleeding from his lungs. He strenuously resisted allowing another doctor to examine him. Yet, he could hardly hold any illusions about his diagnosis. He suffered recognizable symptoms of tuberculosis throughout medical school, and in 1894 he joked with a friend that he would live only five or ten more years. In 1897 a serious hemorrhage from the lungs hospitalized him; he could no longer deny the truth. He sold Melikhovo and built a new house in the warmer climate of Yalta. There, he felt exiled from Moscow and longed for the city as fervently as do his *Three Sisters*.

In 1904 Anton Pavlovich risked one last trip to Moscow, appearing on his name day for the premiere of his last play, *The Cherry Orchard*. He arrived at the Moscow Art Theatre just before the last act and was promptly called to the stage by loud applause. He was emaciated, pale, and hardly able to stand on stage as the company made speeches in his honor.[81] By spring, his condition turned mortal. On the advice of Muscovite doctors, his wife rushed him to the German health spa of Badenwieler. But the trip itself was dangerous for him. He died in the warmth of the resort on 2 July 1904. He is buried in Moscow's Novodevichy cemetery, where his father and his *Three Sisters*' mother had been buried.

LITERATURE

Medicine may have been Chekhov's "lawful wife," as he put it, but his "mistress," literature, proved to be his more publicly visible and more financially lucrative profession. His rise to fame as a writer of short stories was meteoritic. By 1888, at age twenty-eight, Anton Chekhov had

---

[81] Ibid., 587.

already established himself as the greatest living Russian storyteller, second only to the famous novelist Lev Tolstoy (1828-1910), then in his sixties. (See Illustration 6.) Chekhov had begun to write at age fourteen. While still in high school he submitted short comedic stories to popular magazines under various pseudonyms. His first publication dates from 1879. As a medical student, he churned out hundreds of stories. In 1883 alone he published ninety. When he graduated, he kept writing at the same furious pace. In 1885 he published more than one hundred stories. By the end of his life he had written nearly five hundred.

Clearly, Chekhov was driven to write by inclination and talent. Trigorin (*The Seagull*, Act II) comes close to speaking for his author, when he tells Nina:

> There is such a thing as a fixed idea when a person can think of nothing else, day and night, except, say, the moon. I have my "moon." Day and night, one nagging idea obsesses me: I must write, I must write, I must... As soon as I finish one story, I have to write another, then a third, after the third, a fourth... I write constantly, as if I'm riding relay horses, and I can't do it any differently. [...] When I finish something, I run off to the theater or I go fishing; surely there I will relax and forget. But no, a new, heavy, iron ball starts rolling around in my head—a new subject. My desk begins to call to me, and I have to hurry home and write and then write some more. It's always like that. I give myself no peace. (trans. Carnicke, 80)

In fact, Chekhov had written remarkably similar words to Lika a few years earlier.[82]

There is also little doubt, however, that Chekhov's prodigious writing during the 1880s provided significant and necessary additional income. His hasty writing in the earliest years of his career reflects the fact that he was paid per line; the more lines he could write the more money he could earn for his family.

In the early 1880s, Chekhov found a convenient publishing outlet in Russia's cheap, comic journals, such as *Fragments* (*Oskolki*), *The Alarm Clock* (*Budil'nik*), *News of the Day* (*Novosti dnia*), and *The Dragonfly*

---

[82] Donald Rayfield, "Chekhov's Stories and Play," in Vera Gottlieb and Paul Allain, eds., *The Cambridge Companion to Chekhov* (New York: Cambridge University Press, 2000), 207.

(*Strekoza*)—all of which published the young Chekhov. Such rags grew in number and popularity at a furious pace during the 1870s and 1880s, partly because a new readership was growing among the urban poor and partly because Tsarist censorship was severely limiting more politically sophisticated publications. The new readers, like Chekhov himself, were often the children of former serfs and peasants, who had escaped from their parents' economic classes through education; this group came to be known in Russia as the *raznochintsy* ("people of various ranks") because they no longer fit neatly into any of the established classes of imperial Russia's strict social hierarchy. They were from the lower classes, but they were also self-made merchants, teachers, doctors, and intellectuals. Russia's persistent censors were as concerned about the morals of these readers as much as they were about their political discourse. Therefore, censors paternalistically purged the comic journals of graphic sexual images, peasant superstitions, and heretical slurs on Tsarist authority and the Russian Orthodox Church. As Chekhov reports, the censor cut four hundred to eight hundred lines from each issue of *The Alarm Clock*.[83]

Unlike most of the era's authors, who were from aristocratic and intellectual backgrounds, Chekhov knew well how to communicate with this new type of reader.[84] He wrote brief satirical sketches that played on situational jokes and featured characters from all walks of Russian life—students, teachers, postal clerks, petty bureaucrats, people with and without money, peasants, and former serfs. For example, in "On the Train" (1881) Chekhov conjures up the rhythmic atmosphere of a trip in a railroad car where "pickpockets and cold drafts of air" combine. As the story starts, the narrator feels "a hand slip into my [thankfully empty] back pocket," only to realize by story's end that his suitcase has walked off in another's hand. "God," he exclaims as he catches sight of the thief, "it's my suitcase!"[85] In "Joy" (1883), a young office worker rushes ecstati-

[83] Daniel Balmuth, *Censorship in Russia, 1865-1905* (Washington, D.C.: University Press of America, 1979), 207.

[84] For more on Chekhov's class and its effect on his writing, see Williames, *Anton Chekhov, The Iconoclast*, 3-8.

[85] "V vagone," in A. P. Chekhov, *Polnoe sobranie sochinenii i pisem v tridtsati tomakh* [The Complete Works and Letters in Thirty Volumes], Vol. 1 (Moscow: Nauka, 1974), 84-9. This story has been translated into English by Peter Constantine in Anton Chekhov, *The Undiscovered Chekhov* (New York: Seven Stories Press, 1998), 11-20.

cally home to tell his astonished parents that he has become suddenly famous. After work he stopped at a tavern where he got very drunk. When he went back out onto the street in his inebriated state, he slipped and fell under a horse, which bolted in fright and dragged him down the street. The incident was duly recorded in that day's newspaper. "Yes-sir!" he tells his parents, "They wrote about me! Now all Russia knows me."[86] In "The Death of a Clerk" (1883), a lowly clerk accidently sneezes on the bald head of a general while watching a theatrical performance. The clerk is so mortified by the accident that he does not believe the general, who, undisturbed, tells him to forget it. The clerk keeps apologizing so profusely and so many times and in so many ways, that the general finally explodes in real anger—not at the sneeze but at the persistent apologizing: "'Get out!' barked the general, suddenly turning blue and shaking." Frightened by the general's anger, the clerk goes home, lies down, and dies.[87]

Editors of the comic journals could not get enough of Chekhov's brilliantly funny satires; the more he could write, the more he could earn. But, to protect his sober reputation as a doctor he published under a series of pseudonyms—at one count, fifty different names. He signed "On the Train" as "Antosha Ch." He signed "Joy" and "The Death of a Clerk" as "A. Chekhonte." His most persistent pseudonym was "Antosha Chekhonte," a nickname given to him by his favorite high school teacher.

At the end of 1885, he traveled to Russia's cosmopolitan capital, St. Petersburg, in order to visit the publisher of *Fragments* (who had become a major promoter of Chekhov's work). There he was astonished to learn that people not only read his stories avidly, but eagerly awaited his next contributions. His readers, it seemed, were taking him seriously as a writer. "If I had known they were reading me like that," he told his eldest brother, Alexander, "I would not have written on short order" (4 Jan. 1886). Three months later, Chekhov received a long, detailed letter that "surprised me, as if it were a lightning bolt" (to D. V. Grigorovich, 28 Mar. 1886). The nationally famous author, Dmitry Vasilyevich Grigorovich, had written to tell Chekhov that his "real talent," which

---

[86] "Radost'," in Chekhov, *Polnoe sobranie sochinenii* [The Complete Works], Vol. 2, 12-3.
[87] "Smert' chinovnika," in A. P. Chekhov, Ibid., 164-6. See the English translation by Pevear and Volokhonsky in Anton Chekhov, *Stories*, 1-3.

"far exceeds other writers of the new generation," could translate into a literary career of significance. "You are, I am sure, meant to write some exceptional, truly artistic works." But Grigorovich also reprimanded the young writer for obviously hasty and careless writing, telling him to "respect" his own talent or risk "commit[ting] the great moral sin of not fulfilling your calling."[88] Chekhov took heed, began to use his real name for publications, slowed the pace of his writing, and perfected the economical and allusive craft by which he created true masterpieces of short fiction.

Also in 1886, another important figure entered Chekhov's life: Aleksey Sergeyevich Suvorin, the publisher of New Times (Novoe vremia), a strongly conservative and highly influential journal. Suvorin was so impressed with the young writer that he invited him to contribute to New Times and later started a weekly supplement to feature Chekhov's stories. Suvorin was the first publisher in Russia to include illustrations in his journal and to use a high-speed rotary press to increase subscriptions.[89] These innovations placed him at the head of a huge publishing company and made him a millionaire. Publishing in Suvorin's journal meant a significant increase of visibility for Chekhov among Russia's intellectual elite. New Times was one of the so-called "thick journals," where literary figures like Dostoyevsky and Tolstoy had found their readers and where political and social discussions of more complexity occurred. In short, Suvorin had invited Chekhov to enter into the world of serious literature.

Suvorin quickly became Chekhov's most avid publisher, as well as his fast friend. Despite their wide discrepancies in age, class background, and political views, their correspondence is frank, often providing insight into Chekhov's personality and beliefs. There occurred, however, one notable rift in their longtime friendship, which was triggered by Suvorin's pro-government views. In 1897, Suvorin insisted on supporting in New Times the anti-Semitic sentiments that lay behind the conviction of Captain Alfred Dreyfus, who had been falsely accused of spying and treason in France. Chekhov criticized Suvorin for standing up for

---

[88] Grigorovich to Chekhov, 25 Mar. 1886, in A. P. Chekhov, Sobranie sochinenii [Collected Works], Vol. 11 (Moscow: Izdatel'stvo khudozhestvennoi literatury, 1956), 626.
[89] Balmuth, Censorship in Russia, 95.

a corrupt court system and for believing in a false stereotype. Chekhov knew that stereotypes, such as those that colored public opinion about Jews, blinded people to the unique strengths and weaknesses inherent in individuals. Chekhov had known and loved many Jews in his life, among them: the innkeepers he had met on the steppe; his close friend, the noted landscape painter Isaac Ilyich Levitan; and Dunya Efros, Chekhov's first fiancée, a Jewess from a rich Moscow family, who served as his model for Ivanov's wife (*Ivanov*, 1887). Chekhov's anger with Suvorin was serious; the writer broke off all relations with the editor. But, as was Chekhov's wont, he later mended their friendship.

Suvorin's invitation offered Chekhov a venue for exactly the type of writing that Grigorovich was demanding. Chekhov began to write stories of greater subtlety and insight into the human condition. Such stories were also much more likely to catch the eye of the censors. For example, in "The Peasants" (1897)[90] Chekhov explodes the romanticized and unrealistic images of peasants—so prevalent in nineteenth-century Russian literature—by portraying them as people—some good, some bad—who live and struggle in dire poverty. Whereas the aristocratically born Lev Tolstoy saw in the Russian peasantry purity of soul, Chekhov knew firsthand the underbelly of peasant culture. As he tells Suvorin in the mid-1890s, "Peasant blood flows in me, and so it's hard to astonish me with peasant virtues" (27 Mar. 1894). Chekhov's innovation in "The Peasants" was only in speaking the truth without praise or blame and without political commentary. Yet, the censor cut Chekhov's conclusion to the story, frankly admitting that his portrayal was too true and thus "too gloomy" for public consumption.[91]

In October 1888—a scant two years after Grigorovich's reprimand and Suvorin's invitation to publish in the "thick journals"—the Russian Academy of Sciences unanimously voted to award Chekhov the prestigious Pushkin Prize for literature. In another two years, Chekhov would himself become a member of the Academy.[92]

---

[90] "Muzhiki," in Chekhov, *Polnoe sobranie sochinenii* [The Complete Works], Vol. 9, 281-312.

[91] Williames, *Anton Chekhov, The Iconoclast*, 70.

[92] In 1902, the Academy of Sciences welcomed the writer Maksim Gorky as a member and then nullified his membership because of his revolutionary politics. Chekhov proved his loyalty to Gorky (see Illustration 5) and his belief in freedom of speech by resigning from the Academy.

Despite Chekhov's professional attention to his craft from the late 1880s on, he continued to depend upon his writing, not medicine, to provide economic stability for himself and his family. Thus, artistic decisions were sometimes contingent on financial considerations. While he wrote with less haste, he still forced himself to abide by lucrative deadlines. When in 1888 Suvorin criticized Chekhov for rather sketchy character descriptions in "The Name Day Party,"[93] the author responded by confessing his own dissatisfaction with the story (now numbered among his masterpieces). His excuse reveals how little had actually changed for him over the course of his career.

> I understand that I cut and spoil my heroes, that there is good material that I leave out for nothing... Speaking frankly, I wanted to spend half a year on "The Name Day Party." [...] But what can I do? I start a story on the 10th of September, and I must finish it by the 5th of October—a short deadline; and if I break my word and miss the deadline, then I get no money. (to A. S. Suvorin, 27 Oct. 1888)

Chekhov was left especially short of funds after his expensive trip to Sakhalin. He solved the problem by selling the rights to his collected works to Adolf Marks for a mere 75,000 rubles. While the sum seemed enormous to Chekhov, he had in fact made a bad deal for himself. The canny publisher had bought nine volumes of stories for the normal price of four. Sales of Chekhov's works totaled 100,000 rubles for Marks in the first year of publication alone. Moreover, Marks had bought Chekhov's works on condition that the author revise everything anew, thus chaining Chekhov to his older writings and limiting the time he could spend on creating new works.[94] Chekhov reacted by punning on the similarity between his publisher's name and that of the German philosopher, Karl Marx, whose idea of communism was then fuelling Russia's revolutionaries: "At any moment I'll become a Marxist."[95]

---

[93] "Imeniny," in Chekhov, *Polnoe sobranie sochinenii* [The Complete Works], Vol. 7, 167-97.
[94] Rayfield, *Anton Chekhov*, 481-3.
[95] Ibid., 484.

MARRIAGE
TO THE MOSCOW ART THEATRE

In tandem with fiction Chekhov had also been writing plays, but fame as a dramatist came much harder and later than it had from his fiction. He was attracted to the theater from the first. In high school, his father and teachers forbade him from attending the local theater. Such entertainment, after all, could prove a bad influence on a boy. Chekhov still managed to sneak off to see lascivious French farces and operettas, classic Russian plays by Nikolay Vasilyevich Gogol (1823-86) and Alexander Nikolayevich Ostrovsky (1809-52), Shakespeare's classics, melodramas, and broadly comic vaudevilles. Among the first books that Chekhov bought were translations of Shakespeare's *Hamlet* and *Macbeth*.[96] By the time Chekhov was eighteen, he had written at least two plays (a serious one, *Fatherlessness*, and a lost vaudeville, *Why the Hen Clucks*).[97] When he moved to Moscow for Medical School, he built his social life around theater: he attended all kinds of performances, befriended actors of the highest rank, and flirted (and more) with actresses. When he finally married in 1901, as noted above, he married an actress! Like his early stories, many of his plays were short "jokes," as he called them. Staged widely throughout Russia's provinces, these one-acts provided Chekhov with substantial income, so much that he advised his older brother, Alexander, to sit down and write two or three plays. "A play," he said "is a pension fund" (21 Feb. 1889). Chekhov's first major play, *Ivanov* (1887), significantly coincided with his newly honed professionalism as a fiction writer for the "thick journals."

Despite his early infatuation with theater, Chekhov had also begun to criticize the unconvincing melodramatic claptrap and the histrionic acting that was common on nineteenth-century stages. He wanted plays and acting to be "just as complex and also just as simple as in life. People eat their dinner, just eat their dinner, yet at the same time their happiness is taking shape and their lives are being smashed."[98] Put another way, "in real life people do not spend every minute shooting each other,

---

[96] Ibid., 59.
[97] *Bezottsovshchina* and *Nedarom kuritsa pela*.
[98] Spoken words from 1889, translated by Gordon McVay in *Chekhov's Three Sisters* (London: Bristol Classical Press, 1995), 42.

hanging themselves, or making declarations of love." Instead, "they eat, drink, flirt, talk nonsense."[99]

Chekhov began to experiment with dramatic forms that matched his opinions of theater. But these new forms at first only confused the producers and actors who staged and performed his plays. In 1889, the selection committee for the Aleksandrinsky Theatre in St. Petersburg found his play, *The Wood Demon*, to be "a beautiful dramatization of a novella, but not a play."[100] Alexander Lensky (Moscow's leading actor) boldly told his good friend Chekhov to "write [only] tales. You refer too scornfully to the stage and to dramatic form. You esteem them too little to write a play."[101]

Flouting all advice, Chekhov told Suvorin that he would write his next play, *The Seagull*, by "mercilessly doing away with stage conventions" (21 Oct. 1895). At its 1896 premiere, the play was audibly booed. Selected as a benefit performance for a famous comic actress of the Aleksandrinsky Theatre, *The Seagull* opened to an audience of her fans, who expected broad comedy. The subtlety of Chekhov's new play escaped them. Moreover, critics (who had lobbied against Chekhov's plays) further provoked the crowd's guffaws. Chekhov left the theater midway through the performance, walked the streets in despair, and returned to his home, vowing never to write for the theater again. He told his younger brother, Mikhail, that, "The play flopped, collapsed with a thud. In the theater I felt the burdensome tension of perplexity and shame. [...] The moral is: it's not worth writing plays" (18 Oct. 1896). He immediately stopped the play's publication, and told Suvorin, "It wasn't just my play which failed, it was me. [...][102] I will never forget what happened, just as I could never forget, for example, being slapped in the face" (14 Dec. 1896).

---

[99] Translated by David Allen in *Performing Chekhov* (New York: Routledge, 2000), 4.

[100] A. P. Chekhov, *Sobranie sochinenii* [Collected Works], Vol. 9 (Moscow: Izdatel'stvo khudozhestvennoi literatury, 1956), 475. *The Wood Demon* [*Leshii*] can be found in A. P. Chekhov, *Polnoe sobranie sochinenii i pisem v tridtsati tomakh* [The Complete Works and Letters in Thirty Volumes], Vol. 12 (Moscow: Nauka, 1978).

[101] Cited and translated by Simmons, *Chekhov*, 197.

[102] In these words, Chekhov may have been thinking as much about how he had personally handled the people who had been his models for the play as about artistry. See Donald Rayfield's opinion in *Understanding Chekhov* about *The Seagull* as an "an instrument for putting others at a distance" (136-7).

Even so, admiration lurked behind the abuse. At least one member of the selection committee had been thrilled with *The Wood Demon*. The leading St. Petersburg actor, Pavel Svobodin, praised Chekhov's "life-like figures, living speech, and characters, which are beyond the whole Aleksandrinsky trash."[103] At least one playwright saw something new and exciting in *The Seagull*. When Vladimir Nemirovich-Danchenko won the coveted Griboyedov Prize for drama in 1897, "I told the judges that [...] the prize should be given to *The Seagull*. [...] The judges did not agree with me."[104] All the same, Nemirovich-Danchenko's insight into Chekhov's play would soon help turn the tide of opinion, when the new company he founded with Stanislavsky—the Moscow Art Theatre—would match Chekhov's dramatic innovations with fresh new ideas on theatrical production.

The playwright Nemirovich-Danchenko and the actor Stanislavsky co-founded the Moscow Art Theatre in 1897 in order to reform worn-out conventions in nineteenth-century theatrical productions. They had costumes and sets designed to suit the plays they staged instead of using stock items; thus the entire production team brought a unified vision to bear on each play. They rehearsed their productions until they got them right, a discipline rarely found on Russia's other stages which assembled actors only for a few rehearsals prior to first performances. Above all, Nemirovich-Danchenko and Stanislavsky instituted a new commitment to ensemble acting, where stars did not predominate; the Moscow Art Theatre actors played in concert with each other, always striving to serve the artistry of the play.[105]

Beginning in 1898 with a radically innovative production of *The Seagull* directed by Stanislavsky (Chapter 6), the Moscow Art Theatre turned Chekhov into a world famous playwright. Moreover, the company also introduced him to the West. Not only did Russian theater audiences see Chekhov through the eyes of the Muscovite company, but so did European and American spectators. First in 1906, and then in 1923-4,

---

[103] Simmons, *Chekhov*, 198.

[104] Vladimir Nemirovitch-Dantchenko [*sic*], *My Life in the Russian Theatre* (Boston: Little Brown, and Co., 1937), 71.

[105] This company, arguably the most important theatrical enterprise in the twentieth century, was the breeding ground for the now globally famous Stanislavsky System of actor training. For more see Carnicke, *Stanislavsky in Focus*.

the Art Theatre took their Chekhov productions on tour. No wonder that Chekhov's name will forever be linked to that of Stanislavsky and the Moscow Art Theatre!

While Chekhov did not need the Moscow Art Theatre to become a famous writer, he did need them to become an influential dramatist. In return, Chekhov offered precisely what the company's co-founders needed: the financial stability that comes with sold-out houses and a new kind of writing that could make their theatrical ideals stunningly visible. His colloquial language, sound effects taken from daily life, and tightly knit groups of characters were in close sympathy with the newly founded company's goals. Marrying Chekhov's dramatic vision with the Moscow Art Theatre's innovations made theater history. Today, it is as hard to imagine a dramatic tradition without Anton Chekhov as it is to teach acting without reference to Konstantin Stanislavsky.

By 1898 the newly founded Moscow Art Theatre had opened to critical acclaim, but it was struggling financially. Nemirovich-Danchenko realized that *The Seagull*, with its novel structure and a leading character who calls for "new forms" in theatrical art, would be perfect for their company. More significantly, Nemirovich-Danchenko also realized that Chekhov's apparent failure as a playwright had less to do with the author's ignorance of stage convention and more to do with standard productions that did not support his fresh conception of drama. For example, the first production of *Ivanov* (1889) "left not a trace in the theater because there was nothing strictly 'Chekhovian' about it. [...For this production,] the favorite actors had scored a success: it was pleasant to see them again in other attire and in other make-up,"[106] and that was all. In short, Chekhov suffered from "routine success." As Nemirovich-Danchenko writes of an 1897 production of *Uncle Vanya* in the Ukrainian city of Odessa:

> The public applauded, the actors were called before the curtain, but with the end of the performance came also the end of the play's life; the spectators did not bear away with them any intensely lived experience; the play did not awaken them to a new understanding of things. I repeat: there was nothing of that new reflection of life which a new poet had brought to his play.[107]

---

[106] Nemirovitch-Dantchenko [*sic*], *My Life in the Russian Theatre*, 22-3.
[107] Ibid., 50.

In April 1898 Nemirovich-Danchenko began an aggressive campaign to persuade Chekhov to give the Moscow Art Theatre permission to stage *The Seagull*. But Chekhov was unwilling; he was still deeply pained by its St. Petersburg premiere. Nemirovich-Danchenko argued that "a conscientious production" of *The Seagull* "without banalities will thrill the audience." He promised Chekhov just such a production. "Perhaps the play won't get bursts of applause, but a real production with *fresh talents, free of routine,* will be a triumph of art, I guarantee that."[108] Chekhov relented in June and in September Stanislavsky began to create his directorial plan for the play in consultation with his partner.

The Moscow Art Theatre production opened after a record number of twenty-four regular and three dress rehearsals on 17 December 1898. Yet, the company was still not confident in their work. Nemirovich-Danchenko vividly recalls the tense mood backstage as the first act curtain closed:

> There was a silence, a complete silence both in the theater and on the stage, it was as though all held their breath, as though no one quite understood [what they had seen...]. This mood lasted quite a long time, so long indeed that those on stage decided that the first act had failed, failed so completely that not a single friend in the audience dared applaud. [...] Then suddenly, in the auditorium something happened. It was as if a dam had burst, or a bomb had exploded—all at once there was a deafening crash of applause from all: from friends and from enemies.[109]

The performance had made theatrical history, and, to this day, a simple sketch of a seagull brands the Moscow Art Theatre's work.

Following the success of *The Seagull*, the Moscow Art company naturally assumed that Chekhov had joined them. But, unbeknownst to the company, he had submitted *Uncle Vanya* (1899) to their competitor, the Maly Theatre. Only when the Maly rejected it did Chekhov decide to place his fate squarely in Stanislavsky's and Nemirovich-Danchenko's hands. From that point on, Chekhov became a Moscow Art Theatre

---

[108] Nemirovich-Danchenko, *Tvorcheskoe nasledie* [Creative Legacy], letter to A. P. Chekhov, 25 April 1898, Vol. I, 165-6; the italics are Nemirovich-Danchenko's.

[109] Nemirovitch-Dantchenko [*sic*], *My Life in the Russian Theatre*, 187-8.

3. Anton Chekhov and Olga Knipper as newlyweds, 1901.

playwright. With Chekhov's marriage in 1901 to Olga Leonardovna Knipper (1868-1959), who was an acting student under Nemirovich-Danchenko and a founding member of the Moscow Art Theatre, Chekhov forged more than a professional link with the young and enthusiastic company. (Illustration 3) He had first admired her acting in 1897. She then took note of him during rehearsals for *The Seagull*, in which she played the leading role of Arkadina. When she took on the role of the beautiful Yelena in *Uncle Vanya*, their mutual interest in one another turned into a serious relationship. From that point on, Chekhov created his last two plays, *Three Sisters* (1900) and *The Cherry Orchard* (1904), for the company and with specific actors in mind for specific roles. His wife premiered as Masha (*Three Sisters*) and Ranyevskaya (*The Cherry Orchard*).

Like all marriages, however, Chekhov's relationship with the Moscow Art Theatre had its ups and downs. Chekhov often disagreed with the company's two directors about their casting and directorial decisions concerning his plays (Chapter 6). Nonetheless, Chekhov's plays might well have been forever overshadowed by his fiction, had it not been for the Moscow Art Theatre.

To conclude this brief introduction to Chekhov's life and career, I underline a few key points: Chekhov was an utterly private man, making it hard to know him; his family bred in him loyalty, restraint, and compassion; he continued to value his training in and his practice of medicine, even when literature rewarded him more publicly and more lucratively; he enjoyed the stance of distanced observer both in his social life and in his art, even as he actively accomplished a great deal of civic work as a doctor over the years; and his success in drama was harder won than in fiction. These points lay a firm foundation for understanding his radically innovative drama.

Chapter Two

The Literary Soil for Chekhov's Drama

At the turn of the twentieth century, Chekhov created a paradigm shift in drama that is still pertinent today. First, his plays opened the stage door to the notion that characters often think what they do not say. Their unspoken thoughts have come to be called "subtext." In fact, Chekhov's characters often betray themselves more fully through the ways in which they speak (their linguistic behaviors) than in the semantic meanings of their words.

Second, Chekhov puts offstage the obvious moments of crises in his characters' lives—like auctions, murders, and suicides. On the surface nothing much seems to happen in his plays, prompting critics to call his drama plotless with zero-endings. Simultaneously Chekhov concentrates on the subtle, interactive dance that occurs whenever people try to communicate with each other in ordinary circumstances. He makes stage worthy the nearly invisible movements of his characters' minds and souls during the tedium of their daily lives. In other words, he transforms traditional stage action into what the director Stanislavsky calls "inner action."

Third, Chekhov shifts away from traditional nineteenth-century tenets of comedy, tragedy, and melodrama to a uniquely modern perspective that finds absurdity in life's tragedies and humor in the odd eccentricities of people. In so doing, his plays often provoke "laughter through tears," another phrase commonly used to describe the emotional impact of his drama. His famous persistence in calling *The Cherry Orchard* a comedy, when everyone around him insisted upon its tragic dimensions, speaks directly to the shift of genre that he initiated.

These three central Chekhovian notions—subtext, inner action, and laughter-through-tears—launched modern drama with "boldness and originality," two traits that Chekhov claimed as important to his work (citation below).

Chekhov's innovations in fiction provided rich soil for his radical experimentation with drama. Before writing his major plays, he had

already explored in his stories the power of subtext, the interesting tedium of daily life, and the paradoxical mood of laughing through tears.
Moreover, because Chekhov so deliberately crafted his stories, he was
highly aware of his storytelling methods. After the famous critic Grigorovich had provoked Chekhov into taking his talent as a writer seriously
(Chapter 1), he began to value and perfect his craft. "It's not important
what one's views, convictions, or worldview are—everyone these days
has that—it's important to have a *method*," he stressed. "Method constitutes half of talent" (to A. N. Pleshcheev, 6 Mar. 1888). In a letter to his
eldest brother, Alexander, Chekhov describes his "method" as consist-
ing of six primary principles of writing:

> (1) no politico-socio-economic long-winded jargon; (2) utter ob-
> jectivity; (3) truthfulness in the description of people and objects;
> (4) strict brevity; (5) boldness and originality, always fleeing from
> clichés; (6) compassion. (10 May 1886)

When Chekhov turned his attention to drama, he transferred to the
stage the three central notions and the six storytelling principles that
had grounded his fiction. In short, Chekhov's drama was born in part
from his narrative fiction. The producers, directors, and actors of Russia's famed imperial theaters immediately recognized Chekhov's fictional traits in his plays, but they did not value what they saw. He seemed a
good writer with few playwriting skills. The selection committee for the
Aleksandrinsky Theatre found *The Wood Demon* to be "a beautiful dramatization of a novella, but not a play;"[1] and the famous Maly theater actor
Alexander Lensky told Chekhov that "you refer too scornfully to the
stage and to dramatic form [...] to write a play"[2] (Chapter 1). Granted,
Chekhov had not yet perfected his new dramatic vision in the plays
that these theater elites had rejected, but even so they had completely
missed the potential in Chekhov's fiction to unlock something entirely
new for the stage.

In this chapter, I start, as did Chekhov, by examining how his methods in fiction can illuminate his innovations in drama. By doing so, much
that is useful in the staging of his plays can be gleaned, particularly in

---

[1] A. P. Chekhov, *Sobranie sochinenii* [Collected Works], Vol. 9 (Moscow: Izdatel'stvo
   khudozhestvennoi literatury, 1956), 475.
[2] Translated by Simmons in *Chekhov*, 197.

terms of how he used minute but tellingly important details to create the subtexts and inner action of his characters and to prompt ambivalent emotional reactions in his audiences.

But such an examination also means donning the spectacles of a doctor. "I do not doubt that medical science has had a serious influence on my literary work," Chekhov once told a fellow doctor. "It has significantly broadened the field of my observations and enriched my knowledge in ways that only a doctor can fully appreciate" (to G. I. Rossolimo, 11 Oct. 1899).[3] Revisit the six principle points in the method that Chekhov had outlined for his brother (cited above), and you will find that scientific and literary thinking are married in his work.

FROM THE MEDICAL POINT OF VIEW

What is it in Chekhov's stories and plays that "only a doctor can appreciate"? Recently I ran across a book on ballet written by a Russian doctor in the mid-twentieth century. Dr. George Borodin justified his unusual decision to write about art in the following words:

> In his day-to-day work, the doctor is always having to sum up people, to ask himself why this person behaves in this way, and that person in that. It is essential for him—and his patients— that he should know why one individual reacts in a certain way to a certain condition, while another, suffering from precisely the same malady, behaves quite differently. He learns quickly and the lesson is never ended, that there is no limit to human diversity.[4]

Dr. Borodin might well have been speaking for Chekhov by explaining that medical training develops two important habits of mind: the careful observation of symptoms and sensitivity to how each individual patient's case differs from textbook generalizations. Close attention to details and the assumption that every individual is unique are literary perspectives that Chekhov honed in his fiction and also applied to his

---

[3] For reactions of doctors to Chekhov's stories, see "Seminar in Medical Humanities" in Finke and Sherbinin, eds., *Chekhov the Immigrant*, 271-344.

[4] George Borodin, *This Thing Called Ballet* (London: Macdonald and Co, Ltd., 1945), xiv.

drama. Therefore, these two medical habits of mind become as necessary to readers and actors who wish to understand his works, as they are to doctors who treat patients.

In the first case, Chekhov's pleasure in observing others (Chapter 1) and his diagnostic talent as a doctor made him keenly aware of the importance of seemingly insignificant details. These are the sources of two of his six principles: his "utter objectivity" and his descriptive "truthfulness" (cited above). As an artist, he pays attention to things that others might deem trivial. Additionally, in medical school he had become fascinated with advancements in psychiatry, which further prompted him to present to the reader easily overlooked aspects of his characters' language, behavior, and interactions as important clues to their hidden thinking and inner emotional lives. In so doing, Chekhov also invites us to diagnose the ills of his characters' souls in precisely the same way that doctors diagnose physical illnesses, by observing the outward symptoms closely. Examples from his plays abound. Masha's whistle in *Three Sisters* and Masha's snuff in *The Seagull* betoken their heartaches. In *The Cherry Orchard*, Gayev's obsession with playing imaginary games of billiards whenever emotional matters are about to erupt demonstrates his inability to face reality. Andrey's gambling in *Three Sisters*, Astrov's drinking in *Uncle Vanya*, and Lomov's hypochondria in *The Proposal* (Chapter 4) are telling symptoms of their inner lives. As Boris Eichenbaum wrote in 1944:

> The genius of [Chekhov's] diagnoses lay not only in that they were accurate, brilliant, and convincing, but also that he made them on the backs of the most imperceptible, minute symptoms.[5]

In the second case, Chekhov's understanding of how typical diseases can produce different symptoms in individual patients prompted him to avoid stereotypes in his characters, even when he simultaneously saw them as typical of their classes, genders, and professions. From this sensitivity stems his principle of "compassion" for others (cited above). As translator Richard Pevear rightly notes, Chekhov's characters are "sharply observed types—the darling, the explainer, the fidget, the student, the

---

[5] Boris Eichenbaum, "Chekhov at Large," in Robert Louis Jackson, ed., *Chekhov: A Collection of Critical Essays* (Englewood Cliffs: Prentice-Hall, Inc., 1967), 27.

malefactor,"[6] etc. But it is also true that each "type" in Chekhov's mature writing is simultaneously a uniquely surprising individual. Chekhov does not paint generalized portraits of students, landowners, servants, teachers, doctors, Christians or Jews. Instead, he introduces us to specific individuals: Trofimov (*The Cherry Orchard*), a revolutionary student in love with the daughter of a landowner; Lyubov Ranyevskaya (*The Cherry Orchard*), a landowner whose property is as much a burden to her as a joy; Firs (*The Cherry Orchard*), a servant who ironically longs for the good old days of slavery; Kulygin (*Three Sisters*), a pedantic teacher who loves his wife so dearly that he silently forgives her for her adultery; Dr. Astrov (*Uncle Vanya*), whose passion for saving the environment exceeds his dedication to medicine; the Christian theology student, Ivan Velikopolsky ("The Student") who falters in his faith; and the Jewish Anna Petrovna (*Ivanov*), who is disowned by her parents for having married a Christian. Chekhov's men and women are complex, multifaceted people.

Additionally, some scholars have suggested that Chekhov learned his principles of "strict brevity" and "utter objectivity" (cited above) from scientific papers and autopsy reports. As early as 1914, the Russian critic Leonid Grossman observed how Chekhov delights in "the matter-of-fact style of a report, because it interprets elementary things coldly and simply, and like a good textbook tries to be precise."[7] Medical writing and Chekhov's stories alike are characteristically brief and to the point, including only those details that are necessary to the task at hand, and avoiding any indulgence in picturesque or emotional flourishes. There results an extreme economy of means. He always worked with a scalpel's precision, cutting mercilessly any detail he deemed superfluous to his stories and his plays. Those details that remain are densely rich and loaded. Moreover, he explains how he distinguished the necessary from the unnecessary elements in his writings.

> I can write only from memory. I have never written directly from nature. I need to have my memory work on the subject like a filter, so that what remains in my memory, as on a filter, is only what is important or typical. (to F. D. Batiushkov, 15 Dec. 1897)

---

[6] Richard Pevear, "Introduction," in Anton Chekhov, *Stories*, trans. Pevear and Volokhonsky, x.
[7] Leonid Grossman, "The Naturalism of Chekhov," in Jackson, ed., *Chekhov*, 32. See also Williames, *Anton Chekhov, The Iconoclast*, 2.

In Chekhov's stories and plays there is virtually nothing, not one word, that is irrelevant to the whole. Everything comments on something, or expresses something. Everything relates to everything else. For example, during rehearsals for *Uncle Vanya*, Chekhov criticized Stanislavsky for assuming that the title character wears boots and work clothes simply because he manages the estate. "'Listen,' [Chekhov] said getting annoyed, 'everything is written down. You haven't read the play.'" Stanislavsky searched through the text, but could find nothing more than an apparently off-hand comment in a stage direction in Act I about a "stylish tie" (trans. Carnicke, 117). When the puzzled director asked the author to explain, Chekhov said, Vanya "has a wonderful tie; he is an elegant, cultured man. It's not true, that all landowners go around in muddy boots. They are educated people, they dress well, they go to Paris. I wrote all that."[8] This anecdote demonstrates how important the smallest item, like a tie, could be to Chekhov.

I squarely confronted Chekhov's richly dense tapestry of details while translating his plays. The tedious, close, close reading, necessary to the work of rendering Russian into English, reveals how intricately interrelated are all the various details in his plays. This tightly woven fabric is what allows readers and audiences to revisit Chekhov's works (both stories and plays) time after time, always finding something new within them.

I still make discoveries that surprise me, whenever I reread his plays, as do my colleagues. For example, in a recent rehearsal of *Three Sisters*, Milton Justice (Chapter 1) saw Olga's opening remarks about her father's death in a new light, when his cast considered the fact that the traditional mourning period for the loss of a family member is one year long.

> Father died exactly a year ago, this very day, the fifth of May, on your name day Irina. It was very cold. It snowed then. I thought I wouldn't live through it. You fainted and lay there like a corpse. But you see, a year has passed, we can think about it easily, you can wear a white dress already, your face is shining... (trans. Carnicke, 169)

For the first time in one year the sisters no longer need to wear black as a token of their loss; and so Olga wears her blue teacher's uniform and Irina dresses in white. Masha alone remains dressed in mourning.

---

[8] Stanislavskii, *Sobranie sochinenii* [Collected Works], Vol. 1, 300.

In light of this cultural reference, Olga's words no longer seem a sadly self-indulgent, nostalgic recollection, serving merely as expository information for the audience. Her words now become a gentle reminder to Masha or an implicit reproach of her for her inappropriate attire. Olga is embedded from the first in the interactive dynamics of Chekhov's subtle play. The actress who does not recognize how Olga's words are directed toward Masha risks an overly sentimental or bland performance.

4. The character actor, Alexander Artyom, as Dr. Chebutykin in *Three Sisters*, 1901. One of Chekhov's favorite actors, Artyom also played the roles of Shamrayev (*The Seagull*), Telegin (*Uncle Vanya*), and Firs (*The Cherry Orchard*).

Similarly, another of my colleagues, R. Andrew White (Valparaiso University), suddenly realized in rehearsing the same play that the alcoholic Chebutykin (Illustration 4) is so drunk when he breaks the sisters' precious clock in Act III, that later in Act IV he cannot remember having done so. With this realization, one of Chebutykin's most puzzling lines comes into sharp focus: "We are not here, nothing is here on this earth, we don't exist but only think we exist... And so it's all the same, isn't it!" (trans. Carnicke, 230) While one might seek existential philosophy in his words, they can also register as quite literally true to a man whose drunken binges leave him with significant lapses in memory. This latter interpretation, however, only becomes possible when the tapestry of details in the play is closely and thoughtfully examined.

There remains one major way in which Chekhov's medical mind influences his artistic sensibility. Like any good doctor, he examines his characters' outward symptoms, leaving all moralizing about their personalities aside. He avoids intervening in his readers' processes of diagnoses. He does not tell us what to think or how to feel. He merely sets forth his characters' symptoms and their specific traits and lets us draw our own conclusions. Thus, he follows his cardinal principle and sidesteps "politico-socio-economic long-winded jargon" (cited above). When attacked for his habitual lack of commentary by his friend and editor, Suvorin, Chekhov defended himself with the following words:

> You upbraid me for my objectivity, calling it an indifference to good and evil [...]. You want me, when I depict horse-thieves, to say: stealing horses is evil. But surely, everyone knows that without my saying so. Let a jury judge them; my business is only to show them as they are. [... As I write,] I must speak and think in their tones of voice, I must feel as they do [...]. When I write, I rely on my readers, I assume that they will fill in the subjective elements in my story. (1 April 1890)

If we expect literature to illuminate the ills of society or teach us how to live, then Chekhov's stories and plays do indeed seem wanting. If, however we understand that our job as reader and audience is to pay attention to the characters and to "fill in the subjective elements," then Chekhov's works become endlessly fascinating.

In surveying his works, one notices that Chekhov also avoids all obvious emotional commentary. The seemingly objective and unemotional tone of his writing paradoxically creates strong emotional reactions in his readers. Precisely because Chekhov does not indulge in authorial pity for his characters and instead provokes empathy by letting the simple facts of the case speak for themselves, the impact of his stories are all the stronger and more vivid. Chekhov exposes this narrative strategy to the writer Lidia Avilova, who peppered her prose with tears and emotional outbursts. "When you depict a luckless victim of misfortune and want the reader to feel pity for him," Chekhov advises her, "then try to be colder—it provides a kind of backdrop for another's grief against which it stands out like a sculptural relief" (19 Mar. 1892).

Such backdrops are readily visible in Chekhov's stories. For example, in "Misery" (1886), Chekhov describes one night in an old cab driver's life, during which he picks up a number of passengers with whom he attempts unsuccessfully to talk about the recent death of his son. When the cabdriver returns home, all are asleep and so he still cannot speak of his loss. In despair, he goes out to the stable where he at last tells his horse all about how his son died. The cab driver's nearly inexpressible grief registers as all the more heart wrenching in light of Chekhov's lack of emotional commentary.[9]

Chekhov's penchant for avoiding authorial commentary functions especially well in drama, where characters generally speak for themselves from their own points of view without a narrator's intervention. Olga's words at the opening of *Three Sisters* (cited above) serve as a sufficient example. She, like Chekhov, points only to the fact that the year-long mourning period has ended, that time has passed, that she and her sisters are not as they once were, and that Irina now wears white. It is up to her sisters and the audience to infer that Olga's words mask her chiding of Masha.

Chekhov's lack of obvious emotional commentary suits a long tradition in the theater, which teaches actors that tears in one's own eyes are less important than tears in the audience's eyes. As early as 1773, the French philosopher Denis Diderot famously wrote in *The Paradox of the*

---

9 "Toska," in A. P. Chekhov, *Polnoe sobranie sochinenii i pisem v tridtsati tomakh* [The Complete Works and Letters in Thirty Volumes], Vol. 4 (Moscow: Nauka, 1976), 326-30. For an English translation, see "Misery," in Ralph E. Matlaw, ed., *Anton Chekhov's Short Stories: Texts of the Stories, Backgrounds, Criticism* (New York: W. W. Norton and Company, 1979), 12-6.

Actor, "People come [to the theater] not to see tears, but to hear speeches that draw tears."[10] Nearly three hundred years later, John Barton (the director of London's Royal Shakespeare Company) similarly cautioned actors to keep emotion in check, so that the audience might better feel the emotional moment. "If [the actor] goes for passion only, he will almost certainly be overlaying something on top of the text," Barton teaches. "The moral is that it's sometimes more important to make the text resonate than to be moved oneself."[11] Chekhov would clearly concur with both of these theatrical thinkers.

Given the absence of judgment and emotional commentary in his stories, Chekhov can easily strike the reader as somehow absent from his own works. He hides his opinions from us, forcing us to form opinions of our own. His absence is mere illusion, however. The details in his works, like the pieces of a puzzle, fit together into complete pictures that eventually reveal Chekhov's authorial presence within his masterful craft. Ilya Ehrenburg puts it best: Chekhov's "message lies in his art,"[12] that is to say in the patterns, structures, words, juxtapositions of images, etc., etc.—in short, in all the tiny details—that he carefully selects for inclusion in his stories and plays. Seen from this angle, Chekhov is quite present in his writings. His attitudes and opinions can be found in the rich pattern of details that always add up to more than the sum of the parts. As the American theater critic, John Gassner, puts it, "Chekhov is passionate in both his scorn and his sympathy even when he displays a cool surface of naturalistic objectivity."[13]

The hidden Chekhov emerges when the reader fits the individual puzzle pieces together into the whole picture. Indeed, Virginia Llewellyn Smith understates the case, when she writes, "A full appreciation of Chekhov's work requires of the reader a certain degree of involvement."[14] I would say that a full appreciation requires the reader to pay focused attention to everything, absolutely everything that

---

[10] Denis Diderot, *The Paradox of the Actor*, and William Archer, *Masks or Faces?* (New York: Hill and Wang, 1957), 68.

[11] John Barton, *Playing Shakespeare* (London: Methuen, 1986), 138, 145.

[12] Ilya Ehrenburg, *Chekhov, Stendhal, and Other Essays* (London: MacGibbon & Kee, 1962), 13.

[13] John Gassner, "The Duality of Chekhov," in Jackson, ed., *Chekhov*, 177-8.

[14] Virginia Llewellyn Smith, "The Lady with the Dog," in Eekman, ed., *Critical Essays on Anton Chekhov*, 121.

Chekhov put down on paper. Just as Chekhov expected Stanislavsky to pay attention to Vanya's elegant tie, so too does Chekhov expect his readers to do their work. If we want a play to be obvious in its messages and intentions, then indeed Chekhov will leave us cold. If, however, we understand that our job as audience is to pay attention and "fill in the subjective elements" (cited above), then Chekhov's plays become endlessly fascinating.

"THE STUDENT": A READING[15]

I now turn to a case study of Chekhov's devilishly short but richly dense story, "The Student" (1894). I invite you to read it by putting on a doctor's diagnostic spectacles. Bear with me as I take you slowly through the development of the story by tracing some of its most telling details. In the process, you will see how the puzzle fits and the intention behind the story emerges.

While less familiar than stories like "The House with the Mezzanine" (1896) and "The Lady with the Little Dog" (1899),[16] "The Student" contains virtually all of Chekhov's most important narrative techniques. Thus, it serves as an excellent guide to the kind of close reading that Chekhov demands of his readers and his actors.

As with nearly all of Chekhov's works, "The Student" has elicited both positive and negative criticism. While American poet and novelist Conrad Aiken viewed Chekhov as "possibly the greatest writer of the short story who ever lived,"[17] the writer George P. Elliot saw "The Student" as

---

[15] "Student," in A. P. Chekhov, *Polnoe Sobranie sochinenii i pisem v tridtsati tomakh* [The Complete Works and Letters in Thirty Volumes], Vol. 8 (Moscow: Nauka, 1977), 306-9. It was first published on 16 April 1894 in *The Russian News* (*Russkie vedomosti*). I am indebted to two particular analyses of "The Student," which prompted much of my thinking: Nathan Rosen, "Chekhov's Religion in 'The Student,'" *The Bulletin of the North American Chekhov Society* 14, no. 1(Fall, 2006), 1-9; and Rayfield, *Understanding Chekhov*, 131-4.

[16] "Dom c mezaninom" in Chekhov, *Polnoe sobranie sochinenii* [The Complete Works], Vol. 9, 174-92; "Dama s sobachkoi" in Chekhov, *Polnoe sobranie sochinenii* [The Complete Works], Vol. 10, 128-43.

[17] Thomas A. Eekman, "Introduction," in Eekman, ed., *Critical Essays on Anton Chekhov*, 4.

"rank[ing] quite low in the Chekhov canon."[18] In contrast, other Chekhov admirers place the story much, much higher on their lists of favorites. Michael Finke describes it as a "brief masterpiece,"[19] and Donald Rayfield calls it "a perfect example in miniature of Chekhov's art."[20]

In Chekhov's day, Russian critics often reprimanded him for his pessimism. In their eyes, he exposed the ills of society without offering any social solutions in his prose. Chekhov countered their view of him by pointing to "The Student," which is an uplifting parable about the power of storytelling to connect people and create joy. "What kind of pessimist am I? After all, my favorite story, from all that I have written, is 'The Student.'"[21]

A close study of "The Student" readily reveals how Chekhov buttresses his keen observational skills with his deft handling of narrative voice and his careful use of names and literary allusions to broaden the scope of his work. Thus, Chekhov manages to say more in his four-page story than the words would seem to convey upon first read.

The tale begins when a young divinity student feels a chill in the weather as night falls. A woodcock flies by and the sound of a shot rings out, suggesting that a hunt is on. Using an apparently distanced third-person narration, Chekhov seems to be writing a conventional story with a more or less omniscient narrator. But he plants seeds of doubt by using adjectives that imply human judgments: the wind is "unwelcome," the forest "inhospitable."[22] Recall, for a moment, that in "The Lady with the Little Dog," nature's indifference to human life had consoled Gurov (Chapter 1). By contrast, in "The Student" nature seems to care how cold and anxious the protagonist feels. Thus, despite the fact that Chekhov writes the story in a third-person voice, canny readers already suspect that the story's narrator is also its protagonist. Moreover, despite the passive voice that describes the shot as occurring of its own volition, the adverbs "boomingly and merrily" suggest that someone, no doubt

---

18 George P. Elliott, "Warm Heart, Cold Eye," in Ibid., 60.

19 Finke, *Seeing Chekhov*, 160.

20 Rayfield, *Understanding Chekhov*, 134.

21 Chekhov's words as related by I. Bunin, *Polnoe sobranie sochinenii* [Complete Collected Works], Vol. 6 (Petersburg: A. Marks, 1915), 299.

22 In my analysis below, I quote the translation by Pevear and Volokhonsky in *Anton Chekhov, Stories*, 263-6. I do not give the specific pages for quotations because the story is so short that the reader will have no trouble locating them.

the protagonist, has been actively enjoying the hunt. By the end of the story's first paragraph, the reader understands that the title character has been enjoying a hunt until the chill wind curtails his day. "It felt like winter," not only outside but also in the student's chilled mood. Chekhov's use of third person narrative to convey a first-person perspective is one of his most famous storytelling techniques.

A glance at the first paragraph in the Russian original also reveals the great care with which Chekhov uses the simplest words. The verb (*dulo*), which describes an eerie sound like "blowing into an empty bottle," reverberates again later in the paragraph when the icy wind also "blew" (*podul*). Similarly, the verb that marks the passage of a woodcock (*protianul*) also echoes in the movement (*protianulis'*) of the ice. These two small examples already suggest how precisely and musically Chekhov writes. In addition, Chekhov uses the repetition of simple words to characterize an individual's unique voice. The student's mood changes from merry to desolate, but his consistent vocabulary betrays a single mind.

As the student treads reluctantly home, two brief images flash through his mind: his mother on the floor "barefoot" cleaning the empty samovar and his father lying down "coughing" (a common symptom of tuberculosis). These details expose the protagonist's dire poverty, explain why his coat does not keep out the cold, and demonstrate why he travels home reluctantly. The images even imply how his thoughts of home, as much as the wind, may have chilled his mood.

In this second paragraph, we also learn that the story takes place on Good Friday—a holy day in the Russian Orthodox Church that commemorates Christ's death by crucifixion through prayer and fasting from food. The student has been dutifully fasting; he is "painfully hungry." In this hunger he seems a good Christian, as well we might expect from a divinity student. But the fact that he has been out hunting simultaneously undermines him. Would a good Christian go hunting on Good Friday? The skeptical reader now understands that the passive way in which the shot was earlier described exposes the student's sense of his own guilt for having had his fun on this somber holy day. If his conscience were entirely clear, his sentence would have been more direct and active. "He took a shot at a woodcock" would appear in the story instead of "a woodcock chirred by, and a shot rang out boomingly and merrily in the spring air." Given the poverty of his family, coupled with his well-hidden twinge of guilt about having gone hunting, one might even suspect that the student's fast is less ardently religious than one had initially thought. Such suspicion may well bring a Chekhovian smile of irony to our lips.

On his way home, the student encounters two widows in a garden, who are washing a pot and spoons. As he warms his hands by their fire, they converse. After a time, the student tells the women the biblical story of the apostle Peter, who, despite his devotion to Christ, denies knowing Him three times during the night of Good Friday.[23] This story-within-the-story constitutes the central and longest part of "The Student."

The transition from the student's journey home to this garden, however, involves a lapse in narrative continuity. As the second paragraph ends, the student sees the garden in the distance: "Only by the widows' gardens near the river was there a light burning." At the start of the third paragraph, the student is already in the widows' presence. Chekhov has not chosen to describe how the student got there. Is the garden simply on his way? Or has he made a detour? In either case, the student's visit with the widows delays his return, and thus fulfills his desire, stated at the end of the preceding paragraph: "he did not want to go home."

A host of telling details emerges in this central part of "The Student," alas, too many to follow all of them here. There is the garden that recalls the biblical Garden of Gethsemane, where Christ prays before his arrest by Roman soldiers. There is a descending and ascending journey of the student toward his home, recalling not only Christ's crucifixion and resurrection, but also Dante's *Divine Comedy* (with its descent into the abyss and its ascent into joy). There is the fire of hearth, hell and salvation. There are the male workers (*rabotniki*) on the far bank who stand in contrapuntal opposition to the two women. The men recall those in the New Testament, who arrest, beat, and finally crucify Christ; the student makes this specific association when he calls both groups of men "workers" (*rabotniki*). To trace all these details thoroughly would make an all too unwieldy chapter, significantly longer than the story itself. As the Russian writer Korney Chukovsky asserts, "In general every Chekhov story is so laconic and so consistently concentrated, and its forms are so many-layered, that if someone wanted to comment on any of them, the

---

[23] The New Testament references in the story are the following: Luke 22:33-4 and 56-62; Matthew 26:34-5 and 69-75; Mark 14:29-30 and 66-72; and John 18:15-9 and 25-7.

comment would be much longer than the text."[24] I will therefore focus primarily on how Chekhov individualizes the two women and depicts the student's reaction to them.

The women are mother and daughter, both of them widowed. The older woman is tall, stout, and wears a man's coat. She speaks well because she has worked as a nurse for an aristocratic family and has learned manners. Her pasted-on smile is one such manner. The younger woman is "pock-marked" with a "slightly stupid face." She was beaten by her husband (*zabitaia muzhem*) and looks at the student with the uncomprehending expression of a "deaf-mute." In sum, both women carry the visible signs of their sufferings: the older woman's "dignified smile" and oversized coat seem to serve as armor, protecting her from further pain; the younger woman's face is pitted by illness and scarred with a nearly senseless expression caused by her husband's beatings.

Since the narration takes place through the student's consciousness, the selection of details about the two women also reveals further information about him. He seems to think that their washing of a pot and spoons means that they have broken the Good Friday fast. "Evidently," he thinks, "they had only just finished supper." The student obliquely voices his criticism of such unholy behavior by questioning their attendance at church for the day's Bible readings. "I expect," he says, more than asks, "you've been to the Twelve Gospels?" When the older woman replies, "I have," he launches into his story about Peter, which forms a major part of the Good Friday readings. This behavior suggests that the student disbelieves her answer. Why else would he feel the need to reiterate the Gospel lesson? His story seems to chide the women for their lapse of faith. Moreover, by preaching he also demonstrates his knowledge as a divinity student and rehearses his future career as a preacher. The picture that emerges is that of a young, rather arrogant adolescent, drawn by Chekhov's keen sense of comic irony. In short, "The Student" pokes fun at the arrogance of youth.

If the story-within-the story begins as an implicit criticism of the student's listeners, it ends quite differently. Something unexpected happens as the story unfolds. While the student uses traditional biblical language at times (as when he uses the Old Church Slavonic word *petel* for the cock that crows in testimony of Peter's third denial of Jesus), the

---

[24] Cited and translated by Williames, *Anton Chekhov, The Iconoclast*, 66.

student more frequently turns to common Russian words. Notably he refers to the scourging of Christ as a simple beating. They "beat" (*bili*) Christ, says the student twice. At the second repetition, the younger woman "abandoned" her washing "and turned her fixed gaze on the student." The word catches hold of her and echoes her own reality as a "beaten" wife; it unlocks her comprehension. She seems to empathize with the beaten Christ.

Glancing down the page in Russian, one can also see that the student's tone now becomes especially gentle. He uses the double-adjectives and double-adverbs that are common to Russian fairy tales, as if he were speaking tenderly to a child. He describes Peter weeping bitterly-bitterly (*gor'ko-gor'ko*) in the quiet-quiet (*tikhii-tikhii*), dark-dark (*temnyi-temnyi*) garden. The student's now comforting tone provokes his own sigh and sets him "thinking." Perhaps his thoughts have drifted back to his own lapse in judgment that day, when he decided to go hunting. Perhaps he now realizes that he is no better than they who have not fasted. The student, like Peter, seems to realize after the fact that he is weaker in his faith than he professes. As his earlier arrogance cedes to compassion, his tender tone also releases the older woman's "big, abundant tears," as if witnessing her daughter's attentive reaction to the student's story had pierced her armor. All three characters share a deeply felt emotional moment. This communion of shared feeling directly reflects Chekhov's deep compassion for people from all walks of life.

The emotional moment also triggers the epiphany, which the student then experiences at the climax of the story after he bids the women good-bye. As he continues home, "joy suddenly stirred in his soul, and he even stopped for a moment to catch his breath." The fact that Peter's story had visibly moved both women seems to prove to the student that human experience over the centuries is somehow of a piece. Past and present are palpably linked to each other. This insight is not in itself a new thought. Before meeting the women, he had related his cold and hungry state to the cold and hunger that people in Russia had experienced since the country's founding. "And now, hunching up from the cold, the student thought how exactly the same wind had blown in the time of Rurik [Russia's legendary founder], and of [Ivan] the Terrible, and [Tsar] Peter [the Great, who had opened a window onto Western culture], and in their time there had been the same savage poverty and hunger." Now, in light of the women's reaction to Peter's story, the student reframes his previously oppressive thought more optimistically. "The past, he thought, is connected with the present in an unbroken chain of events flowing one out of the other. And it seemed to him that he had just seen both ends of the chain: he touched one end, and the other moved." One can make a difference, however small it may be, whenever one touches the soul of another in true communication.

Chekhov also points his story toward the future by setting "The Student" on Good Friday. The student's "joy" anticipates Christ's resurrection on Easter Sunday. Chekhov even makes true the prediction in the Russian superstitious saying with which the older widow had first greeted the young man: "You'll be a rich man." Poverty, after all, could be seen in the student's initial state of mind, as readily as in his thin coat. By story's end, however, his coat may still be poor, but he has become rich in spirit: "...and a feeling of youth, health, strength—he was only twenty-two—and an inexpressibly sweet anticipation of happiness [...] filled [him] with lofty meaning."

Only now does Chekhov mention the student's age, prompting the reader to see the student anew. The portrait that now emerges is of a young man full of potential with his whole life ahead of him to do good. In this newly painted portrait Chekhov's deep humanistic belief shines. The student's initial arrogance may be the common sin of youth; but his visit with the two widows shows his ability to learn compassion. He is indeed a "student," not only of theology but also of life.

The reader might now feel that Chekhov's story speaks about how the commonality of human experience can console and lift the spirit. But there is still more to uncover in his dense four-page story.

On closer examination, the student's ability to generalize his experience seems somehow faulty. He concludes that, "If the old woman wept, it was not because he was able to tell [the story] movingly, but because Peter was close to her and she was interested with her whole being in what had happened in Peter's soul." However, earlier details contradict this conclusion. The student has actively changed some of the Bible's original Old Slavonic language into simple Russian, like his substitution of "scourging" with "beating." Moreover, the student has made Peter's state of mind more obviously emotional than in the biblical story through slight distortions of the liturgical texts, which the protagonist (as a divinity student) and Chekhov (as his father's son) would know letter perfect. For example, in the New Testament Christ turns to look at Peter, causing him to remember the prediction that he would betray his Lord. But the Student reverses this gaze. Instead, Peter "look[ed] at Jesus from afar" and then "remembered" the prediction. In the liturgy Christ's look prompts Peter's tears; in the student's story Peter weeps without a prompt. Thus, the student's Peter seems more actively aware of his transgression than does Peter in the Bible.[25]

By choosing words and changing his source, the student has indeed told the story "movingly." It is his word "beaten" (not Peter) that reminds the young widow of herself. Moreover, it is the power of the student's story to move the young widow that brings tears to her mother's eyes, not Peter's historical sufferings as the student surmises. The old woman reacts because her daughter reacts, and neither reaction would have occurred without the student's ability as storyteller. By planting details that contradict the student's conclusion, Chekhov makes us aware that the student himself does not fully appreciate his own gifts.

Chekhov's selection of details further suggests that the student is also unaware of how his own life feeds his creative storytelling. Chekhov has implied throughout his story that the student identifies with Peter's faltering faith. Moreover, in the student's story-within-the-story the sharply drawn emotional portrait of Peter seems more imaginatively alive for both storyteller and listeners than in the Gospel. Consequently, it is not the young widow (as the student thinks) who feels "close" to Peter and "was interested with her whole being in what happened in Peter's soul," but the student himself who feels this particular closeness to Peter. The student went hunting on Good Friday, felt guilty about it, and transmuted his feeling into his art. This additional layer of meaning in "The Student" depends upon Chekhov's trust in his readers to know and interpret literary references to the bible.

But Chekhov also relies upon his readers and audiences to know and interpret literary references more generally. Russian culture actively supported that trust; nineteenth and twentieth-century Russians had an unusually wide and deep familiarity with literature and poetry, often memorizing extensive passages from their favorite works. An émigré teacher of mine would often sit back in her armchair, close her eyes, and recite long passages from *Eugene Onegin*, a novel in verse by the father of modern Russian poetry, Alexander Sergeyevich Pushkin (1799-1837).

---

[25] Rosen, "Chekhov's Religion in 'The Student'," 4.

She was not alone in this pleasurable talent. As Richard Peace writes: "Far more, perhaps, than in any other culture, a writer in Russia can play upon the literary memory of his audience or his readers."[26] Moreover, Tsarist and then Soviet censorship prompted Russian artists to speak through hints and associations; in turn, their audiences developed the ability to find unstated but associative meanings in art. Thus, Russians "have long been attuned to the finer points of oblique statements and innuendo."[27]

In his plays, no less than in his stories, Chekhov employs literary references to great effect. A few examples, such as those to Shakespeare's *Hamlet*, should suffice to illustrate Chekhov's usage.[28] In *The Seagull*, Treplev and Arkadina's arguments over her current sexual relationship parallel those between Hamlet and his mother Gertrude; and Nina presents a clear analogue with Ophelia. Just before Treplev's play-within-the-play, he spars with his mother using quotations from *Hamlet*. Arkadina "recites" from the play accurately: "My son! Thou turnst my eyes into my very soul, and there I see such black and grainèd spots, as will not leave their tinct!" Treplev returns her blow with a distorted version of Hamlet's line: "Why did you then surrender to vice, and seek love in the depths of crime?" (trans. Carnicke, 63) Chekhov could not have made his reference clearer. In *The Cherry Orchard*, he again uses Hamlet and Ophelia as an analogue, this time for Lopakhin's ineffectual behavior with Varya. Lopakhin now distorts Hamlet's lines as he teases Varya: "Ohmelia, get thee to a hermitage..." and "Ohmelia, oh, nymph, remember me in thy prayers!" (trans. Carnicke, 273)

---

[26] Richard Peace, "An Introduction to Chekhov's Plays," in Eekman, ed., *Critical Essays on Anton Chekhov*, 129.

[27] Ibid., 130. Memorization by readers often preserved whole works of literature that were banned from publication and dissemination by Tsarist and Soviet censorship. In the case of Chekhov's premiere director, Konstantin Stanislavsky, whose late experiments in acting were banned by Stalin after 1934, actors' memories of his workshops preserved his ideas until they could re-emerge publicly in the 1960s during Khrushchev's so-called "thaw" in the arts. See Carnicke, *Stanislavsky in Focus*, 94-109.

[28] In my translations of Chekhov's plays, *Chekhov: 4 Plays and 3 Jokes*, I identify literary references in footnotes in order to assist readers, actors, and directors in the interpretation of his texts. Alas, there are far too many to mention them all in this book.

References to other European and Russian authors also abound in Chekhov's plays. In *The Seagull*, Arkadina's lover, the fictionally famous writer Trigorin, is compared to two actually famous authors with whom Chekhov himself was often compared: the French naturalistic writer, Guy de Maupassant (1850-93) and the Russian realistic novelist Ivan Sergeyevich Turgenev (1818-83). In the first case, Dr. Dorn reads a passage aloud to Arkadina from Maupassant's diary of his Mediterranean cruise, *On the Water* (*Sur l'eau*, 1888), about the specific machinations that a woman used to seduce him, machinations that uncomfortably mirror Arkadina's own with regard to Trigorin. No wonder she asks Dorn to stop reading! In the second case, Trigorin, like Chekhov himself, bristles at the comparison with Turgenev. As Trigorin tells Nina, "And when I die, my friends will walk around my grave saying: 'Here lies Trigorin. A good writer, but not as good as Turgenev'" (trans. Carnicke, 82). In *Uncle Vanya*, Professor Serebryakov's craving for the old-fashioned poet Konstantin Nikolayevich Batyushkov (1781-1855, whose lyrics harken back to the eighteenth century) marks the professor as hopelessly out of step with his wife's younger generation. Finally, when Masha in *Three Sisters* recites the opening lines of Alexander Sergeyevich Pushkin's fairy tale poem, *Ruslan and Lyudmila* (1820), about a hero whose wife is abducted by a wizard on their wedding night, she hints at her feelings of oppressive boredom toward her marriage. On stage, she recites under her breath, "On a curved seashore a green oak stood. A golden chain upon that oak. A golden chain upon that oak..." (trans. Carnicke, 174). She speaks no more, but a Russian audience could easily fill in the rest: "...and to the chain is tied a learned tom cat, who circles round and round, day and night. When he moves to the left, he sings a song; when he moves to the right, he tells a tale" (trans. Carnicke, 174 n. 10). Masha, like my émigré teacher and like Chekhov's contemporary audiences, knew much of Pushkin by heart.

By puzzling through all the details (literary and otherwise) in "The Student," by seeing them in relationship to each other, and by considering how some details seem to contradict others, one begins to understand Chekhov's carefully crafted story as a parable about the communicative power of art and its often intuitive creation by the artist. Through the bits of information in his story, Chekhov deftly leads his reader to a conclusion that seems inevitable. Yet his manipulation of the details is so subtle that we can easily feel as if we had reached the conclusion on our own. In this narrative sleight of hand, Chekhov reveals the full mastery of his craft and how he and his point of view can be fully present within the story despite his avoidance of commentary and his much-hailed objectivity. Chekhov employs the same kind of masterful manipulation of details in his plays (Chapter 3) as his caution to Stanislavsky about Vanya's stylish tie demonstrates.

Yet, there is still more to say about Chekhov's craft. Consider his selection of characters' names, sometimes themselves literary references. The student is Ivan Velikopolsky, which can be translated as "John Greatfields." "John" makes him seem at once a common man and an Evangelist (recalling "John" of the New Testament). His surname suits his journey over the fields toward home and simultaneously implies the broad scope of his vision by story's end. The old widow is Vasilisa, a name reminiscent of the Russian fairy tale, "Vasilisa the Beautiful," about an orphaned girl who is comforted by the doll given to her by her late mother.[29] Her name, together with the student's use of fairy tale language to comfort the younger woman, underlines the student's entry into the long tradition of storytelling. The young widow is Lukerya—a common peasant name (and most peasants—as Chekhov well knew from his childhood—beat their wives). Her name also recalls another of the Evangelists, Luke. In short, Chekhov uses both literary references and meaningful names to broaden the associative resonances in his concise writing.

He does the same in his plays. In *The Seagull*, Treplev's surname sounds like the Russian verb "to chatter," and thus his name undercuts his idealistic, but rather pompous, pronouncements on art. In *Uncle Vanya*, the beautiful Yelena, who inspires love from all the key men in the play and consequently disrupts their lives, shares her name (in its Russian variant) with another famous beauty who also wrought havoc in her family—Helen of Troy. In *Three Sisters*, Vershinin means "pinnacle" or "summit"; Vershinin's grand thoughts about the future possibilities of human life seem eminently worthy of his name. In *The Cherry Orchard*, Ranyevskaya's first name is Lyubov, or "love"

---

[29] "Vasilisa The Beautiful," in *Russian Fairy Tales*, trans. Norbert Guterman (New York: Pantheon Books, 1973), 439-47. This volume translates the stories that were recorded from oral traditions by Alexander Afanasyev.

in Russian; and she surely understands love if not business. In short, it always behooves one to consider the names that Chekhov gives his characters.[30]

Finally, one last look at narrative voice completes my commentary on "The Student." As already noted, Chekhov uses conventional third-person narration to convey the thoughts and perceptions of his central character. Adjectives and adverbs that betoken human opinion along with phrases like "he thought" position the reader within the student's mind. But nowhere in "The Student" is this narrative technique more obvious than in the last paragraph. It is one long chain of run-on thoughts with multiple dependent clauses, twice punctuated by dashes rather than commas. The very structure of this sentence embodies the student's excitement. His words race toward the future with optimistic anticipation. The run-on form of his thoughts mirrors his uncontainable joy. This sentence comes very close to the kind of self-revelatory dialogue that Chekhov uses so masterfully in his plays.

Consider, for example, Lopakhin's speech in Act III of *The Cherry Orchard* about how he bought the Ranyevskaya estate at its auction. On one hand the speech gives important expository information. On the other hand, Lopakhin's language reveals how his great joy wars with his childhood affection for Ranyevskaya, and how his past conditions his ambitious desires for the future. His speech careens from one concern to another, creating a sense of emotional ambivalence that emulates a drunken state. For ease of analysis, I quote the speech in full:

> I bought it! Wait a minute, ladies and gentlemen, be so kind, my head is swimming, I can't talk... (*Laughs.*) We got to the auction. Deriganov was there. Leonid Andreyevich had only fifteen thousand and Deriganov had already put down thirty thousand over and above the debt. I saw how the business stood, so I jumped in and put down forty... He put down forty five. I made it fifty five. You see he kept adding five thousand and I added ten each time... Well, it came to a finish. I put down ninety thousand over and above the debt, and it was mine. Now the cherry orchard

---

[30] Chekhov's use of meaningful names derives from Russian satire generally and French vaudeville specifically (Chapter 4). I give the meanings of the names in Chekhov's plays in *Chekhov: 4 Plays and 3 Jokes.*

is mine! Mine! (*Laughs out loud.*) My God, Lord in Heaven, the cherry orchard is mine! Tell me that I'm drunk, not in my right mind, that I've imagined all of this... (*Stamps his feet.*) Don't laugh at me. If my father and grandfather were to get up out of their graves and look at everything that's happened, how their Yermolay, their beaten, half-literate Yermolay, who ran around barefoot in the winter, how this very same Yermolay bought an estate, the most beautiful one in the whole world. I bought the estate where my grandfather and father were slaves, where they weren't allowed into the kitchen. I'm asleep, this is a mirage for me, it only seems to be... This is the fruit of your imagination, hidden by the darkness of the unknown... (*Picks up the keys, smiling tenderly.*) She threw down the keys, wants to show that she's no longer the housekeeper here... (*Jingles the keys.*) Well, it's all the same. (*The orchestra is heard tuning up.*) Hey musicians, play, I want to hear you! Everyone, come look at how Yermolay Lopakhin will take the ax to the cherry orchard, how the trees will fall to the ground! We'll build summer houses and our grandchildren and their grandchildren will see a new life... Music, play! (*The music plays. Lyubov Andreyevna lowers herself to a chair and bitterly cries. To her reproachfully.*) Why, why didn't you listen to me? My poor, good woman, you can't go back now. (*With tears.*) Oh if only all this would pass quickly, if only our incoherent, unhappy lives would change quickly! (trans. Carnicke, 288)

Like the student's joy at story's end, Lopakhin's words embody a man caught off guard by heady joy. In buying Ranyevskaya's estate, Lopakhin has overcome the serfdom into which he was born. He cannot fully trust the amazing truth of that triumph; it seems an unbelievable "mirage," which will soon disappear. He revels in his present success through outsized pride, drunken frenzy, even a revengeful sense of having overcome those who had once oppressed his family. He takes charge of the moment by ordering the musicians to play. He takes charge of his purchase by looking forward to the future of the estate and its possibilities with relish. Yet, he also experiences this joy uncomfortably. Before him are those whose lives he now disrupts. Varya throws the keys to the house at his feet; Ranyevskaya collapses into a chair in tears. Seeing them, Lopakhin struggles with the guilt he feels for having betrayed them. He tries but fails to express compassion; and finally, he simply prays for the painfully joyous moment to pass. In short, the speech is far more self-revelatory than expository.

CHEKHOV'S LITERARY INNOVATION IN CONTEXT

By completing this slow, thoughtful examination of "The Student," one can see how Chekhov's fiction functions as "the magic of trifles."[31] What may be less apparent is how he breaks away from the storytelling modes of his countrymen. The simplicity of his stories, lacking in obvious didactic social commentary and moral outrage, stands in stark contrast to Fyodor Mikhailovich Dostoyevsky's passionately extreme novels. Chekhov's perspicacity about human psychology makes his characters even more concretely specific than those in the poetically crafted novels of Ivan Sergeyevich Turgenev (with whom Chekhov is often compared). Chekhov's strict selectivity and economy of detail also sets him apart from the epic novels of Lev Nikolayevich Tolstoy, with their broad and expansive panoramas of Russian life and culture. In short, as the Ukrainian scholar Dmitri Chizhevsky put it, Chekhov was "an innovator, and consequently a dangerous destroyer of the then accepted cannon of poetics."[32]

As Chizhevsky further asserts, Chekhov's innovative prose made him "the object of attacks by nearly all recognized and established critics" of his day.[33] However popular his stories might be among readers, critics objected to him on two significant counts. First, he did not participate in the expected political and social discourse of his day. Second, he did not honor the realism of his literary predecessors. Below I will address each of these counts in turn.

First, given the late nineteenth-century Russian context, Chekhov's persistent avoidance of authorial commentary elicited especially harsh criticism from the literary establishment. The abolition of serfdom, greater freedom of the press, reforms in the court system, and a broadening of educational opportunities during the 1860s affected all classes of Russian society from the aristocratic landowners to the lowliest of peasants. The fabric of Russia's economic and cultural life was rapidly

---

[31] Vladimir Nabokov, "Chekhov's Prose," in Eekman, ed., *Critical Essays on Anton Chekhov*, 31.

[32] Dmitri Chizhevsky, "Chekhov in the Development of Russian Literature," in Jackson, ed., *Chekhov*, 50.

[33] Ibid. For an interesting overview of contemporary views of Chekhov's artistry, see Alevtina Kuzicheva, "'Breaking the Rules': Chekhov and His Contemporaries," in Clayton, ed., *Chekhov Then and Now*, 269-84.

changing. Moreover, these changes released strong revolutionary desires among the educated classes, manifest in student riots at universities, terrorist activities against governmental officials, the failed revolution of 1905, and the successful communist revolution of 1917.

Literary critics in Russia—whether they were liberal, overtly radical, or conservative in their politics—expected artists to weigh in on the burning questions of the day and to take political sides. The most influential critic of the 1840s was Vissarion Grigoryevich Belinsky (1811-48), who effectively propagated the doctrine of civically engaged literature. His influence remained so pervasive during the second half of the nineteenth century and into the first decade of the twentieth that the leading Russian émigré literary historian, Dmitry Mirsky, baldly states that, "Belinsky, more than anyone else, [...] poisoned Russian literature by the itch for expressing ideas."[34] From Belinsky's time and arguably throughout the history of the Soviet Union, literature with political purpose was highly valued. Setting the scene for Chekhov's own critical reception were two groups of thinkers. Progressive intellectuals (the Westernizers—*zapadniki*) looked to Europe for innovative political models of reform; they wanted their arts to point the way toward social change. Conservative thinkers (the Slavophiles—*slavianofili*) stressed a return to the roots of nationalism in the cultures of Old Russia and the Russian Orthodox Church; they also expected their arts to engage with social issues of the day by supporting traditions.

Chekhov's inclinations ran counter to the trend. "In my opinion," he tells Suvorin, "it is not the writer's job to solve such problems as the existence of God, pessimism, etc. The job of the artist is only to record who under which circumstances said or thought what about God or pessimism" (30 May 1888). In short, Chekhov seemed out of step with the literary scene. Consequently, the Russian critical expectation that art engage in social causes and politics poisoned his reception. Despite his undisputed popularity among readers, most critics—even the admiring Grigorovich (Chapter 1)—faulted Chekhov for lacking opinions and convictions. Liberal thinkers wanted Chekhov to use his stories to promote freedom of the press, civic reforms, the creation of a parliamentary structure within the Tsar's autocratic reign, etc. Radicals hoped that his stories would provide fuel for the various revolutionary movements to

---

[34] Mirsky, *A History of Russian Literature*, 176.

overthrow the Tsar. However much his left-leaning friends (like the revolutionary writer Maksim Gorky) prodded Chekhov to take a stand in his
writings, and however much he openly proved his liberal views through
his civic activism (building hospitals and schools for peasants, donating
books to community libraries, supporting the prisoners in Sakhalin, resigning from the Academy of Sciences in support of Gorky, etc.), Chekhov
staunchly refused to preach reform or revolution in his writings. Thus,
the leading populist critics were left to bemoan Chekhov's "talent [as]
being lost in vain!"[35] Similarly, however much conservative intellectuals
(like his close friend and editor, Suvorin) pleaded for Chekhov to preach
morality alongside his descriptions of crime, prostitution, alcoholism,
etc., Chekhov always refused, eschewing all political parties equally.

> I am not a liberal, not a conservative, not an evolutionist, not a
> monk, but neither am I indifferent. I would like to be a free artist,
> and I only fear that God has not given me the strength to become
> one. I hate lies and coercion in any form. [...] My holy of holies is
> the human body, health, the mind, talent, inspiration, love, and
> the most absolute freedom, freedom from coercion and lies, in
> whatever ways these might be expressed. (to A. N. Pleshcheev,
> 4 Oct. 1888)

No wonder critics in Chekhov's own day shared a common refrain in
regard to his work! He was talented, perhaps the most talented writer of
his generation, but he had "no definite aim" as an author. So said two of
his strongest admirers, Grigorovich and Tolstoy;[36] so said the critics one
after another. In *The Seagull* (Act I) Chekhov echoes what he heard so
often about himself, when Dr. Dorn first encourages and then cautions
Treplev about his writing. "I very much liked your play. [...] It has left
a strong impression on me. You are a talented person, and you must
continue." But, Dorn adds, "A work of art must have a clear and definite
point. You must know why you write. Otherwise, if you travel down the
road of art without a definite aim, you will lose your way, and your talent
will destroy you" (trans. Carnicke, 70).

---

[35] Cited and translated in Williames, *Anton Chekhov, The Iconoclast*, 57.
[36] L. N. Tolstoi in A. S. Melkova, ed., *L. N. Tolstoi i A. P. Chekhov: Rasskazyvaiut sovremenniki, arkhivy, muzei* [L. N. Tolstoy and A. P. Chekhov: In the Words of their Contemporaries, Archives, and Museums] (Moscow: Nasledie, 1998), 47.

As the close reading of "The Student" proves, however, Chekhov did indeed have aim behind his writings. "If an author were to boast to me that he wrote a story without having thought about his intention beforehand, [...] then I would call him a madman," says Chekhov to Suvorin (27 Oct. 1888). Chekhov merely hides his intentions deep within the details of his stories, expecting his readers to find answers to the questions posed within his fiction on their own. "If one doesn't pose a question for oneself from the beginning," he continues, "then there's nothing [for the reader] to figure out" (27 Oct. 1888).

Chekhov's overarching authorial aim derives from his deep belief in humanism, so beautifully stated in the letter cited above, in which Chekhov places his "holy of holies" within the "human body." As Eichenbaum insightfully observes, Chekhov seeks to convey humanity's potential to do "great things." "Chekhov [deals] with the everyday petty side of life—not in order to expose or to express indignation directly, but in order to show how incompatible this life is with people's inherent possibilities."[37] While traveling to Sakhalin, Chekhov's awe was voiced in his letters home to his sister, Masha: "My God," he exclaims, "how rich is Russia in good people!" (17 May 1890) Just as Chekhov avoided stereotypes in his descriptions of these peoples, so too did he eschew political labels for their actions:

> I believe in individual people; I see salvation in individual people scattered through Russia—be they of the intelligentsia or the peasants; in them is our strength, even if they are few in number. They are the true prophets in our country. And these individual people, of whom I speak, go unnoticed in society. [...] But nonetheless their work is visible. (to I. I. Orlov, 22 Feb. 1899)

This appreciation of the individual's power to promote social change seems in perfect sympathy with his literary approach to the creating of complex, multifaceted characters. It registers in "The Student" when the protagonist's epiphany suggests that the small, unnoticed activities of individual people in the present form a continuum of past and future. In short, Chekhov believes small steps lead to social and political change.

Chekhov's second major challenge to the Russian literary elite involves his subversion of standard forms of realism. While Chekhov's

---

[37] Eichenbaum in Jackson, ed., *Chekhov*, 24.

fictional world is as all-encompassing of Russia's diversity as Tolstoy's, Chekhov developed methods that constitute "a complete break with sacred realism."[38] In light of the fact that many theater directors and actors still try to force Chekhov into the mold of realism, Chekhov's unique aesthetic style bears special attention.

The objectivity and care with which Chekhov describes the specific details in his stories and plays seem to argue for his place in the history of realism. Moreover, one can easily find statements in his notebooks and letters that seem to function as calls for realism. For example, he says that he only writes about subjects that he knows well in order to ensure that his details are accurately depicted. "Knowledge of the natural sciences and scientific method always put me on guard, and I tried whenever possible to take account of scientific fact, and when that wasn't possible, I preferred not to write" (to G. P. Rossolimo, 11 Oct. 1899). In fact, much as he admired Tolstoy, Chekhov did not hesitate to criticize the elder writer for getting his facts wrong, as in *War and Peace* (*Voina i mir*, 1869) when Prince Andrey dies of non-fatal wounds. "Had I been near Prince Andrey, I would have cured him," Chekhov joked to Suvorin (25 Oct. 1891). After reading Tolstoy's medically inaccurate description of syphilis in "The Kreutzer Sonata" ("*Kreitzerova sonata*," 1889), Chekhov even called the otherwise "artistically admirable" Tolstoy an "ignorant man, who did not trouble himself in the course of his long life to read two or three books written by specialists" in order to get the "truth" of his facts straight (to A. N. Pleshcheev, 15 Feb. 1890).

Indeed, the word "truth" reverberates throughout Chekhov's letters, also sounding suspiciously like a call for realism in art. For example, he warns a young writer who seeks beauty in art, that art's "aim is truth—unconditional and honest. It would be perilous to restrict its function to something so specialized as digging for 'pearls' as it would be to require [the painter] Levitan to paint a tree without including its dirty bark or yellowing leaves" (to M. Kiselyova, 14 Jan. 1887).

Modern and contemporary critics who currently argue for Chekhov's place within realism most often compare him to the French naturalists, particularly Guy de Maupassant and Émile Zola, because they, like Dr. Chekhov, believed in using scientific methods for literary craft.[39] Che-

---

[38] Chizhevsky in Ibid., 50.
[39] See, for example, Grossman in Ibid., 32-48.

khov's medical precision and the scientific objectivity in his literary descriptions make this comparison seem strong. As Chekhov says:

> To a chemist nothing in the world is impure. The writer must be just as objective as the chemist; he must free himself of everyday subjectivity, and he must know that manure plays a most respectable role in nature and that evil passions are just as much a part of life as virtues. (to M. Kiselyova, 14 Jan. 1887)

From this perspective, Chekhov seems to represent "the supreme achievement of the naturalistic movement in modern theater," as J. L. Styan would have it.[40]

In sum, because Chekhov's telling details are true (insofar as they accurately depict reality) and objective (in that they do not mask the less than beautiful in life), Chekhov seems to belong to the school of realism. However, those who so label him miss the ways in which his truthful details also subvert realism's literary norms.

Consider for a moment what Chekhov left out of "The Student." Despite the many, many carefully crafted details in his story, he never describes what Ivan Velikopolsky looks like, or whether he has any coins in his pockets, or whether he carries a bible or an empty gun, details that most nineteenth-century realists would consider important. Chekhov does tell us something about the widows' looks, but nothing about how or when their husbands died. He does not even tell his readers whether Ivan's assumption about their having had dinner is an accurate surmise. They might be washing someone else's bowl and spoons. Omniscient narrators in traditional realistic novels would surely describe all these things. Chekhov also does not tell us anything about the motives behind his protagonist's decision to go hunting. Was it a desire to entertain himself out of boredom, or a serious hunt for food?

Clearly "The Student" does not provide a complete picture of reality so much as a selective one. The story is filtered through the consciousness of a single mind and purged of anything that is extraneous to Chekhov's artistic intent within the story. Because Chekhov masks the first-person perspective with a third-person narrative voice, however, the subjectivity of the story remains hidden. The details may be realistic in and of

---

[40] J. L. Styan, *Chekhov in Performance: A Commentary on the Major Plays* (New York: Cambridge University Press, 1971), 239.

5. Chekhov with the writer, Maksim Gorky, in Yalta, 1901.

themselves, presenting a surface that seems stylistically realistic, but Chekhov's selectivity also moves the narrative method away from standard realism. "Do you know what you are doing?" Maksim Gorky asked his friend Chekhov in 1900; "You are killing realism, and you will finish it off—finally and for a long time."[41] (Illustration 5)

---

[41]   Quoted by Chizhevsky in Jackson, ed., *Chekhov*, 50.

If Chekhov's carefully detailed prose, which seems at first glance realistic, is not realism, then what is it? Tolstoy, who admired Chekhov's "mastery at the highest level," saw in Chekhov's fiction something "completely new, which I have encountered nowhere." (Illustration 6) In struggling to define Chekhov's originality, Tolstoy writes:

> He has a particular manner, somehow like the impressionists. You see, a man without any apparent effort throws on a canvas some very vivid colors, which fall with no apparent relationship from one vivid spot to the next, but the general impression is surprising; before you is a vivid and incontrovertibly effective painting.[42]

In short, Tolstoy likened Chekhov to an impressionist painter whose medium is not paint but words.

Tolstoy's metaphor is apt. The pattern within Chekhov's writing—be it his stories or his plays—rarely appears with a first reading, because his details (like splashes of color) seem random or inconsequential during a first encounter with them. Only after working carefully through a Chekhov text does the full pattern emerge, much as one can see the subject of an impressionist painting only by stepping back and looking at it from a distance. In "The Student," for example, two details—the woodcock passing by and the booming, merry sound of a shot—initially seem to provide little more than atmosphere. Only when later juxtaposed with other details within the story—such as the protagonist's religious studies, the fact that the story takes place on Good Friday, and the student's choice to tell of Peter's betrayal of Christ—do the two initial details acquire their full significance. They are tokens of the narrator's own guilty behavior. Yet one can easily miss the student's sense of guilt in this pattern of details, because Chekhov builds significance into his story so subtly. Similarly, only after the reader works carefully through all the details does the story's full subject reveal itself. One can only admire such carefully hidden craft.

Chekhov's key fictional methods proved equally efficacious in drama. The Russian literary specialist Nicholas Rzhevsky states the obvious, but often overlooked, fact that "when [Chekhov] began to write plays

---

[42] Tolstoy in A. S. Melkova, ed., *L.N. Tolstoi i A.P. Chekhov* [Tolstoy and Chekhov], 250-1.

6. Chekhov and the novelist, Lev Tolstoy, in Yalta, 1901.

actively, the tradition-breaking stage simplicity, understatement, and plot-lines he offered theater were all long-standing elements of his literary work," proving "that theater could be as complex as literature."[43] There are within his plays the same devilish use of detail and the same rich patterns, woven from these details, which form meanings that exceed the semantic content of the dialogue. Similarly, in the careful craft of his plays Chekhov reveals the same ironic smile of amused compassion for the foibles, joys and sufferings of his characters, the same sensitivity to the character's unspoken thoughts and the inner action of their souls. In short, he invokes the same laughter-through-tears in his audiences as he does in the readers of his stories.

---

[43] Nicholas Rzhevsky, *The Modern Russian Theater: A Literary and Cultural History* (London: M. E. Sharpe, 2009), 31-2.

Chapter Three

The Devil in the Details
of Chekhov's Plays

As a close reading of "The Student" reveals, Chekhov employs tiny details of all sorts to deepen his portrait of Ivan Velikopolsky (Chapter 2). Moreover, when one recalls Chekhov's expectation that Stanislavsky read *Uncle Vanya* through its most minute and apparently insignificant details (Chapter 2), it becomes utterly clear that Chekhov builds depth into his plays in the same way that he does in his stories. His drama, like his narrative oeuvre, registers as serious, sad, comic, compassionate, or ironic only so far as seemingly trivial details coincide or collide with each other.

Chekhov's drama also bears the same ambiguous relationship to realism as do his stories. Realistically described moments from daily life and colloquial speech bring his characters to life; but Chekhov does not actually write realistic plays any more than he writes realistic stories. He carefully selects lifelike details and places them into artfully structured patterns, so that realistic moments suggest more than surface reality. This aspect of his dramatic art was visible in Stanislavsky's productions of the plays, and noticed by the theater critic Edmund Wilson during the 1923 Moscow Art Theatre tour to the United States. As Wilson wrote in his review of *The Cherry Orchard* in January 1923:

> [The Russian actors] bring out a whole set of aesthetic values to which we are not accustomed in the realistic theater: the beauty and poignancy of an atmosphere, of an idea, a person, a moment are caught, and put before us without emphasis.[1]

The British director, Peter Brook, noticed the same break with artistic tradition in Chekhov, this time contrasting his use of detail with that of naturalism:

---

[1] Cited in Emeljanow, ed., *Chekhov*, 236.

It is an easy mistake to consider Chekhov as a naturalistic writer, and in fact, many of the sloppiest and thinnest plays of recent years called "slice of life" fondly think themselves Chekhovian. Chekhov never just made a slice of life—he was a doctor who with infinite gentleness and care took thousands and thousands of fine layers off life. These he cultured, and then arranged them in an exquisitely cunning, completely artificial and meaningful order in which part of the cunning lay in so disguising the artifice that the result looked like the keyhole view it had never been.[2]

Struggling to identify Chekhov's break with tradition, Tolstoy likened his fellow writer's narrative style to impressionism (Chapter 2). Most theater folk today prefer to call it poetic realism. Neither term, however, satisfactorily describes the full impact of Chekhov's dramatic style, especially when his realistic details escape the spatial and temporal limits of the present to speak of eternal matters, as they do in "The Student," where a momentary experience of epiphany offers a glimpse of the indomitable human spirit and the deeply communicative power of art.

During Chekhov's life, a group of writers, who came to be known as symbolists, were also struggling to get beyond realism in order to express the transcendent mental and spiritual aspects of the human condition. No wonder they recognized Chekhov as a kindred soul! The poet and dramatist Andrey Bely (1880-1934) was one of these, and his views on Chekhov are eloquent and enlightening. In a 1904 critique of *The Cherry Orchard*, Bely notices that whenever a realistic artist looks at a particular moment of life as if through a microscope, that moment seems "torn" from reality and has the potential to "become a door to eternity." "Such realism crosses imperceptibly into symbolism." In Bely's view, "Such is Chekhov," who takes full and remarkable advantage of this potential for symbolism in his work.

His characters are sketched with external strokes, but we understand them from within. They walk, drink, talk nonsense, but visible in these are their souls' abyss. They speak as if they were imprisoned by life, but we have recognized something about them that they have not noticed about themselves. The trivial

---

[2] Brook, *The Empty Space*, 72.

details of their lives are for us a secret code—and thus the trivial is no longer trivial. The triteness has been neutralized, as the trite details reveal something grand. Isn't this seeing through the triteness? And *seeing through* something is exactly what it means to be a symbolist.[3]

In 1888, one of Chekhov's fictional characters says something more mundane but quite similar to Bely. In the story "A Nuisance," Dr. Ovchinnikov slaps his medical assistant in a fit of temper, because the assistant has come to work hung over. The doctor's anger, however, has more to do with his own grinding burden of routine work than with his assistant's transgression; nonetheless neither of the two men can swallow enough pride to apologize. Instead, both escalate the battle: the doctor calls upon the regional District Board to fire his assistant, who in turn takes the doctor to court. For one moment within the story, however, Dr. Ovchinnikov admits the truth of their situation to the head of the Board:

> You smile! In your opinion it's all trifles, petty details, but understand this; there are so many of these trifles, and together they make up the whole of life, as grains of sand make mountains![4]

Chekhov did indeed strain the bounds of realism by borrowing from the emerging school of symbolism in drama. Critics and admirers who expected realism from him reacted negatively to the symbolist aspects of his plays. After seeing *Uncle Vanya* at the Moscow Art Theatre in 1900, Tolstoy told his diary that he "was indignant" over the play. While he had been able to accept the impressionism in Chekhov's stories, Tolstoy now complained to the theater's co-director about the growing symbolic trend in Chekhov's plays. "Oh please," Tolstoy complained to

---

[3] Andrey Bely, "*Vishnevyi sad*" [*The Cherry Orchard*] in A. P. Kuzicheva, ed., *A. P. Chekhov v russkoi teatral'noi kritike* [Chekhov in Russian Theatrical Criticism] (Moscow: Chekhovskii poligraficheskii kombinat, 1999), 343-4. The translation here is mine, but a full English translation of this article is also available in Laurence Senelick, trans. and ed., *Russian Dramatic Theory from Pushkin to the Symbolists: An Anthology* (Austin: University of Texas Press, 1981), 149-70.

[4] "Nepriiatnost'," in Chekhov, *Polnoe sobranie sochinenii* [The Complete Works], Vol. 7, 155.

Nemirovich-Danchenko, "a guitar, a cricket—all that is fine and good, but why look for other meanings behind these things?"[5]

Chekhov's admiration for turn-of-the-century symbolism is as easily documented as his disdain for symbolist excesses. Pejoratively called "decadent" by critics in Russia and by Arkadina in Act I of *The Seagull*, symbolism was already challenging nineteenth-century platitudes about realism and the necessity for writers to create politically engaged art (Chapter 2). As early as 1895 while writing *The Seagull*, Chekhov was telling his friend and editor Suvorin about the works of Maurice Maeterlinck (1862-1949), the Belgian symbolist poet and playwright, who would win the Nobel Prize for literature in 1911. In 1897, Chekhov reported having read three of Maeterlinck's plays: *The Blind* (*Les Aveugles*, 1891) about a group of blind people whose caregiver has taken them out to the country, died without warning and without their knowledge, and left them stranded and unable to return home; *The Intruder* (*L'Intruse*, 1891), about a family who waits through one long night for the arrival of Death; and *Aglavaine and Selysette* (*Aglavaine et Sélysette*, 1896), a romantic story of selfless and supernatural love set in the imagined landscapes of Arthurian legend. "All of them," Chekhov tells Suvorin, "are strange, wonderful pieces, and the impression they make is huge; if I had a theater, then I would absolutely stage *The Blind*" (12 July 1897). Maeterlinck's influences on Chekhov are easy to find.

The most glaringly symbolist detail in Chekhov's work is arguably the mysterious and ultimately unidentified sound in Acts II and IV of *The Cherry Orchard*, that he describes as "faraway" and "as if from the sky" (trans. Carnicke, 272; 301). Something like the snapping of a string, or an owl hooting, or a bucket falling loose in a mine shaft, the unidentifiable sound first intrudes upon the characters' trivial pleasantries while they are relaxing in an abandoned graveyard as if in a park. The setting, which includes a view of a chapel in the distance, offers a grim counterpoint to the flirtations and conversations that take place among the gravestones. This atmospheric setting is in perfect sympathy, however, with the otherworldliness of the sound that stops the action for a brief but significant moment. The characters' unsettled

---

[5] Both cited in Melkova, ed., *L. N. Tolstoi i A. P. Chekhov* [Tolstoy and Chekhov], 49; 166.

reactions suggest how much the eerie sound has shaken them. Perhaps it marks a confrontation with their souls' abyss, to borrow Bely's image. Perhaps it is a reminder of the inevitability of death as surely as is the setting. Shortly thereafter, a passing beggar interrupts and unsettles them in just the same way, as if suggesting that physical and spiritual poverty are akin.

At the end of the play, all but the old servant Firs have left the house; ill and weak, he has been accidently forgotten. He enters the once lively room to find its doors locked. "Life has passed by as if it were never lived..." (trans. Carnicke, 301), he mutters and lies down. It is as if he waits for death, much as do the family members in Maeterlinck's *The Intruder*. Speaking to himself, Firs then notices that, "You don't have your strength now, do you? Nothing's left, nothing... Ah you... Nincompoop!..." With this self-reprimand, the same unsettling sound from Act II reverberates through the empty house—a "distant sound... as if coming from the sky—the sound of a snapping string, dying away, sad" (trans. Carnicke, 301). Is this a death knell? If so, Chekhov has ended his play with the arrival of death, just as Maeterlinck ends *The Intruder*.

Read any of Maeterlinck's short plays from the 1890s, like those that Chekhov specifically mentions or *The Seven Princesses* (*Les sept princesses*, 1891, a play that tells a nightmarish fairy tale), and you will better understand Chekhov. Maeterlinck uses eerie images and sounds to create transcendental atmospheres. He repeats simple sentences to emphasize them and to suggest that the depths of human experience lie behind even the simplest of statements. He uses atmospheric settings to mirror the emotional landscapes of his characters' souls. Chekhov, too, uses off-stage sounds, as the mysterious snapping string in *The Cherry Orchard* demonstrates. Chekhov, too, uses patterns of repeated dialogue, images, and sounds to create mood. Instances include: Chebutykin's repeated refrain, "It's all the same," and the taking of a photograph to stop time at Irina's name day party in *Three Sisters*; the killing of a gull and Nina's consequent identification with it in *The Seagull*. Chekhov, too, creates atmospheric landscapes for his characters, like the magical lake in *The Seagull*, and the beautiful, blossoming trees at the opening of *The Cherry Orchard*.

Despite Chekhov's attraction to symbolism, however, he actively rejected the movement's interest in obvious abstraction. Treplev's play in *The Seagull* is a brilliant parody of a symbolist drama that has lost its moorings in reality. It is indeed "decadent" as the author's mother calls it. Thus, while Maeterlinck draws his refrains from the abstract world of poetic imagery, Chekhov transforms the details of ordinary life into symbolic images.[6]

In the end, Chekhov's stylistic use of detail remains his alone. No literary label, including "symbolism," seems inclusive enough. The familiar trivialities that create the illusions of reality, the splashes of color in impressionistic pictures of life, and symbolic codes to the mysteries of human existence—these and more describe the many ways that Chekhov uses details in his works.

TYPES OF DETAILS

I have created a typology of details below as a guide to the close reading of Chekhov's plays.[7] Far from comprehensive, my catalogue only begins to suggest the kinds of dramatic details within Chekhov's plays and the multiple ways in which they can acquire meaning and resonance from contextual associations and juxtapositions.

Some of the details I include rely upon what characters actually say, hence upon their use and abuse of language. Such verbal details can easily be found in both Chekhov's stories and plays.

Other kinds of details, however, depend upon the physical and material reality of the stage. Unlike narrative prose that creates a rich experience for readers solely through words, a dramatic text functions like a blueprint from which the director, actors, and designers build a production, which in its turn creates the spectators' experience of

---

[6] For more on this topic see Laurence Senelick, "Chekhov's drama, Maeterlinck, and the Russian Symbolists," in Jean-Pierre Barricelli, ed., *Chekhov's Great Plays: A Critical Anthology* (New York: New York University Press, 1981), 161-80.

[7] Natalia Pervukhina creates a fascinating catalogue of the many types of telling details that Chekhov uses in her book, *Anton Chekhov: The Sense and the Nonsense* (New York: Legas, 1993). I am indebted to her for her insights and have been inspired by her to create this typology of my own. See also Cathy Popkin, *The Pragmatics of Insignificance: Chekhov, Zoshchenko, Gogol* (Palo Alto: Stanford University Press, 1993).

the play (Chapter 6). In performance, Chekhov's texts are embodied by specific actors, the sound of their voices, and their gaits as they move across the stage. These living people collaborate in the creation of Chekhov's dramatic worlds by using actual furniture and other material objects as their props. They enter into and exit from designed spaces, enhanced by visual and sound effects made by stage technologies. Chekhov's careful descriptions of the environments and the physical objects in his plays suggest that he was utterly cognizant as he wrote of the ways in which the material reality of productions could enrich his work. In short, every time a Chekhov play is produced, the spectator encounters his dramatic details both verbally and as they are materially presented.

1. Apparent non sequiturs in conversations and behavior.
Sometimes conversation in a Chekhov play seems comedic because it appears to flow illogically. One famous example of a non sequitur is Charlotta's entrance line, "My dog eats nuts," in *The Cherry Orchard* (trans. Carnicke, 246). While irrelevant to the onstage action, her words presumably make sense in terms of the offstage conversation that is in progress when she enters. Chekhov does nothing new here; Shakespeare had used the same technique to make his plays seem as continuous as real life.

But occasionally, Chekhov has a more insidious strategy in mind. He also uses non-sequential remarks to comment on the wider action of a scene. For example, when Chebutykin, Solyony and Tuzenbach first enter in *Three Sisters*, they interrupt Olga's reminiscence about her father's military funeral. She has just described how his high status as a general entailed real pomp. Just as she remembers that, "I wanted passionately to go back home," the three local military men enter. Not only do their ranks (clearly inferior to her father's) visually point to her family's lowered status since his death, but their first lines also appear to debunk her lofty words: "The devil you say! [...] Of course, it's nonsense" (trans. Carnicke, 170). While the men have been arguing offstage and their lines are part of that argument, the audience can hear their exclamations as inadvertently appropriate criticisms of Olga. After all, her sister Irina has just expressed annoyance with Olga: "Why remember!" (trans. Carnicke, 170).

Another excellent example of Chekhov's strategy occurs in the last act of *The Cherry Orchard*. Anya is comforting her mother: "Mama, you'll come back soon... Isn't that true? [...] Mama, you'll come back..." Lyubov Andreyevna, in turn, reassures her daughter with a hug: "I'll come back, my precious." Next the governess, Charlotta, decides to perform a feat of ventriloquism, which registers on the surface as irrelevant to the prior action. She "picks up a bundle and holds it to look like a baby wrapped in a blanket." The baby cries, and Charlotta comforts the imaginary child with "I'm so sorry for you!" Then she abruptly "throws the bundle down" (trans. Carnicke, 295). In actuality, Charlotta has just debunked Lyubov Andreyevna's motherly reassurance.

Then again, Chekhov sometimes uses non sequiturs to suggest multiple levels of meaning within his play. For example, whenever Firs answers questions illogically because he is hard of hearing, we might laugh, but we also might come to understand that clear communication between people is always difficult. In some sense, we are all hard of hearing.

2. Apparent irrelevancies. Details that appear irrelevant can function as creatively as do non sequiturs in Chekhov's world. For every such detail, consider its context within the play. For example, in *Uncle Vanya* Chekhov draws special attention to a specific prop in his description of the set: "On the wall there hangs a map of Africa, clearly of no use to anyone here" (trans. Carnicke, 156). The only character who pays any attention to this map is Dr. Astrov. Near the play's finale, as he gets ready to leave the estate for the winter, he "goes to the map of Africa and looks at it," saying, "There must be a heat wave in Africa now—a terrible thing!" Vanya replies indifferently: "Yes probably" (trans. Carnicke, 165). Astrov is preparing to leave reluctantly but dutifully, because he has learned that Vanya's niece, Sonya, is hopelessly in love with him. Is Astrov's irrelevant remark just something to say at an awkward moment? Perhaps so. He had also reverted to a conversation about the weather earlier in the play when caught by Vanya making hot, sexual advances to Sonya's stepmother, Yelena.

But the map of Africa and Astrov's remark may not be as irrelevant as they seem. There is another map in the play, and Chekhov implicitly invites us to compare the two. In contrast to the useless map of Africa, Dr.

Astrov has lovingly drawn a detailed chart of the local region in hopes that it will be of use to those who live nearby. In depicting how the flora and fauna are disappearing, he hopes his map will spur civic development. Within the confines of the play, however, he uses it only to seduce Yelena. (Illustration 7) But for Vanya's interruption, an emotional heat wave might well have hit the estate. Does Astrov look at the map of Africa and think about what might have been? Does Vanya himself do the same? When earlier he had inadvertently interrupted Astrov with Yelena, Vanya had arrived with a bouquet for her, hoping to seduce her himself. His indifferent response to Astrov's remark about Africa's heat wave suggests his own failure with her. Comparing the two maps in *Uncle Vanya* prompts a flood of such associations concerning the play's tight web of relationships. But then again, perhaps the map of Africa merely reminds the audience that there is a world of concerns outside this claustrophobic little estate.

While at first glance, Gayev's penchant for playing imaginary billiards in *The Cherry Orchard* seems as irrelevant as the map of Africa, it is actually a symptom of his psychological desire to escape painful reality. Yet another look proves Chekhov's full savvy as playwright. Gayev's obsession with billiards also provides a significant image for Chekhov's handling of action throughout the play.

7. Dr. Astrov (Konstantin Stanislavsky) and Yelena Andreyevna (Olga Knipper) look at one another, not at Astrov's regional map in *Uncle Vanya*, 1899.

Characters in *The Cherry Orchard* tend to avoid direct confrontations with each other, preferring to step away from fights. Thus, open conflicts are rare in Chekhov's plays generally. Furthermore, over the course of his career, he tended to write fewer and fewer scenes in which conflict takes center stage. *The Cherry Orchard* represents the pinnacle of this trend in his writing. Central to the play are Lopakhin's two attempts to persuade Lyubov Andreyevna to build summerhouses in order to save her estate from auction and Lyubov Andreyevna's two attempts to persuade Lopakhin to propose to Varya. In all four scenes, persuasion is met by indirect rebuttal. When confronted by Lopakhin about the auction, Lyubov Andreyevna changes the subject. In Act I, she appears to engage with Lopakhin for a moment but then quickly drifts off into remarks about Paris. In Act II, when Lopakhin demands that she "answer in one word," she immediately deflects him: "Who's been smoking those revolting cigars here..." (trans. Carnicke, 265). When Lyubov Andreyevna raises the idea of marriage to Varya, Lopakhin's mode of rebuttal is different but still indirect. He always agrees with Lyubov Andreyevna, but so halfheartedly that it is difficult to take him at his word. In Act II, he says: "Well? I'm not against it... She's a good girl" (trans. Carnicke, 268). In Act IV, he even agrees with Lyubov Andreyevna, when she tells him that she doesn't understand why he has not yet proposed: "I have to admit I don't understand it either" (trans. Carnicke, 296).

Their interactions with each other have become a game of indirection[8] that mirrors the game of angles in billiards. Rarely does a billiard player use the cue ball to hit his actual target square on; instead, he reaches his target by hitting a by-standing ball that sets a number of other balls into motion until the target is reached and a point is finally scored. Events do occur in Chekhov. Lyubov Andreyevna loses her orchard and returns to her lover in Paris; Lopakhin loses Varya and buys the cherry orchard. Yet these events come about in much the same way that billiard balls score points: through indirection, leaving characters feeling sideswiped and audiences wondering what the characters' actual targets of desire really were all along.

---

[8] The first scholar to write about Chekhov's "plays of indirect action" was David Magarshack in *Chekhov the Dramatist* (London: John Lehmann, 1952), 159-73.

3. Puns and word play. Chekhov delights in playing with words, as is obvious in the one-act plays that he called "jokes." In *The Bear*, Smirnov challenges the young widow Popova to a duel in the standard way: "I demand satisfaction!" (trans. Carnicke, 17). These words register as double entendre when he ends by begging for sexual satisfaction instead. In *The Proposal*, Lomov's explicit hypochondria reaches a level of literal absurdity, when he asks, "Where's my shoulder?" (trans. Carnicke, 33). Chekhov also puns in *The Cherry Orchard* when Lyubov Andreyevna asks Gayev to lend money to their neighbor for his mortgage debt. "Give it to him, Leonid," she says. He ironically answers, "I'll give it to him all right!" (trans. Carnicke, 258). His sarcasm also echoes Varya's earlier comment on Lopakhin's maddening passivity toward her: "If only I could give it to him..." (trans. Carnicke, 248).

My favorite instance of word play in *The Cherry Orchard* is Firs' devilishly untranslatable word, *nedotyopa*. He mutters it whenever he criticizes Dunyasha and Yasha for their flightiness; Lyubov Andreyevna quotes it when she reprimands Trofimov for not acting like a grown-up; and Chekhov uses it as the very last word in the play when Firs applies it to himself as he lies down in the empty house. Some scholars think the word might be Ukrainian for "incompetent." Some think that it is slang that Chekhov heard while working as a doctor in Russia's provinces. Russian dictionaries cite Chekhov as its originator.[9] Translators have rendered it in many different ways: "good for nothing," "addle pate," "job-lot," "pathetic old fool," "you old fool," "flibbertigibbet," and "sillybilly." My solution is "nincompoop,"[10] because it picks up the Russian word's nonsensical quality as well as its percussive sound.

---

[9] Laurence Senelick, *Anton Chekhov* (New York: Grove Press, 1985), 133-4.

[10] The translators of these options (in the order given in the text above) are Constance Garnett (*Four Great Plays by Anton Chekhov*, New York: Bantam Books, 1958), Ann Dunnigan (*Chekhov: The Major Plays*, New York: Signet, 1964), an anonymous translator (*Plays by Anton Chekhov*, New York: Concord Books, 1935), Carol Rocomora (*Chekhov: Four Plays*, Lyme: Smith and Kraus, 1996), David Mamet (*The Cherry Orchard by Anton Chekhov*, New York: Grove Press, 1985), Paul Schmidt (*The Plays of Anton Chekhov*, New York: Harper Perennial, 1999), and Michael Frayn (*Chekhov: Plays*, London: Methuen Drama, 1991). Ronald Hingley (*Five Major Plays* by Anton Chekhov, New York: Bantam Books, 1977) and Jean Claude Van Itallie (*Chekhov: The Major Plays*, New York: Applause, 1995) also use "nincompoop."

4. Verbal tics, meaningless phrases, and eccentric grammar.
Chekhov's linguistic play includes repeated phrases that fill the air
but carry no semantic meaning; these verbal tics often individualize
characters. For example, Lomov's would-be father-in-law, Chubukov,
blusters through his lines with "etc." and "so forth and so on." In
The Seagull, Sorin's "and all that" suggests his desire to say more than
he can. In *Three Sisters*, Chebutykin's "it's all the same" adds a refrain
of absurd futility to the experience of the play. Through these linguistic
habits, Chubukov becomes a character who always chatters too much,
Sorin betrays his inarticulate dissatisfaction with his lot in life, and
Chebutykin dismisses his own bad behavior (his drunken stupors and
his participation in Solyony's duel) with empty philosophizing.

Chekhov also willfully distorts logic, word usage, and even grammar
when it suits him. For example, Telegin in *Uncle Vanya* and Yepikhodov
in *The Cherry Orchard* speak awkwardly and ungrammatically, sometimes illogically, getting tangled up in long, convoluted sentences and
big, elegant, but incorrectly used, words. For example, in Act I Telegin
asserts that, "Anyone who betrays a husband or wife, you see, is an
unfaithful person, and might even betray his country!" He makes this
unusual connection, because "My wife ran off with the man she loved
the day after our wedding because of my unattractive appearance." He
salvages his self-esteem, however, by holding to his principles: "After
that I never broke my vows to her. I love her to this day, I help her
however I can. I gave her my property, so that she could raise the prog-
eny she bore for the man she loved. Happiness may be denied me, but
I still retain my pride" (trans. Carnicke, 120). Similarly, the clumsy
Yepikhodov bemoans his fate in Act II in broken language: "I am a
well-developed person, I read various marvelous books, but somehow
I can't understand the direction in which I personally feel like going, to
live or to shoot myself, personally speaking. But just in case, I always
carry a revolver on me. Here it is..." (trans. Carnicke, 263). A few moments later, he continues, "Personally speaking, not referring to other
objects, I must express myself, by the way, on the subject that fate
treats me without compassion, like a storm treats a small ship" (trans.
Carnicke, 263). Telegin's and Yepikhodov's speech alone marks them
as among Chekhov's most comic characters, his vaudevillian clowns
(Chapters 4 and 5).

5. Fractured foreign languages. Having studied and often failed at languages in school, Chekhov enjoys peppering his plays with the elegance of French, the educational elitism of Latin, and flourishes from Italian. Furthermore, in the Russian context where nineteenth-century aristocrats often learned French before their native language and where English and German politics set the tone for social change, foreign languages provided rich material for Chekhov to mine. The self-important bank manager, Shipuchin, in *The Anniversary* uses French to demonstrate his appreciation of the finer things in life, but, in so doing, he exposes his pretensions. In *Uncle Vanya*, the aging feminist, Maria Vasilyevna, uses French to show her education, while Dr. Astrov's Latin demonstrates his medical training. In *Three Sisters,* Kulygin's pedantic overuse of Latin suggests not only his approach to teaching, but also his ability to impress, at least initially, the bright schoolgirl, Masha, who became his wife. In contrast, his sister-in-law Natasha's atrocious French reveals her peasant background and her ambitious desire to compete with her husband's overeducated family. When the youngest sister, Irina, breaks down, she sees her inability to "remember the Italian for window or ceiling" as proof of her despair. As her brother says, "my sisters and I know French, German, and English. And Irina even knows Italian. But what is it worth!" (trans. Carnicke, 182).

6. Grandiloquent speech and philosophizing. While it is tempting to take the beautiful passages in Chekhov's plays as genuine insights into life, the careful reader may also begin to suspect that sometimes philosophy reveals the underbellies of would-be heroes. Do Vershinin's seductive musings about the future in *Three Sisters* signify wisdom or mask his inability to solve the problems caused by his all too present and unhappy marriage? Talk, in and of itself, can hide a character's flaws.

For instance, in *The Cherry Orchard* Trofimov waxes poetic about Russia's genuine need for revolutionary reform. Because history would later prove him right, Trofimov seems prophetic. No wonder interpreters of the play often position him as Chekhov's spokesman![11] But Chekhov undercuts the young revolutionary as much as he applauds him.

---

[11] See, for example, Maurice Valency, *The Breaking Sting: The Plays of Anton Chekhov* (New York: Schocken Books, 1983).

For example, Trofimov reaches the apex of fine political rhetoric in an inappropriate setting. Consider his only love scene with Anya in Act II. He made his love for her clear to the audience at the end of Act I, but when he finally gets her alone, he launches into a fine political speech, that includes his most frequently cited line, "All Russia is our orchard." His eloquence seems no more to the point than does Gayev's pompous salute to a bookcase earlier in the play. Why does Trofimov not speak of his love? Anya responds with "How well you speak!" (trans. Carnicke, 275). Her words may be filled with awe, but they also draw attention to his speechifying. In Act III, Anya's mother accuses Trofimov of not yet understanding love. "You must become a man," she tells him, "at your age, you should understand those who love. And you yourself must love…" (trans. Carnicke, 282). She seems correct in her appraisal, as her accusation throws him literally off-balance. He exits only to fall down the stairs, and this literal fall seems to be exactly what he needs. In Act IV, Trofimov says relatively little; instead, he forgives the teasing of others, comically looks for his galoshes, silently helps Anya pack, and finally ushers her into the future as they exit together. It seems that he has learned sympathy and the ability to express love through the ordinary actions of daily life.[12]

7. Clothing as commentary. In the famous opening lines of *The Seagull*, Masha tells her suitor that she wears black, not because it is a mysteriously attractive color, but because "I am in mourning for my life" (trans. Carnicke, 54). Her response already makes clear her propensity for self-dramatization, most explicitly demonstrated later in the play when she suggests that Trigorin write a story about her life. Her words also demonstrate how Chekhov uses costume to shed light upon the personalities of his characters. From Masha's seductive black mourning dress and Natalya Stepanovna's work apron in *The Proposal*, from Vanya's stylish tie to the bookkeeper's inappropriate wearing of slippers at the office in *The Anniversary*, examples abound of Chekhov's clever use of clothes.

---

[12] See Bernard Beckerman, "Dramatic Analysis and Literary Interpretation: *The Cherry Orchard* as Exemplum," *New Literary History: A Journal of Thought and Interpretation* 2, no. 3 (Spring 1971), 391-406.

When the curtain opens on *The Cherry Orchard*, spectators see a man dressed in an elegant white waistcoat and expensive, but gaudy yellow shoes; he seems a fine gentleman who flaunts his wealth. A well dressed and perfectly coifed woman then enters to join him; she seems his match. Their apparel suggests that they might well be the owners of the orchard, but their words soon belie their clothes. Lopakhin feels that, however fine his clothes, he is still an uneducated peasant underneath. "You can't make a silk purse out of a sow's ear" (trans. Carnicke, 244), he says. Then eying Dunyasha's fashionable appearance, he brusquely observes that she should dress like the servant she is. "You ought to remember your place" (trans. Carnicke, 244), he tells her. Thus, Chekhov begins his play with a costuming sleight of hand, as deft as the card tricks that Charlotta (a former circus performer) will later use to entertain her masters. Through Lopakhin's and Dunyasha's inappropriate clothing, Chekhov expresses their upwardly mobile aspirations and also warns his audience that all is not always what it seems in the world of his play.

Chekhov continues to play with clothing and social roles throughout *The Cherry Orchard*. If Lopakhin wishes to overcome his peasant roots by donning expensive clothes, how can he then marry a woman like Varya, who chooses to dress below her station? As the landowner's adopted daughter, she might well don Dunyasha's fancy dress, but instead Varya chooses the dour clothes of a servant, with keys hanging at her waist like a nun's rosary. Indeed, she looks, as her mother says, "like a nun" (trans. Carnicke, 244). Similarly, if Dunyasha aspires to a lady's delicacy of feelings by putting on the latest fashion and primping her hair, then how can she agree to marry the oaf, Yepikhodov,[13] who lacks all style? No wonder Dunyasha prefers the dandified cad, Yasha, who so drenches himself in patchouli (the latest French perfume) that people can tell when he has been in a room by the smell.

Moreover, Chekhov's playful use of inappropriate clothing alerts his astute spectators to other kinds of discrepancies. For example, before the play begins the seventeen-year-old Anya has travelled to Paris to fetch her runaway mother. Despite news of the impending auction and numerous pleading telegrams, Lyubov Andreyevna kept delaying

---

[13] Yepikhodov's name derives from the Russian verb *khodit'*, "to walk," but, being accident prone, he trips more often than he walks.

her return until finally escorted home by her daughter. In short, the child plays the role of the parent to her errant mother. Similarly, when their home is finally sold at auction, the child comforts and reassures her parent, again turning audience expectations inside out. (Illustration 8) While Anya and her mother are appropriately dressed, they have exchanged behavioral roles as surely as Dunyasha and Varya have exchanged dresses.

8. Anya (Maria Zhdanova) mothers her mother, Ranyevskaya (Olga Knipper), in *The Cherry Orchard*, 1912.

8. Stage settings and the emotional progression of a play. In all four of his major plays, Chekhov uses the changing of sets from act to act to create an emotional journey through the play. Akin to the pathetic fallacy (which uses the weather to mirror a character's internal state of mind), Chekhov's atmospheric sets suggest pervasive moods, which sometimes coincide and sometimes counterpoint the moods of those onstage. *The Seagull* begins outside in a park with a vista on a lake. But nature, which is so often associated with healing peace in Chekhov (Chapter 1), is here significantly "obstructed from view by a stage" (trans. Carnicke, 54). The set thus reflects the fact that the artistic struggles and jealousies among the play's two writers and two actresses similarly obstruct their natural proclivities for love and generosity. This obstruction of nature becomes destruction with Treplev's killing of the seagull in Act II, the play's most famous and familiar symbol.

Act IV ends the play inside Treplev's study, its close atmosphere further intensified by a storm which rages outside. The young man's domain is used for more than writing; during the act it becomes a sick room for his uncle and a gaming room for the entire household, among whom are his mother and his rival Trigorin who have just arrived from her latest acting tour to visit his ailing uncle. The set visibly expresses how Treplev's writing has been pushed to the side and how he has been marginalized by those who surround him. Has he been victimized by them? Or has he allowed them to do so through his own inaction? The study's use as a sick room and his uncle's proximity to death also suggest how fleeting are life and artistic success, prompting questions about whether or not one should sacrifice the simple joys in life, like love, for art and fame. Additionally, as the household plays lotto, which is a game of chance, the audience might well wonder how much of what has already happened within the play has resulted from the operations of chance. Do people have the power to change their fates or not? Or does blaming fate merely provide justification for one's own inaction?

When the schoolteacher Medvedenko remarks that the stage from Act I still stands outside, battered by the storm and now "naked, ugly, like a skeleton" (trans. Carnicke, 96), he underlines the fact that all the old obstructions from Act I are still in place. Like the stage, the emotional obstacles that stand in the way of honest interaction should have been torn down long ago; but instead the characters' pasts continue to intrude upon the present. During the last moments of the play, Treplev confronts his past directly in the person of Nina. She began her acting on that very stage before leaving him for Trigorin, who later abandoned her, pregnant and alone. She enters Treplev's study, cold and wet from the storm. In order to keep Trigorin out and to steal a private moment with Treplev, she asks that the room be locked. As she recalls the past, she seems more like the battered stage from Act I than the dead seagull from Act II with which she is more obviously compared throughout the play. The stage and she, both abandoned and battered by the passage of time, confront Treplev with his lost hopes and unfulfilled ambitions. She then leaves him, strengthened in her resolve to continue with her life. He does not follow her; he does not choose to continue on; he remains alone and imprisoned in this locked room. He turns to his latest manuscript, reads a bit, and finally destroys it as prelude to his destruction of himself. His marginalization within the room, as evidenced in the atmospheric set and its usage as other than a study, along with the storm of despair raging in his soul (as strong as the storm outside that batters the abandoned stage and the abandoned Nina) are as symbolic as anything one can find in a Maeterlinck or Bely play.

Uncle Vanya too moves from outside into a claustrophobic inner room. Act I takes place in an orchard, where the characters gather to enjoy their tea; Act IV ends in Vanya's inner office, where he and his niece all but bury themselves in the work of running the estate. As the play ends, Sonia comforts herself and her uncle with the fact that death will ultimately release them from their emotional burdens as well as from their work. As the whole household sits quietly together, working, knitting, reading, the picture is strongly reminiscent of the family in Maeterlinck's *The Intruder*, which sits and waits for the arrival of Death. The progression from sunny orchard to the lamp-lit study in *Uncle Vanya* mirrors the emotional shift from hope to despair over the unrequited love, experienced by both Sonya and Vanya. This progression, far from inexorable through the course of the play, has been briefly interrupted by the passing of a storm in Act II, which brings fresh air to the estate and new hope to the characters. As the storm ends, it seems the right atmospheric moment for Sonia and her stepmother, Yelena, to clear the air between them and pledge everlasting friendship. This respite, however, is brief. The stormy relationships in the house explode again in Act III, with an especially comic anti-climax as Vanya tries but fails to shoot his brother-in-law. Within the claustrophobic atmosphere of Act IV, Chekhov contrasts the earlier storm's promise of fresh air with the coming winter snows, which threaten the estate with further isolation from the surrounding world.

In contrast to both *The Seagull* and *Uncle Vanya*, *Three Sisters* moves from inside the Prozorov house to outside into the yard, making visible the fact that Andrey's marriage to Natasha and his accumulating gambling debts have effectively evicted his sisters from their home.

Unlike the changing sets in these three plays, *The Cherry Orchard* begins and ends in the same room—the family's former nursery. The changes that occur within this room measure the effect of time passing in the characters' lives. In Act I, the room is furnished for life. By Act IV, it is stripped of all décor, as if readied for death. As a former nursery, it represents birth and yet also betokens death, in that it serves as a constant reminder of Lyubov Andreyevna's drowned little boy. She herself grew from child to adult in this room, thinking all the while that her nursery, like her orchard, remained "just the same" (trans. Carnicke, 256). The visible changes from Act I to Act IV, however, prove her perceptions about room, orchard, and herself to be mere delusions. However much she and her brother Gayev might wish to hold on to the way things once were, they cannot. Chekhov's use of the room draws our eyes to the fact that even if his characters could stand in one place without moving, circumstances would change around them simply because time passes and bodies age.

The orchard outside the house is drawn as an imaginary landscape, never actually seen by the audience. As described in the play, it is visible to the characters through the windows of the nursery, but remains largely invisible from the auditorium. The writer Ivan Alekseyevich Bunin has also explained that orchards in Russia might well contain sections devoted to cherries, but none were exclusively cherry orchards.[14] Thus, Chekhov's orchard may seem realistic at first glance, but it soon becomes primarily symbolic through the associations that it accrues over the course of the play. Its presence is a continual reminder that there is a world beyond the confines of the house. As Trofimov tells

---

[14] I. A. Bunin, *O Chekhove* [About Chekhov] (New York: Chekhov Publishing House, 1955), 209.

Anya, "All Russia is our orchard. The world is big and beautiful, and there are many wonderful places in it" (trans. Carnicke, 273). For Lyubov Andreyevna it represents eternal youth because it blossoms anew every spring: "Oh my childhood, my purity! [...] Happiness awoke with me every morning, and the orchard was just the same then, nothing has changed!" (trans. Carnicke, 256). But for Lopakhin, its beauty is no longer meaningful, because the orchard is no longer productive: "You get cherries only once every two years and then you can't get rid of them, nobody buys them" (trans. Carnicke, 253). Overall, the changes that take place in the orchard with each passing season emphasize the development of the play's story. At the start, it is May and the orchard is in bloom; the estate's auction in August seems far away. By play's end, in October, the axes chop down the trees, forever ending their cycle of growth. August and auction have slipped into the past. Time, Chekhov seems to say, inevitably changes everyone and everything.

9. Furniture and inanimate objects. Chekhov uses his characters' interactions with the things that surround them as creatively and variously as he uses their speech peculiarities (sections 3 to 6 above) to reveal their individualities and inner traits. Thus, in *The Cherry Orchard*, Yepikhodov (nicknamed "Twenty Two Troubles") owns squeaking boots and breaks billiard cues as physical evidence of his clumsy nature, while Gayev shows himself to be a windbag when he makes an elaborate and inappropriate speech to the family's one hundred year old bookcase. In *The Bear*, when the retired army officer Smirnov visits the widow Popova to collect the debt owed him by her late husband, her unexpected refusal to pay causes him twice to grab the backs of chairs so strongly that each chair in turn "trembles and breaks." "Such delicate furniture you have, the devil knows" (trans. Carnicke, 17), he exclaims, leaving little doubt that he is the bear of the title. When he later challenges Popova to a duel, she unexpectedly agrees. But her late husband's dueling pistols are as much a mystery to her as her parlor furniture is for him. As he draws close to her to show her how to cock, aim, and shoot her revolver, the pistol itself becomes the unwitting matchmaker. In such intimate proximity to her, he cannot help but notice her charms: "Her eyes, her eyes! A fiery woman!" It thus becomes a short step from the challenge of a duel to his marriage proposal.

10. Food and drink as commentary on the symptoms of heartache. Chekhov once said he wanted the acting in plays to be "just as complex and also just as simple as in life. People eat their dinner, just eat their dinner, yet at the same time their happiness is taking shape and their lives are being smashed."[15] He structures Act I of *Three Sisters* in exactly this way. Lunch is served in celebration of the youngest sister's name day, and while the sisters and their guests eat and drink, their brother Andrey proposes to Natasha, whose peasant background and personal greed will ultimately push the Prozorov sisters from their home. Thus, the lunch provides a backdrop for the happy start to her brother's unhappy marriage, which will ultimately have repercussions for all who sit at the table.

Elsewhere, food and drink function as props, and the ways in which characters use these often suggest important things about their inner lives. In Act I of *Uncle Vanya*, when Dr. Astrov is unexpectedly called away from the Serebryakov estate to tend a patient, he asks for vodka, not because he wants it, but because he wants to stall his exit. From early morning, he has been hanging around waiting to catch a glimpse of Serebryakov's young wife, the beautiful Yelena. He wants to ask her to visit his forestry in hopes that an affair might develop between them. Yet he has lacked so far the confidence to ask her, as his anxious comments to the old nurse Marina about losing his looks and his unseemly moustaches reveal. But now, under pressure to leave, he acts fast, or at least as fast as the delay for a glass of vodka allows. As the play progresses further, he and Vanya get drunk as much on the thought of Yelena's beauty as on alcohol. (See Illustration 11.) Moreover, her and her husband's move to the estate so disrupt the household routine, that, as Marina complains, orderly meals and comfort foods have been abandoned. As the couple prepares to leave, Marina breathes a sigh of relief: "We'll go back to our old ways again. Have tea at eight in the morning, lunch by one, and in the evening we'll sit down to supper. [...] Ah, it's been a while, sinner that I am, since I've eaten noodles" (trans. Carnicke, 157).

In *The Cherry Orchard*, Lyubov Andreyevna's addiction to coffee and pills mirrors her brother's constant indulgence in candy and her footman's love of cigars and good champagne. What they eat and drink suggest that all three are, in some measure, self-indulgent people. Among

---

15 Spoken words from 1889, translated by McVay in *Chekhov's Three Sisters*, 42.

my favorite instances of Chekhov's use of food for comic effect are two in this, his last play. First, Yasha repeatedly and lasciviously compares Dunyasha to a "juicy little cucumber" (trans. Carnicke, 264); when the governess Charlotta then pulls a cucumber from her jacket and takes a bite, her action mocks his lust. Second, when it seems like Lopakhin is finally ready to propose to Varya, he notes the happy coincidence

9. Yepikhodov (Ivan Moskvin) eyes Yasha (Nikolay Aleksandrov) as he finishes off the champagne that Lopakhin needs for his proposal to Varya in *The Cherry Orchard*, 1904.

that champagne is "at the ready" to toast her acceptance (trans. Carnicke, 297). But once he discovers that Yasha has drunk it all (Illustration 9), Lopakhin's will seems as empty as the celebratory bottle.

11. The pause. Chekhov often calls for moments of silence in his plays by directing his characters to "pause" or by adding ellipses to their lines. In my translations I have scrupulously retained every devilish "..." that Chekhov uses in his Russian texts. Pauses and ellipses can suggest many different things: a thought that remains unspoken, the interruption of one character by another, a momentary lapse, confusion, embarrassment, or a willful refusal to speak. But whatever the function, during every pause or ellipsis something unspoken happens. As Nemirovich-Danchenko explains, "a pause is not something that is dead, but is an active intensification of experience."[16]

Consider the last scene between Irina and Baron Tuzenbach in *Three Sisters* (Act IV). While she has accepted his proposal of marriage, she has also frankly admitted that she cannot return his deep love. In this scene, he tells her, "I have to go into the city for... to say goodbye to my friends" (trans. Carnicke, 232). In fact, he is going to fight a duel over her. His pause marks his desire to protect her from the truth with a credible lie. Yet, even though he withholds information about the duel, he still tries to prepare her for the possibility of his death:

> Look there, that tree has dried up, but it's still waving in the breeze with the others. So I think that if I die, I too will still participate in life in some way or other. Goodbye my darling... (trans. Carnicke, 233)

His comforting words are expressed in full and complete sentences, but his broken farewell hangs in the air between them. Tuzenbach clearly finds it hard to leave her. Sensing that something is wrong, she offers to go with him. "No, no..." he says in alarm, stopping her. He then "walks away quickly" only to stop short with "Irina!" (trans. Carnicke, 233). What does he want to say? His impulse to speak goes nowhere. "Not knowing what to say," he says: "I didn't have any coffee today. Ask them

---

[16]   Nemirovitch-Dantchenko [*sic*], *My Life in the Russian Theatre*, 163.

to make me some..." What remains unspoken seems almost palpable. Then he "exits quickly" (trans. Carnicke, 233).

While one cannot know for certain what happens in such moments of silence, one can infer from the scene's context and character's situation. Pauses create an illusion that Chekhov's characters are engaged in continuous thinking beyond what they actually say. Although words on a page are two-dimensional, the illusion that something lies underneath them has come to be known as the subtext.

Such moments challenge actors to decide why their characters stop speaking and to create the unspoken thoughts. The Moscow Art Theatre actors went on a "quest" to find the meanings behind each Chekhovian pause; they used "persistent and involved research, not merely external, but also psychological."[17] This struggle led Stanislavsky to redefine both acting and the notion of a play. Actors became active collaborators with the playwright by filling in the textual gaps with their artistry. No longer could a director view a dramatic text as a finished work of literary art; it became for Stanislavsky (and is for actors and directors today) a blueprint from which to construct a finished performance (Chapter 6). Thus, Chekhov's importance to the development of modern acting cannot be underestimated. His pauses prompted the most important acting theory of the twentieth century, Stanislavsky's System, and new attitudes toward directing.

12. Soundscapes and the music of everyday life. Quotations from songs of all sorts, including operatic arias, abound among Chekhov's characters. In *The Bear*, Smirnov quotes lines from a gypsy ballad as he challenges Popova to a duel. In *The Anniversary*, Tatyana tells of being serenaded from the opera, *Eugene Onegin*, whose heroine is her namesake. In *The Seagull*, Dorn hums romantic ballads, while Treplev plays soulful waltzes. In *Three Sisters*, Masha and Vershinin communicate their adulterous secrets by singing a duet, while Chebutykin's final refrain from the British music hall adds a flippant counterpoint to an otherwise tragic ending. At times, Chekhov even makes the absence of music significant. Yelena in *Uncle Vanya* and Masha in *Three Sisters* are trained pianists, whose marriages deny them their music.

---

[17] Ibid., 153.

In *The Cherry Orchard*, Chekhov ironically uses music in the same way that standard nineteenth-century melodrama had, even as he subverts the genre's conventions (Chapter 5). As Lyubov Andreyevna confesses her sins in Act II, a distant orchestra underscores her words. Do violins match or mock her sentimental story? In Act III, she hires the same orchestra for her inappropriately timed party. As the orchestra merrily plays, the estate is being sold at auction.

Inspired by symbolism, Chekhov also makes his own music from the sounds of dialogue and daily life. His compositions are unique and startlingly beautiful, but easily missed in a quick read. For example, during Act II of *Three Sisters*, Chebutykin quotes an entirely irrelevant fact from the newspaper he is reading: "Balzac was married in Berdichev." Irina sits next to him, playing a game of solitaire; she "sings softly." Chebutykin continues: "I'll make a note of that in my notebook." He writes, "Balzac was married in Berdichev." Irina, "lost in thought," picks up his phrase and repeats, "Balzac was married in Berdichev" (trans. Carnicke, 199). The rhythmic repetition and alliteration of the sentence function as a meditative duet between the two. Clever actors might use the rustling of the newspaper, the scratching of Chebutykin's pen as he takes a note, and Irina's shuffling of the cards to orchestrate the dialogue. The effect creates a stunning moment of intimate quietude between them.

An extended instance of Chekhov's music occurs at the end of *Uncle Vanya*. From the moment when harness bells signal that the professor and his wife have left the estate, Chekhov begins to write operatically. If you read aloud from this point in the play until the end, making the sounds described in the stage directions as you go (trans. Carnicke, 164-7), Chekhov's extraordinary musicality will become crystal clear. The word "left" echoes anew with each new voice. Astrov begins with "They left." The nurse Marina enters with her knitting and with "They left." Moments later, Vanya's mother enters with her book and "They left." The ending periods make the statements sounds final and percussive. This repetition plays against the sounds of the nurse's knitting needles, Vanya's shuffling of papers, and his clicking of the beads on the abacus as he calculates the estate's accounts. Sonya's pen on paper also plays its part in the orchestra. It is "quiet," Astrov says. "The pens scratch, the cricket chirps. It's warm, cozy." When the harness bells sound again, they serve as Astrov's cue to leave. At his departure, the word "left" echoes again, repeated by the various voices in the scene.

Hearing the jingle of the harness bells on Astrov's horses as they depart, Marina says, "He left..." Then Sonya re-enters, having seen him off, with "He left..." Their sentences now trail off in ellipses, suggesting an unsettled emotion prompted by unfinished business. "Left" is the same note, now played in a different key. Vanya adds percussion to the music as he recites numbers from the estate's accounts: "The total is... fifteen... twenty five." At this point, the nurse introduces a new melody: "Oh, forgive us our sins." Sonia picks up this melody and embellishes it with a fantasy of future forgiveness and grace. Her final monologue ends the play. The sound of her refrain, "We'll rest!" sounds in Russian like an exhalation: *otdokhnyom*!

These twelve items are intended only to whet your appetite for more. They merely suggest the range of what is possible to find within Chekhov's plays. While the verbal details demonstrate the close linkage between his innovations in fiction and in drama, the material ones show how stage production offered him even more options. The overall conclusion is inescapable. For Chekhov's plays, the devil is always in the details.

Chapter Four

Dramatic Innovations
Part One: Vaudeville

While Chekhov's delight in devilish details illuminates much about his literary, dramatic, and comic sensibilities, the microscopic analysis of such details in his plays misses a bigger picture. Chekhov's paradigm shift in drama emerges as much from his passionate theatergoing as from his innovations in fiction. He went to the theater often, sometimes admiring and sometimes criticizing what audiences of his day cheered; in his own plays he adopted some of what he saw, parodied some, and in the process forged an entirely new type of drama from aspects of the older standard fare. Thus, one also needs to take a broader look at the popular theater that he knew.

When Chekhov the schoolboy first visited Taganrog's theater, and later as an adult, when he built his social life around Moscow's theatrical entertainment, French and German vaudevilles and melodramas dominated Russia's stages. True, one could find performances of other kinds, like Shakespeare's plays and Russia's classics, among them satirical comedies by Griboyedov and Gogol and ethnographically realistic depictions of society by Ostrovsky. For the most part, however, audiences thirsted for the imported theatrical confections, often thinly disguised as Russian plays through mediocre adaptations by local playwrights.

Chekhov too enjoyed such entertainments. The first books he purchased may have been Shakespeare's tragedies (Chapter 1), but the first production he saw in Taganrog was Jacques Offenbach's *La Belle Hélène (Beautiful Helen,* 1864), a titillating and farcical re-telling of the story of the Trojan war.[1] Offenbach's work is an *opera bouffe*—a light musical theater genre that derived from the French comic vaudeville. Its risqué treatment of Helen's seduction by Paris made it arguably

---

[1] Donald Rayfield, *Anton Chekhov,* 27.

the most performed theatrical piece of any kind in Russia during the 1870s.[2]

Chekhov laughs at the mediocrity inspired by Russia's theatrical dependence upon foreign imports in a story from 1886, entitled "The Playwright."[3] A man complaining of "shortness of breath, belching, heartburn, melancholy, and a bad taste in his mouth" visits a doctor, who immediately suspects that his new patient is "no stranger to alcoholic spirits." Thus, the doctor asks the man about his profession and lifestyle. "I am a playwright," says the man, who then describes his daily routine of dissipation. He rises at noon, "smokes a cigarette, and drinks two shots of vodka, sometimes even three." He gets dressed and goes out for breakfast, which, he complains, is "modest" because he lacks appetite. He can only manage a "cutlet and sturgeon with horseradish," followed by "two or four" shots of vodka, chased with some beer or wine. He spends the afternoon playing billiards with his friends until dinner, when again a bad appetite limits him to "six or seven" shots of vodka. He ends the day with a trip to the theater, which "upsets [his] nerves." "When do you write your plays?" asks the doctor. "That all depends on circumstances," explains the patient:

> First of all, there might fall into my hands, by accident or through friends [...] some sort of French or German piece. If it's suitable, then I take it to my sister or hire a student for five rubles... They translate it, and then, you see, I adapt it to Russian ways: instead of foreign names I put in Russian ones, and so forth... And that's it!... It's hard! Oh, so hard![4]

Chekhov exposes his theatrical criticism through comic irony in "The Playwright"; yet, he also demonstrates his interest in vaudevilles and melodramas by the adaptations and parodies of these forms within his own plays. On the one hand, he liberally borrows from and then adapts

---

[2] Laurence Senelick, "Offenbach and Chekhov; or, *La Belle Yelena*," *Theatre Journal* 42, no. 4 (December 1990), 455-67. In this article, Senelick makes a strong case for Offenbach's work as a source for Chekhov's *Uncle Vanya*.

[3] Chekhov first published "Dramaturg" in the journal *Sverchok* [The Cricket] in 1886, under the pseudonym "The Man without a Spleen." The standard edition of the story is in Chekhov, *Polnoe sobranie sochinenii* [The Complete Works], Vol. 5, 629-32.

[4] Ibid., 632.

French vaudevillian conventions for the one-act plays that he called "jokes," transforming his love of situation comedy into character driven works. On the other hand, he turns traditional melodrama inside out in his full-length plays, using his criticisms of it to reinvent entirely the notions of dramatic action and genre in the twentieth century. As the critic Eric Bentley once speculated, "Maybe any man only parodies what he is secretly fond of."[5] Without examining Chekhov's fondness for and criticisms of the wildly popular nineteenth-century conventions of vaudeville and melodrama, one cannot fully understand his innovations. Therefore, in this chapter and the next, I focus on his use and abuse of these theatrical forms in his own plays.

CHEKHOV'S LOVE OF FRENCH VAUDEVILLE

In 1888, Chekhov reported:

> Having nothing to do, I wrote a silly little vaudeville in the French style entitled *The Bear* [...] Ah, if they knew in [the literary offices at the journal] *The Northern Messenger* that I was writing vaudevilles, there would be hell to pay! But what can I do if my fingers itch with desire to turn out some tra-la-la? However much I try to be serious, nothing ever comes of it and I always end up alternating the serious with the trivial. (to Ia. P. Polonsky, 22 Feb. 1888)

Not to be confused with variety shows in the American tradition, the French vaudeville is a short comic play that uses convoluted and often implausible situations to entertain audiences. "You go to the theater for relaxation and amusement, not for instruction or correction," said France's most prolific writer of vaudevilles, Eugène Scribe (1791-1861), in defense of his highly successful but thoroughly improbable plays.[6]

---

[5] Eric Bentley, *The Life of the Drama* (New York: Atheneum, 1975), 212.

[6] Cited and translated by Stephen S. Stanton, "Introduction," in Stephen S. Stanton, ed., *Camille and Other Plays* (New York: Hill and Wang, Inc., 1957), n.2, vii. For an excellent treatment of the conventions of French vaudeville, see also Stephen S. Stanton's *English Drama and the French Well-Made Play, 1815-1915* (Ann Arbor: University Microfilms, 1955).

Taking inspiration from the ancient Roman comedies of Plautus, the Italian traditions of the *commedia dell'arte*, and French comedies of intrigue, vaudevilles were initially created for Paris' boulevard theaters in the 1790s, including *Le Théâtre de Vaudeville* (The Vaudeville Theatre) which opened in 1792. During the nineteenth century, vaudeville was perfected by a series of writers led by Scribe, who alone wrote two hundred and sixteen one-act vaudevilles, in addition to his other forty seven plays of varying types. No wonder Scribe said in 1814 that vaudeville is "the only genre to which I am utterly devoted"![7]

Initially, vaudeville combined spoken dialogue with popular songs. By the end of the century, however, the form had bifurcated, with vaudeville relying more upon dialogue (as in Chekhov's one-act plays) and its music inspiring new forms (like comic opera and operetta, including Offenbach's popular *opera bouffe*). At this junction, Scribe became highly influential in operatic incarnations of the vaudeville, producing innovative *libretti*[8] for eighty six comic operas, twenty eight grand operas, and nine ballets.

Usually in vaudeville a young couple who wishes to marry must face obstacles that block their happiness. Parents or guardians might object to the match. Financial considerations might present economic difficulties; a young woman's family cannot afford a dowry or a young man lacks an attractive income. The attentions of a competing but less attractive suitor (favored by the parents or in better financial circumstances than the romantic lead) might further complicate the lovers' desires. On the way to a happy ending, there occur misunderstandings, mistaken identities and unexpected complications. These difficulties are often untangled in a single thrilling, climactic scene.

In short, vaudevilles are situation comedies *par excellence*. They revel in well-engineered plots and theatrically exciting climaxes, leaving little stage-time for the development of complex characters. No wonder vaudevilles are peopled largely by one-dimensional stock characters! At the beginning of the play, the cast announce themselves as lover, crafty servant, stern parent, or mischief-maker; and these stereotypes remain intact until the end. As the critic Stephen S. Stanton explains, "The will

---

[7] Karin Pendle, *Eugène Scribe and French Opera of the Nineteenth Century* (Ann Arbor: UMI Research Press, 1979), 4.

[8] The Italian word for "little books" is commonly used for texts of operas.

of the characters in this type of drama is always subordinate to the exigencies of the plot and to the artifices employed by the author."[9]

Vaudevilles were introduced into Russia in the first decades of the nineteenth century. By the 1830s, Russian writers and comic actors alike were trying their hands at the form. For example, actor Dmitry Lensky-Vorobyev (1805-60), who had become famous for his portrayal of Molière's *Tartuffe* at Moscow's Maly Theatre, wrote over seventy vaudevilles. His most famous was *Lev Gurych Sinichkin, or The Provincial Debutante* (1840), about a father and his precious daughter. This play became such a successful vehicle for comic actors that it was staged regularly in Russia until the mid-twentieth century.[10] Such French-styled comic one-acts reached their peak of popularity in Russia during the 1890s, when Chekhov was attending Moscow's theaters.

Two factors made this frothy type of entertainment particularly suited to Russian theaters at the turn of the twentieth century. First, tsarist censorship encouraged light, non-controversial fare over more satirical and serious productions; vaudevilles were safe bets when passing through the hands of the censors.[11] Second, actors frequently chose vaudevilles for their benefit performances, because comedies guaranteed strong ticket sales. At that time, theaters allowed stars to stage periodic benefits for themselves in lieu of bonuses. The actors would choose their material and keep the profits from the first night's tickets. Because vaudevilles frequently included roles that allowed for star turns, actors often found these plays to be especially good vehicles for demonstrating their talents. In fact, Chekhov wrote some of his most innovative vaudevilles for particular actors and their benefit performances.[12]

---

[9] Stanton, "Introduction," *Camille and Other Plays*, xv.

[10] Marc Slonim, *Russian Theatre: From the Empire to the Soviets* (New York: The World Publishing Company, 1961), 50-1.

[11] Vera Gottlieb, *Chekhov and the Vaudeville: A Study of Chekhov's One-Act Plays* (Cambridge: Cambridge University Press, 2000), 27-8.

[12] Ironically, the well-known comic actress Elizaveta Ivanovna Levkeyeva (1851-1904) chose Chekhov's *The Seagull* for her benefit at the Aleksandrinsky Theatre, St. Petersburg, in 1896. By some accounts, the premiere went badly because the audience was comprised largely of her fans, who expected vaudevillian comedy instead of subtlety. Moreover, in the character of Arkadina, played by Levkeyeva, the audience saw only a cruel parody of their idol. See Rayfield, *Anton Chekhov*, 388.

Chekhov got his itch for writing comic vaudevilles early on. During his school days, he wrote, acted in, and then tore up several, including the lost play, *Why the Hen Clucks* (*Nedarom kuritsa pela*).[13] As an adult, he continued to enjoy this type of theater, despite the fact that most vaudevilles were written on demand by resident playwrights for the imperial theaters in St. Petersburg and Moscow and were consequently of low literary quality. As scholar Marc Slonim notes:

> While some of those "dramatists in residence" had a certain dexterity in presenting stereotyped stage effects and situations, all of them were so alien to "great literature" that their plays did not appear in print and were turned down by periodicals and publishers.[14]

Chekhov's comic criticism in "The Playwright" demonstrates that his passion for contemporary Russian vaudevilles did not blind him to their faults; rather, his passion impelled him to improve the genre. He enlivened both content and form in his clever one-act plays, expanding the range of possibilities within the traditional conventions of vaudeville.

As his guilty remarks in 1888 suggest, Chekhov understood that the intellectual elite saw the writing of such frothy little plays as literary slumming. Nonetheless, he worked on the popular genre with zest. As he told his friend Suvorin:

> When I have written myself out, I will still be able to write vaudevilles and live on the income from them. It seems to me that I could write about a hundred a year. Subjects for vaudevilles pour out of me, like oil from the wells of Baku.[15] (23 Dec. 1888)

Alas, Chekhov only found enough time to turn out nineteen, all of which are extraordinarily funny and stageworthy. In print, however, he did not label all his short plays "vaudevilles." He used various generic subtitles from "jokes" to "dramatic etudes." By whatever subtitle they are called, they clarify the comic sensibility that underpins Chekhov's full-length

---

[13] Ibid., 33.

[14] Slonim, *Russian Theatre*, 83.

[15] The city of Baku is located on the Black Sea near Chekhov's last home in Yalta and is well known for its oil wells.

plays and they successfully challenge his undeserved reputation as a writer who dwells on tears instead of laughter (Introduction). Chief among the one-acts are the following plays.

On the Harmfulness of Tobacco (*O vrede tabaka*, 1886-1903) is a "scene and monologue in one act;" it depicts a pseudo-scientific lecture given for a women's social club, during which the speaker—a hen-pecked husband of one of the club's members—unwittingly airs his family's dirty laundry. Chekhov first created this monologue for a popular comic actor at the Korsh Theatre in Moscow, Leonid Ivanovich Gradov-Sokolov (1846-90), who had played a small role in the premiere of Chekhov's full-length *Ivanov* (1887). However, Chekhov kept tinkering with the solo performance piece until one year before his death, ultimately revising it five times. With each revision, the central character gains more and more psychological complexity.

Chekhov called four of his vaudevilles "jokes." In *The Bear* (*Medved'*, 1888) a blustering, retired soldier comes to collect a debt from a widow with dimples in her cheeks. She refuses to pay; he challenges her to a duel; and when she accepts his challenge, he unexpectedly finds himself proposing instead of shooting her. In *The Proposal* (*Predlozhenie*, 1888-9) a hypochondriac tries unsuccessfully to propose marriage to the daughter of a neighboring landowner. (See the extended analysis below.)

Chekhov wrote his next "joke," *A Tragedian In Spite of Himself* (*Tragik ponevole*, 1889-90)[16] for Konstantin Aleksandrovich Varlamov (1848-1915), a major star of the imperial Aleksandrinsky Theatre in St. Petersburg, who played comic, operatic, and tragic roles. In this play, a businessman is on his way to visit his wife in the country. He carries with him an absurd assortment of objects, which she wants for their summerhouse: a new globe for her lamp, a bicycle for their son, and various gourmet groceries. On his way to the station, he stops by a friend's home to complain about his wife's burdensome requests, only to acquire yet two more items for his pile. In the course of the conversation, his sympathetic friend learns that a mutual acquaintance is also staying in the country, very close to the businessman's wife; and this acquaintance had unfortunately forgotten to take her bird and birdcage with her

---

[16] Note that Chekhov's title echoes that of Molière's comedy, *The Doctor in Spite of Himself* (*Le Médecin malgré lui*, 1666).

when she left for the country. So, it only makes sense for the business-man to take these along with him to the country as well. Thus, by play's end, he has only added to his burden. In Chekhov's fourth "joke," *The Anniversary* (*Iubilei*, 1891), multiple disturbances from a gallery of eccentric characters derail a pompous ceremony to commemorate a bank's centennial jubilee.[17]

Also falling into the vaudevillian tradition are three other short plays by Chekhov, in which comedy registers more ambiguously than in the one-act jokes. The first of these is *The Swan Song* (*Lebedinaia pesnia*, 1887-8), "a dramatic etude" about an old comic actor named Svetlovidov, who confronts his failed ambitions to become a great tragic actor in an empty theater in the middle of the night. Like the story from 1886 on which it is based,[18] Chekhov initially entitled the play *Calchas*, after the hypocritical Trojan oracle in Offenbach's comic opera, *La Belle Hélène*. This initial title refers to the fact that Svetlovidov wears Calchas' usual costume—a short tunic and tights. By his dress and manner, the audience understands that the old actor had performed Offenbach's role that evening, gotten drunk before changing out of his costume, and fallen asleep in his dressing room. When he wakes up several hours later, the theater is empty of sets and audience. Its dark, cavernous atmosphere shocks him into a realization of how he has wasted his talents. Alone but for the company's prompter, who feeds him cues from all the roles that he would have most liked to play, including Shakespeare's King Lear, Svetlovidov lives out his fantasy of being a serious actor. As he performs, these classic roles are visually out of joint with his silly, clownlike attire. Chekhov's final choice of title suggests that, like the dying swan who sings only at the end of life, Svetlovidov's performance marks the end of his hopes and career. How ironic that the actor gives what might well be his best performance for an empty house! Not only does Chekhov brilliantly use an empty stage as his set, but he also creates further irony by naming his character

---

[17] This play is based on the story, "A Defenseless Creature" ("Bezzashchitnoe sushchestvo," 1887). See A. P. Chekhov, *Polnoe sobranie sochinenii i pisem v tridtsati tomakh* [The Complete Works and Letters in Thirty Volumes], Vol. 6 (Moscow: Nauka, 1976), 87-91.

[18] "Calchas" ["Kalkhas"] in Chekhov, *Polnoe sobranie sochinenii* [The Complete Works], Vol. 5, 389-94. See Senelick, "Offenbach and Chekhov; or, *La Belle Yelena*."

Svetlovidov, which means in Russian "one who sees the light." In both his comic role as Troy's hypocritical seer and in his tragic swan song, Svetlovidov makes good on his name.

Chekhov created *The Swan Song* as a vehicle for Vladimir Nikolayevich Davydov (1849-1925), an especially versatile actor who played both at the imperial Aleksandrinsky Theatre in St. Petersburg and at Moscow's most popular private theater, the Korsh. Davydov originated the phleg-matic and suicidal title role in *Ivanov* in 1887. One can easily imagine Davydov's performance of Svetlovidov as at once hysterically funny and astonishingly beautiful, registering in just the paradoxical way that Che-khov might have wanted.

The second of these last three ambiguously comic vaudevilles is *Tatyana Repina* (1889), "a drama in one act," which Chekhov wrote as a parodic response to a full-length melodramatic play of the same title written by his friend and editor Aleksey Sergeyevich Suvorin (Chap-ter 1). While Suvorin's play depicts the real-life tragedy of an actress who poisoned herself during a performance because she had been spurned in love, Chekhov turns the sensational suicide into a fashionable fad, with women everywhere responding to their failed love affairs by commit-ting a "Tatyana Repina." The third vaudeville is *The Wedding* (*Svad'ba*, 1889-90), a nearly absurdist "play in one act" about a family who hires a general to preside over their daughter's wedding reception in order to give the event added prestige. Instead of an impressive military man, however, there arrives a deaf naval officer who cannot understand why he has been brought to the party.[19]

Chekhov's first unequivocal hit as a playwright was *The Bear*, which he had written for publication, not performance. When this one-act joke appeared in *New Times* in August 1880, his friends were so taken with its humor that they persuaded him to submit the script to the censor for permission to get it staged. The censor denied the request: "The unfavorable impression produced by this more than strange

---

[19] *The Wedding* is based on three of Chekhov's short stories: "The Wedding Season" ("Svadebnyi sezon," 1881), "Marrying for Money" ("Brak po raschetu," 1884), and "A Wedding with a General" ("Svad'ba s generalom," 1884), in A. P. Che-khov, *Polnoe sobranie sochinenii i pisem v tridtsati tomakh* [The Complete Works and Letters in Thirty Volumes], Vol. 3 (Moscow: Nauka, 1975), 449-52, 98-102, and 107-12.

subject is magnified owing to the coarseness and indecent tone of the whole play."[20] But this initial decision was overturned by the head of the censorship ministry on a second review: "I read the play. It seems to me, that several coarse phrases should be struck from it, but as for the subject, it contains nothing reprehensible, only sheer nonsense."[21] *The Bear* premiered on 28 October 1888 at the Korsh Theatre in Moscow, where the full-length *Ivanov* had also premiered. *The Bear*'s immediate success guaranteed its production all over Russia, with major actors often choosing its roles for their benefits.[22] Moreover, it proved such a financial success that Chekhov had it specifically in mind, when he advised his brother Alexander to write two or three plays, because "a play is a pension fund" (21 Feb. 1889). His next one-act joke, *The Proposal*, proved just as successful and lucrative.

Chekhov's zest for writing vaudevilles was coupled with seriousness of purpose. He crafted each of his short plays with the same care that he used for all his writings. "In one-act pieces, you have to write nonsense—that's their strength," he explained to Suvorin. But, Chekhov continued, "it is much easier to write a play about Socrates than about a young girl or a cook, which merely shows that I do not regard the writing of vaudeville as a frivolous occupation" (2 Jan. 1894). In light of the subtlety in Chekhov's full-length plays, however, his one-acts appear at first glance simple and obvious in their dramatic means. The Russian formalist critic, Sergey Dmitrievich Balukhaty, who spent much of his career analyzing Chekhov's innovations in drama, observes that in the vaudevilles, "he did not establish any kind of original stylistic principle, but only mirrored the vaudevillian conventions of his day."[23] Consequently, few scholars have seriously studied Chekhov's dramatic jokes. Vera Gottlieb is the exception, and she too speculates that, "It is, perhaps, because of the apparent conventionality of his vaudevilles that Chekhov's short plays have been largely neglected by critics."[24] A closer

---

[20] S. I. Donaurov, cited in Chekhov, *Polnoe sobranie sochinenii* [The Complete Works], Vol. 11, 427.
[21] E. M. Feoktistov, cited in Ibid.
[22] Laurence Senelick, in Anton Chekhov, *The Complete Plays*, trans. Laurence Senelick (New York: W.W. Norton and Company, 2006), 415-6.
[23] S. D. Balukhatyi, *Voprosy Poetiki* [Questions of Poetics] (Leningrad: Izdatel'stvo Leningradskogo Universiteta, 1990), 238.
[24] Gottlieb, *Chekhov and the Vaudeville*, 16.

look at his one-acts reveals that their conventionality is indeed only apparent. As Ronald Hingley, who translated all of Chekhov's short plays, insightfully observes, his "vaudevilles are improvements as well as adaptations."[25] Moreover, as Gottlieb's detailed study also makes clear, Chekhov transfers much that he learned from his experiments with vaudeville into his major plays.

Thus, I invite you to compare one of Eugène Scribe's vaudevilles, *A Peculiar Position*, with one of Chekhov's jokes, *The Proposal*, particularly with regard to their differing treatments of situation and character.

A VAUDEVILLE BY SCRIBE AND A JOKE BY CHEKHOV

A Peculiar Position (*La Frontière de Savoie*) was Scribe's 183rd vaudeville.[26] It premiered in Paris in 1834 and presents an excellent example of the genre. In fact, as Stanton observes, in this play "Scribe invented nothing. He used the technical methods of the great writers of comedy, but he kept all their tricks in use all the time in his plays. He was the theatrical juggler supreme."[27] *A Peculiar Position* takes place in a castle in Savoy near the border of France. Savoy was initially an independently governed dukedom that was later annexed by the French government. The play's action occurs during the decade of political unrest before Savoy's annexation. In the first scenes of the play, the audience learns that the Count of Novara (who never appears onstage) is suspected of membership in a secret revolutionary society and is thus in jeopardy of arrest by the Savoyard army. As the play begins, soldiers have been sent to the border to ensure that the Count be prevented from crossing into

---

[25] Ronald Hingley, "Introduction" in Anton Chekhov, *Twelve Plays*, Ronald Hingley, trans. (New York: Oxford University Press, 1992), viii.

[26] Scribe listed his fellow vaudevillist Jean-François Bayard as his co-author for *La Frontière de Savoie* [literally *The Border of Savoy*] but this attribution may mean little. Scribe often gave credit to those who merely supplied a clever idea that sparked the creation of a play. See Pendle, *Eugène Scribe and French Opera of the Nineteenth Century*, 13. In the following analysis, I use an English translation that was created in 1837 by J. R. Planché, published in Stanton, ed., *Camille and Other Plays*, 3-32. All quotations are taken from this edition and page numbers are given in parentheses within the text.

[27] Stanton, "Introduction," *Camille and Other Plays*, xiii.

France. Despite this historical context, the play itself deals little with politics. Rather Scribe focuses on interrelated stories of love, betrayal, and mistaken identities, loosely tied together by the Count's need to cross the border to evade arrest.

First, the Count's young servant Barbara, who is "very pretty" (6), indeed "uncommonly pretty" (14), is in love with Carlo, a soldier for Savoy. Barbara's mother (who never appears on stage) objects to her daughter marrying a military man and insists that Barbara choose Pepito, a conniving servant with few scruples. Thus, Barbara's story is conventional; she prefers one suitor while her parent prefers another. To wiggle out of her situation, Barbara lies to Pepito, telling him that she is already married. Her lie soon leads to a case of mistaken identity within the play, when she buttresses her lie by claiming for her husband a bumbling, middle-aged French grocer who happens to be visiting the castle in order to solicit the Count's business.

Second, Pepito reveals to Barbara that a cloaked man (who never appears onstage) has snuck into the bedroom of the "magnificent" (10) Countess de Novara in the middle of the night, apparently compromising her honor. Thus, he sets into motion a second conventional story about an apparently adulterous marriage. However, Barbara correctly guesses that the mysterious man is none other than the Count in disguise.

Next, when the Countess learns that the grocer is a French citizen with a proper passport, she realizes how she can help her husband escape arrest. She surreptitiously exchanges the grocer's passport with the Count's, thus leaving the unsuspecting merchant with the passport of a wanted man. Scribe has contrived yet another opportunity for mistaken identities. When a major from the Savoyard army arrives in search of the Count and finds the wanted man's passport in the hands of the grocer, the Countess ensures the success of her ruse by treating the grocer as if he were her husband, much to the delight of the lusty, overweight merchant. Thus, Scribe has also contrived to turn the most unattractive man in the play into the apparent love interest of the two most beautiful women in the castle, Barbara and the Countess.

From this point on, complications begin to multiply at a furious pace. Thinking that the grocer is the Count and wanting to be kind to the married couple, the Major allows them a moment alone before the arrest. To avoid the intimacy of this favor, the Countess invites the Major to join them for dinner. In conversation over a glass of wine, the Major relates how he was once in love with a woman named Adolphine, who left him to marry a wealthy tradesman. At this moment, Barbara's true love, Carlo, arrives to challenge Pepito to a duel, only to learn that he must now challenge another rival as well, the grocer as her alleged husband. As the frightened grocer cowers in a corner, refusing to duel, his actual and very jealous wife, named Adolphine, arrives. The grocer's wife immediately recognizes the Major as her former lover and seeks his help in dealing with her apparently unfaithful husband. At this moment of crisis, the Major further reveals that the arrest warrant for the Count has become an execution order. The news leaves the grocer, who still holds the Count's passport, cowering in even greater fear for his life. Scribe uses the accelerating pace of these farcical complications to intensify the action of the play and create comic suspense.[28]

All the misunderstandings are resolved simultaneously in a final climactic scene. As soon as the Countess learns that her husband has safely arrived in France with the grocer's stolen passport, she reveals her ruse, freeing the grocer from the execution order. The Major then learns by messenger that the government has cleared the Count of all suspicion and voided the warrant. In turn, Barbara also admits to having lied about being married to the grocer to protect her love for Carlo. Thus, circumstances are happily untangled and the grocer ends the play by asking as much for the audience's applause as for the Count's grocery business: "Ladies and gentlemen, I feel I cannot serve this chateau unless I obtain your approval" (32).

In a play of half an hour or so, much has happened. "In this kind of comedy," explains Stanton, "all the structure of complication and reversal that sustains suspense and delays the resolution, dominates everything else."[29] Scribe successfully juggles the characters' circumstances and secrets through frequent use of expository statements in the dialogue, character asides, and soliloquies that continually remind spectators of the confusing facts. For example, in dialogue Barbara frankly tells Carlo: "Yes; my mother insists upon my receiving the addresses of Pepito, a nasty little mischief-making, tattling, babbling fellow; one of the new servants that the Countess hired just after I came here" (5).

---

28   Pendle, *Eugène Scribe and French Opera of the Nineteenth Century*, 105.
29   Stanton, "Introduction," *Camille and Other Plays*, xi.

When the Countess learns that the grocer is a Frenchman and determines to exchange his passport for her husband's, she makes plain her scheming in an aside that precedes her actual exchange: "What an idea! If I could but manage—" (12). When the grocer then understands that he has been the victim of both Barbara's lie and the Countess' scheme, he vents his anger in an extended soliloquy. Locked in a room by himself so that he cannot escape, he first recounts all the ins and outs of what has happened to him and then vows "vengeance" on all of womankind for having been victimized by female wiles. "There is no atrocity I am not prepared to commit; I will employ all the powers of fascination I possess to victimize the whole sex" (27). Not only does his soliloquy make his reaction all the more comic; it also assists the audience in following the dexterous juggling of action, which marks Scribe as an excellent writer of vaudeville.

Scribe's fast-paced storytelling is only possible, however, by sacrificing character development. Barbara is little more than a pretty servant, the Countess a loyal and loving wife, Carlo a soldier in love, and the Major a responsible representative of the Savoyard government. They are stock characters with behavior always in consonance with their established roles. Barbara follows the Countess' orders; the Countess hides and then saves her husband; Carlo challenges all rivals to duels; and the Major carries out the government's will.

Scribe further delineates his characters by using shorthand techniques. First, names can convey a character's profession, class, or basic nature. For example, the grocer is appropriately named Champignon, the French word for *mushroom*. His name marks him as both a Frenchman and a dealer in gourmet foods. Moreover, "mushroom" suggests his physical appearance and his general cowardice; like his namesake he is squat, round, soft, and without backbone. The phallic shape of a mushroom also comically underlines the women's apparent desire for him and his actual lust for them.

Second, Scribe includes explicit statements about a character's traits that can be taken at face value, such as Barbara's description of Pepito as "a nasty little mischief-making, tattling, babbling fellow" (5). Similar statements about Pepito abound in the play; and he consistently proves the characterization to be true by his behavior.

Third, Scribe also uses "speech peculiarities" to make characters "immediately recognizable to an audience as typical of a particular class or profession."[30] The two women in *A Peculiar Position* speak in a refined manner, using old-fashioned words and romantic phrases in consonance with their beauty. Thus, instead of telling Carlo that she is happy to see him, Barbara more colorfully says: "Dear Carlo, [...] I never dreamed I should [see you] whilst you were quartered at Lans-le-bourg" (5). When the Major arrests the grocer thinking him the Count, the Countess reassures herself that her scheme is working with a conventionally melodramatic phrase: the "unfortunate passport has discovered all" (17). Language too characterizes the clownlike Champignon. In false modesty, he begins nearly every statement about himself with "if I were a vain man." He also peppers his speech with the adjective "peculiar." For example, he repeatedly tells others, "I have a peculiar way of doing business," and then tells himself that circumstances in the castle have placed him in "a peculiar position." These linguistic repetitions so characterize him that, when the Countess finally admits that she and Barbara have been responsible for his difficulties, she acknowledges his right to be angry by quoting him: "'If he had been a vain man' he certainly might have presumed [on us] in his 'peculiar position'" (31).

Chekhov's *The Proposal* turns a vaudeville like Scribe's on its head. Chekhov shifts the center of gravity away from the deft juggling of complexities in plot toward the comic complexities of human nature. On the surface Chekhov seems to mirror Scribe closely. The Russian's situations seem as improbable as anything in Scribe. An estate owner named Lomov attempts to propose to his neighbor's daughter, but faints before he can say the intended words. Natalya Stepanovna, in turn, is so desperate to get married that she faints when she thinks her potential fiancé has died of a heart attack while proposing. Chekhov's characters also define themselves as explicitly as do Scribe's. The would-be bridegroom seems little more than the hypochondriac that he reveals himself to be in his first soliloquy. Natalya Stepanovna observes that she prefers to speak forthrightly and proves it throughout the play with short, direct statements. As she tells Lomov, "I don't like it when a man says what he doesn't think" (trans. Carnicke, 30). Her father, Chubukov, also characterizes himself by saying "I'm quick tempered" (trans. Carnicke, 32). He then proves the accuracy of his statement by jumping into argument after argument with Lomov.

---

[30] Gottlieb, *Chekhov and the Vaudeville*, 29-30.

Scratch the surface, however, and one soon notices that Chekhov's characters develop into credible (if silly) people who escape the bounds of their stock labels. Take Lomov, for instance. His behavior surely fits his comic type, but his hypochondriacal fears have real consequences within the play. He is a healthy-looking man whose every emotional upset leads to a physical manifestation. His dread of proposing and his escalating anger over irrelevant arguments with his intended fiancée make him feel cold, cause his eye to twitch, induce a racing heart, provoke a fainting fit, etc., etc. These physical manifestations of fear derail him from his intention to propose. Surely Dr. Chekhov knew that such symptoms, however extreme and laughable, occur in real life. Chubukov and his daughter are also grounded in a familiar kind of stubbornness, that keeps them arguing with Lomov even when their arguments are at odds with what they actually want. Such counterintuitive behavior rings true to human nature. In other words, in *The Proposal* we meet three eccentric but credible characters whose personal proclivities make it impossible for them to keep from arguing with one another. In short, Chekhov has transformed situation comedy into character comedy by "'humaniz[ing]' the 'stock' characters and [making] them realistic, complex individuals."[31]

CHEKHOV'S COMIC SENSIBILITY

A more detailed look at *The Proposal* demonstrates how Chekhov manages this transformation by working on two fronts: (1) he foils audience expectations of vaudeville; and (2) he concentrates his use of stage-time on extended interactions, which reveal the characters' complex and multi-dimensional natures.[32]

---

[31] Ibid., 44.

[32] Ibid., 63-78. In the following analysis of *The Proposal*, I am indebted to Vera Gottlieb's more detailed reading of the play. I also draw your attention to the work of Peta Tait, who argues in "The Proposal Reconsidered: A Biography of Love," that "Gottlieb's comments about Chekhov's play are analogous to the approach taken by some commentaries on Chekhov and Knipper's relationship." Tait's article is in Clayton, ed., *Chekhov Then and Now*, 301-11 (quotation on 303).

On the first front, Chekhov aggressively overturns audience expectations. In *The Proposal* there are none of the usual obstacles that keep a pretty young woman from marrying her one true love. Unlike Barbara, who is pursued by three men in *A Peculiar Position*, Natalya Stepanovna has only one suitor. Additionally, at twenty-five she is already past the age when rivals would be likely to duel for her sake. Neither does Natalya Stepanovna seem particularly worried about her appearance when she arrives on stage in her apron. True, her father has told her that "a merchant's come for his goods" (trans. Carnicke, 22), but in similar circumstances, Barbara, no doubt, would have taken an offstage moment to remove her apron and fix her hair. Chekhov also sets aside the convention of an obstinate parent who blocks his child's happiness. Unlike Barbara's mother who objects to Carlo, Chubukov is delighted to learn that their neighbor seeks his daughter's hand. "This has been one of my fondest wishes for a long time now," he tells Lomov (trans. Carnicke, 20). Chekhov even does away with the usual financial obstacles that occur in standard vaudevilles. The match between Lomov and Natalya Stepanovna would unite two viable estates and thus create a lucrative life for both of them. In short, this is a good match. Finally, Chekhov does away with all the sentimental vagaries of love. Lomov is far from a standard leading man. At thirty-five years of age he swallows the notion of marriage as if it were a bitter tasting but efficacious medicine: "If you think about it too long, if you hesitate, if you talk too much and keep waiting for an ideal, a true love, then you'll never get married..." (trans. Carnicke, 21). He chooses his neighbor for eminently practical reasons: "Natalya Stepanovna is a wonderful housekeeper, not bad looking, educated... What more do I need?" (trans. Carnicke, 21).

Chekhov draws attention to his overturning of audience expectation by giving his play an ironic title; after all, Lomov never actually proposes. He stumbles nervously over his words and inadvertently into one argument after another. As the play continues, the arguments only escalate until the lovers fall, not into each other's arms, but into faints of exasperated anger. When Chubukov wakes them up, he takes matters into his own hands and simply declares them engaged: "You better get married quick, and—well, what the hell! She's agreed!" (trans. Carnicke, 34). The romantic story promised by the title has been replaced by the couple's prematurely domestic arguments and a father's clever intervention. In short, *The Proposal* seems as much a parody of vaudeville as vaudeville in its own right.

On the second front, Chekhov radically cuts back on the number of circumstances that condition the development of his story by focusing on a single situation with multiple instances of how it gets out of hand. Whereas Scribe multiplies the occasions for misunderstandings and mistaken identities in his play, Chekhov limits himself to Lomov's botched attempt to propose which unfolds in two equally silly arguments that distract him from his intention.

Chekhov uses the stage time that he saves through this simplification of circumstances to create opportunities for extended interactions, which reveal the characters' personalities. In the case of *The Proposal*, the escalating arguments between Lomov and his neighbors are exactly such opportunities. Without the usual vaudevillian obstacles imposed upon them by external circumstances, the characters generate a new kind of inner obstacle. All the difficulties that block Lomov's proposal arise from the silly and sad complexities of the characters themselves. Additionally, because the audience follows the ins and outs of each onstage argument, Chekhov allows his characters to reveal themselves in real time to the audience. In short, Scribe's love of story cedes to Chekhov's fascination with people; and hence, Chekhov has re-made situation comedy into the comedy of "characters in action," to borrow Gottlieb's apt phrase. "In *The Proposal* [...] it is evident that the characters of Chekhov's farce-vaudevilles are not created by or for the situation but create a situation simply by being themselves."[33]

An examination of the arguments in *The Proposal* makes Chekhov's crafting of interpersonal dynamics all the more clear. Secondary remarks in the conversations between Lomov and Natalya Stepanovna spark both arguments. The first clash begins when Chubukov plays a little joke on his daughter by telling her that "a merchant's come for his goods" (trans. Carnicke, 22). While this joke picks up Lomov's rather mercenary view of marriage, it also sets Natalya Stepanovna up for the argument. (Illustration 10) Ignorant of Lomov's intention to propose, she is understandably taken aback by his fancy dress and searches for a reason for his formal attire. As Lomov nervously lists all the practical reasons for their union, she seizes upon his mention of a valueless

---

[33] Gottlieb, *Chekhov and the Vaudeville*, 44; 63-4.

piece of land as belonging to him. Thinking the Ox Field her family's property, she jumps to the conclusion that Lomov has come to contest its ownership. As the argument builds, Chubukov defends his daughter and Lomov turns litigious, threatening to take them to court over the land. Of course, the audience knows that if they were to marry, the argument would be entirely moot.

10. This book's author as Natalya Stepanovna in *The Proposal*, 1978.

143

Only after driving Lomov from their house does Natalya Stepanovna learn the real reason for his visit and then only from her father's off-hand comment: "this... blind dolt...dares to make a proposal, etc. Humph! A proposal!" (trans. Carnicke, 27). Appalled at her lost opportunity, Natalya Stepanovna pleads with Chubukov to bring Lomov back.

The second argument arises from Natalya Stepanovna's inept attempt to make Lomov comfortable through small talk about hunting. As a forthright person, she simply does not know how to flatter him. Thus, Lomov's pride in his hunting dog triggers Natalya Stepanovna's stubborn and defensive insistence that her father's dog is better. When Chubukov again intervenes by backing his daughter, Lomov's hypochondriacal ire leads him to collapse in an apparent heart attack. The intensity of the argument takes its physical toll on Natalya Stepanovna as well, who faints at the realization that she has lost her last chance at marriage.

While the content and intensity of their arguments are unquestionably funny, Chekhov's characters emerge as believably stubborn people who cannot let slide anything that strikes them as amiss. The forthright Natalya Stepanovna simply does not have the tact to concede ownership of a valueless piece of land; nor does she have enough social grace to flatter Lomov for his taste in dogs. Honesty above all else remains her highest principle: "First you say the field is yours, then that Diviner's a better dog than Rover. I don't like it when a man says what he doesn't think" (trans. Carnicke, 30). Chubukov too cannot help arguing his own case, even at the expense of his daughter's happiness. In his turn, Lomov cannot keep his highest priority in mind when challenged. Leaving aside all consideration of his hypochondria, one notices that he is easily distracted and as quick tempered as his would-be father-in-law. Argument is the stubborn way that all three manage to cope with others.

Moreover, Chekhov lets his audience know that marriage will change nothing in their natures. As Chubukov calls for champagne to seal their engagement, Natalya Stepanovna and Lomov continue arguing about their dogs. "Well, the familial happiness has now begun!" exclaims Chubukov (trans. Carnicke, 34). With this exclamation, Chekhov melds a happy ending to Lomov's proposal with an unhappy beginning to his marriage. Unlike Scribe, where the twists in a complicated story are always happily untangled by the end of the play, Chekhov ends on an ambivalent and unresolved note.

Chekhov's newly styled, unconventional vaudevillian situations migrate wholesale into his full-length plays. Pointless arguments that recall those in *The Proposal* are found in *Three Sisters* (Act II) when the disaffected Captain Solyony argues for the sake of argument, first about the name of a Caucasian vegetable (which he has actually confused with a similar sounding name of a roast) and then about whether or not there are two universities in Moscow (a debate that is also a theatrical in-joke, because the imperial Maly Theatre was often called Moscow's second university). Chekhov also transplants Lomov's non-proposal into *The Cherry Orchard* (Act IV), when Lopakhin attempts at long last to propose to Varya. From the beginning of the play, everyone has assumed that the two will marry, but, like Lomov, Lopakhin cannot speak the necessary words. However, unlike Lomov who is assisted by a helpful new father-in-law, Lopakhin is left alone by Varya's mother to fend for himself, despite his accurate prediction to her that "without you I feel that I won't propose" (trans. Carnicke, 297).

Solyony's arguments and Lopakhin's non-proposal retain their comic heritage, while being newly played in a minor key. Solyony's argumentativeness reveals his inability to cede to others; the same trait ultimately prompts him to kill Tuzenbach in a duel over Irina in Act IV. As Solyony warns her in Act II, "I will not allow any fortunate rivals... I will not... I swear to you by all that is holy, that I will kill any rival..." (trans. Carnicke, 207). Lopakhin's failure forever closes the door on the possibility of a future life for Ranyevskaya's family on her former estate, which his marriage to her adopted daughter may have offered. This finality is echoed in the words repeated by both Lopakhin and Varya as they face each other: "life in this house is finished..." (trans. Carnicke, 297).

The ambiguity with which *The Proposal* ends also sheds light on the seamless blending of comic and sad elements in Chekhov's later full-length plays. Compare, for example, how two couples—Lomov and Natalya Stepanovna and Anya and Trofimov in *The Cherry Orchard*—begin their lives together. For the first of these couples, the happy engagement comically promises more arguments. For Anya and Trofimov, the sad loss of her home promises a happy future. "Goodbye, house! Goodbye, old life!" says Anya as she exits with Trofimov. "Hello, new life!" he responds (trans. Carnicke, 300). As they exit into the future, their last lines bring sadness and joy together as surely as does the end of *The Proposal*. In both cases happiness and sadness are merely two sides of the same coin.

While ambiguity registers in the vaudevilles as predominantly comic, Chekhov more forcefully undermines the humor in his longer plays by drawing stronger attention to the consequences of the behavior that makes us laugh. For example, Solyony's silly arguments lead to his fatal duel with Tuzenbach; Lopakhin's failed proposal metaphorically locks the door to Ranyevskaya's estate; and Anya's and Trofimov's hopeful lines do not end *The Cherry Orchard*. Their exit into the future is followed by two more scenes: the painful goodbyes of Ranyevskaya and her brother and the shocking last entrance of the old servant Firs, who has been accidentally left behind in the locked house to die. These last two scenes draw our attention to the consequences of inaction.

However focused on character complexity Chekhov may be in his vaudevilles, he still finds value in the shorthand techniques that Scribe used for quick characterizations. In both writers one finds asides and soliloquies to keep the audience aware of the developing situations among the characters. There are explicit statements about a character's stock traits (as observed above), meaningful names, and speech peculiarities to individualize characters. These techniques place Chekhov's work squarely into vaudevillian tradition, even though he uses them unconventionally to deepen and complicate his characters' psychologies and inner lives.

Chekhov's use of asides, for example, paves the way for the implied subtextual thoughts that he creates in the pauses that punctuate all his major plays ("The pause" in Chapter 3). In *The Proposal*, Chubukov greets Lomov with socially acceptable good cheer, even as he concludes from Lomov's formal dress that "he's come for money" (trans. Carnicke, 20). This spoken aside shares Chubukov's thought with the audience, while hiding it from Lomov. Chubukov's initial reaction also sheds ironic light on his later exuberant about-face, when he finally learns that Lomov has actually come for Natalya Stepanovna's hand. In the full-length plays, such asides become silent pauses, recorded by ellipses, in which a character's thoughts run in parallel with or in contrast to the dialogue. For example, in Act I of *Three Sisters*, Masha reveals her disaffected mood when she puts on her hat and prepares to leave her youngest sister's name day party. When challenged Masha responds, "It's all the same... I'll come back in the evening. Goodbye, my pretty one... (*Kisses Irina.*) One more time, let me wish you health and happiness..." (trans. Carnicke, 174). One can almost hear asides in her pauses: "I can't bear the boredom;" "I can escape gracefully now;" "How much better our parties once were!" Later, as she listens to the decidedly interesting ramblings of their unexpected military guest, Lieutenant-Colonel Vershinin, she takes off her hat and announces, "I'm staying for lunch" (trans. Carnicke, 182). Her about-face in this moment is as radical and funny as Chubukov's.

Extended soliloquies allow Chekhov to develop his characters' psychological complexities with wit and perspicacity. Lomov's first moment alone brings the audience into his private fears as a hypochondriac:

> But the worst thing is going to sleep. I hardly lie down and begin to doze off, when suddenly a spasm shoots through my left side! And then it moves directly to my shoulder and my head... I jump up, like a madman, walk around a little and then lie down again. (trans. Carnicke, 21)

What a wonderful marriage such nightly behavior promises! While true soliloquies (when a character speaks alone) are rare in Chekhov's full-length plays, he sometimes slips them into scenes in clever ways. For example, in Acts II and IV of *Three Sisters*, Andrey all but soliloquizes about his lost ambition to become a professor to the deaf clerk, Ferapont. "If you heard well perhaps I wouldn't talk to you," says Andrey (trans. Carnicke, 192). In Act III, when he attempts to justify his wife's behavior to his oldest sister, Andrey again finds himself soliloquizing, since Olga has shut the curtain on him and effectively left him alone in the room.

Chekhov's use of meaningful names clearly derives from his love of the vaudeville. Yet, unlike Scribe who tends to use names to reflect directly upon a character's traits (as with Champignon in *A Peculiar Position*), Chekhov uses names variously. For example, in *The Proposal*, "Lomov" is both directly and ironically suggestive. *Lom*—the Russian word for crowbar—accurately describes the character's stubborn approach to argument within the play. Similarly accurate is the association of his name with the common phrase, *telo lomit*, which describes how one's body is wracked with fever and hence emphasizes Lomov's hypochondria. Yet, *lomovoi*—a farm horse used for carting heavy loads—ironically emphasizes how his healthy body contradicts his sense of himself as weak and sickly.[34]

---

[34] Ibid., 65. I thank Andrei Malikov for suggesting the association with *telo lomit*.

Chekhov also uses meaningful names liberally in his long plays. In *The Cherry Orchard*, Ranyevskaya's first name—"Lyubov"—means "love;" and she seems the nexus of love in the play. She expresses familial love as she hugs her seventeen-year-old daughter and weeps for her drowned six-year-old boy; she also embodies sexual love as she struggles against her desire to return to her lover in Paris, a desire provoked anew with each of his telegrams. Moreover, different types of love coincide in her lecture to Trofimov in Act III. She begins by criticizing him for his lack of basic human sympathy toward her (the kind of love that links us all), then turns to her wish that he and Anya might someday marry (creating a new link in familial love), and finally upbraids him for his prudish opinions about physical love:

> You must become a man, at your age you should understand those who love. And you yourself must love... You must fall in love! (*Angrily*.) Yes, yes! You have no purity, you're only a prude, a ridiculous freak, ugly... [...] 'I'm above love!' You're not above love, as Firs would say, you're just a 'nincompoop.' At your age not to have a lover!... (trans. Carnicke, 282)

Her expertise in love is matched only by her lack of talent in managing her money, as evidenced in her ordering of expensive meals, scattering coins on the ground, giving a beggar gold, and losing her family's estate. It is as if her name limits her to one special realm of knowledge.

Even so, Chekhov's irony peeks through in the details of her behavior. What does it really mean to be named "Lyubov" when, despite her avowals of familial love, she has clearly ignored her family's repeated requests to return to the estate prior to the opening of the play? But for her daughter traveling to Paris to fetch her, she might well have remained abroad with her lover. Similarly, what does her final promise to return to her daughter and homeland really mean, when weighed against her actual return to her lover in Paris? Her behavior seems to suggest that familial love takes second place to sexual love. Actions do indeed have the potential to speak louder than words, especially in theatrical productions that depend upon actors acting, and not merely reading, the texts.

In *The Cherry Orchard*, Lopakhin seems a negative photographic image of Lyubov Andreyevna. He is as expert in finance as she with love and as talentless in love as she with money. Moreover his name, which derives from two Russian words—"shovel" (*lopata*) and "to gobble up" (*lopat'*)—is as coarse as her name is sentimental. Thus, when he calls himself nothing but a peasant, he seems to be speaking of his personality as much as his past as a serf. In Act I, he points out the discrepancy between his clothes and his manner: "I have a white waistcoat, and yellow shoes. [...] Still you can't make a silk purse out of a sow's ear..." (trans. Carnicke, 244). He may indeed dig up the foundation of Lyubov Andreyevna's estate and gobble up her cherry trees, but Chekhov's contrarian spirit also shines in those details that obviously contradict the coarseness of Lopakhin's name. He seems genuinely sympathetic to Lyubov Andreyevna when he suggests that she create an income through the rental of summerhouses in order to hold onto her estate. He also seems genuine in his offer of a fifty-thousand-ruble loan to put the plan into action. Mixed into his joy of having purchased the property himself is his true sympathy for her loss. When he asks her why she didn't listen to his advice, he seems as shaken by her situation as he was joyful over his purchase only a moment before (Chapter 2). He even admires beauty as much as do Lyubov Andreyevna and Gayev. The blossoms of their cherry trees become Lopakhin's poppies in Act IV when he tells Trofimov:

> In the spring I planted two thousand seven hundred acres of poppies and now I've made forty thousand clear profit from them. But when my poppies were in bloom, what a picture that was! (trans. Carnicke, 292)

Thus, Trofimov's response to Lopakhin rings true: "You have fine, tender fingers, like an artist, you have a fine, tender soul..." (trans. Carnicke, 291).

Finally, following Scribe's vaudevillian conventions, Chekhov uses speech peculiarities to function as verbal tics for his comic characters. Thus, Chubukov repeats "etc." and "so forth" as readily as Scribe's Champignon uses the word "peculiar." However, unlike Scribe, who uses speech as shorthand to mark the social classes, professions, and one-dimensional proclivities of his stock characters, Chekhov uses speech to individualize the people in his plays. As Gottlieb observes, the way a character speaks is "a means of [...] self-revelation which is often comic in effect, partly because it is unconscious. It arises, however, naturally and organically, always motivated by three-dimensional characterizations."[35]

In *The Proposal*, Chubukov's hypocritical desire to curry favor is expressed through his overly sweet forms of address and his use of empty phrases that keep him talking without saying anything substantive. Thus, he greets Lomov: "But my dearest, dearest, dearest friend, why are you dressed so officially? A frock coat, and gloves, etc. Surely you must be going somewhere, my treasure?" (trans. Carnicke, 20). And later, even in the heat of argument, Chubukov pushes back at Lomov more carefully than does his forthright daughter: "In fact, young man, I am not used to anyone talking to me in such a tone of voice, etc. I'm twice as old as you, young man, and I'll ask you to talk to me without such agitation, and so forth" (trans. Carnicke, 26). In contrast, Natalya Stepanovna always speaks in short, direct sentences, without ornament, reflecting her blunt nature. As the multiple examples in Chapter 3 of the use of verbal tics, meaningless phrases, eccentric grammar, fractured foreign languages, grandiloquent speech, and philosophizing prove, speech peculiarities abound and are always psychologically revelatory in Chekhov's plays.

In summary, by examining Chekhov's love for vaudeville, one can see how its conventions ground his comic sensibility and help him draw attention to the ironic inconsistencies inherent in human nature. Furthermore, his transformation of situation comedy into plays about characters in action illuminates his primary approach to characterization through self-revelatory comic behavior. These aspects of his writing take us one step beyond the study of his applications of literary innovations to drama (Chapters 2 and 3) and into the realm of dramatic genre per se. There remains, however, one more step to take toward a full understanding of Chekhov's unique conception of drama. As Chapter 5 will demonstrate, Chekhov writes his most characteristic plays by bringing vaudeville together with nineteenth-century melodrama.

---

[35] Ibid., 30.

Chapter Five

Dramatic Innovations
Part Two: Melodrama

In this chapter, I examine Chekhov's use and abuse of melodrama, which, alongside his unique approach to vaudeville, illuminates the full scope and impact of his dramatic sensibility. Jean-Jacques Rousseau coined the term *melodrama* for his play *Pygmalion* in 1766, because he used melodies to accompany its dramatic dialogue. Chekhov cleverly recalls this heritage, when he underscores Lyubov Andreyevna's monologue in Act II of *The Cherry Orchard* with the sound of distant music from the town's Jewish orchestra. As she speaks of her sins, her loves, and her attempted suicide by poison, the faintly heard violins ambiguously mark and mock her tale of woes. Today, every time directors underscore chase scenes with pounding music or romantic trysts with softly flowing chords they similarly draw from melodramatic tradition, which is arguably as alive today in televised soap operas, films, and popular plays as it was in Chekhov's day.[1]

TRADITIONAL MELODRAMATIC WRITING AND ACTING

Three major playwrights developed melodrama's central conventions: Guilbert de Pixérecourt (1773-1844) in Paris, who is generally considered to have fathered melodrama with one hundred and twenty plays; the German writer August von Kotzebue (1761-1819), who visited Russia as Prussia's ambassador to the Tsar; and Dion Boucicault (1820-90), the Irish-born actor, playwright, and theater manager, who made his career in England and the United States. Also popular in Russia were the melodramas of the French novelist and playwright Alexander Dumas, *fils* (1824-95).

---

[1]   See Ben Singer, *Melodrama and Modernity: Early Sensational Cinema and Its Contexts* (New York: Columbia University Press, 2001).

A typical melodrama focuses on a morally uplifting and action-packed story, told in an exciting manner that features suspenseful cliffhangers at the end of each act and thrilling spectacles, often staged through astonishing theatrical effects. The stories tend to involve extreme circumstances. Innocent young women and children are brought low by villainous men, who are driven by greed or lust. Helpless widows face eviction from their homes, as their late husbands' rivals or financiers buy up their mortgaged property. Fallen or adulterous women face the loss of their virtue either by committing suicide or through acts of self-sacrifice that allow them to rise above their immoral pasts and thus die with purified souls.

In all cases, good comes face to face with evil; and this direct conflict stands at the moral heart of the genre. For example, in *The Daughter of the Exile* (*La Fille de l'exilé*, 1818), Pixérecourt shows the sweet sixteen-year-old Elizabeth as she meets her nemesis Ivan, who earlier caused her father's ignominious exile. Despite the villainy he has done to her family, she proves her virtue by saving his life and shaming him into contrition.[2] In Dumas fils' *The Lady of the Camellias* (*La Dame aux camélias*, 1852), Marguerite is a prostitute, dying of tuberculosis, who breaks off her relationship with Armand to save him from the social scandal of his loving a fallen woman. She decides upon this course of action, when his father confronts her with the truth of how her immoral behavior threatens Armand's reputation. Only on her death bed does Armand finally realize that Marguerite has not betrayed him for another man, but sacrificed her own happiness to ensure his. Thus, her vice has been purged by the virtue of her love.[3]

As the struggle between good and evil ensues, characters are swept up in fast action, designed to astonish the audience. There occur murders, deaths, suicides, auctions, duels, chases, and natural disasters (floods, storms, fires, avalanches, etc.).[4] Boucicault, for example, draws

---

[2] Peter Brooks, *The Melodramatic Imagination: Balzac, Henry James, Melodrama, and the Mode of Excess* (New Haven: Yale University Press, 1976), 24-5. See also Daniel Gerould, "Russian Formalist Theories of Melodrama," *Journal of American Culture* 1, no. 1 (Spring 1978), 152-68.

[3] This play became the basis for Giuseppe Verdi's opera, *La Traviata* (1853).

[4] See Brooks, *The Melodramatic Imagination*, Chapter 2, "The Aesthetics of Astonishment," 24-55.

attention to the extreme consequences of human actions in *The Octoroon* (1859): an innocent bystander, who has inadvertently overheard the villain's nefarious plan, is murdered; the heroine, who has African blood in her veins, must step up onto a public auction platform to be sold into slavery; and the villain sets fire to a boat in full view of the audience in order to destroy the physical evidence of his larceny. Pixérecourt, in contrast, looks to a fearful storm with lightning and thunder to infuse the awesome power of nature into *The Daughter of the Exile*. Just after Elizabeth saves Ivan's life, she gets trapped by a river that rises during the storm and threatens to drown her. Now in an about-face, her enemy Ivan is the only one able to save her.

Astonishing action was usually supported with spectacular stage effects; realistic illusions of dangerous gunshots, thunder, floods, and fire sent audience heartbeats racing. Because many authors of melodrama were themselves actors and theater managers, as was Boucicault, their love of spectacle prompted great strides in the design and mechanics of stage illusion. For example, Boucicault invented new fire-retardant stage materials for his Broadway production of *The Poor of New York* (1857), so that he could bring onstage the heat of an enormous historic blaze that burned to the ground a whole city block of tenement housing.

Finally, melodrama appeals directly to the heart. On the one hand, it plays upon its audience's fears and anxieties, instigating the desire for revenge of the innocent. On the other hand, it appeals to sympathies and passions that arouse unbridled sentimentality. As the story unfolds, strong emotions are expressed through tears and grandiose statements about feelings, beliefs, and sentiments. The spectator roots for heroes and heroines, boos villains and scoundrels, and cries for those victimized by the machinations of evildoers and cruel fate. "What is the least that anyone would ask of a melodrama? As apt an answer as any is: a good cry," quips Bentley.[5] In brief, melodramas are tearjerkers. We weep for dear, sweet Elizabeth, caught by the flood and in danger for her life in Pixérecourt's *The Daughter of the Exile*. We mourn with Armand at the foot of Marguerite's bed in Dumas' *The Lady of the Camellias*. We cry to see Boucicault's heroine take poison when she believes that her slave heritage dooms her planned marriage. We

---

[5]   Bentley, *The Life of the Drama*, 196.

recoil when the good news, that she has been legally freed and can now marry, arrives too late to save her, much as Juliet awakens too late to save Romeo.[6] In short, nineteenth-century melodrama, like opera, revels in excess of all sorts: from stories that engage the polar opposites of good and evil to the thrills of theatrical spectacle, from emotional outbursts to the vindication of virtue.

Melodrama's excess of moral outrage, action-packed adventure, and high emotion begs for performances that are equally histrionic and expansive. Thus, nineteenth-century gestural acting suited the genre admirably. Beginning in France during the Enlightenment at the famed Parisian theater, the *Comédie Française*, and extending into the silent film era, gestural acting taught actors to craft strong physical and vocal gestures that explicitly express characters' emotional experiences. While there has been much variation in this school of acting over the centuries, actors who work this way generally share common assumptions about performance. They tend to see themselves akin to portrait painters, who select visible details to convey their characters' inner emotional states. Thus, Hyppolite Clairon (1723-1803) advises actors "to study the works of the most eminent painters and sculptors," and then "to fill up the [stage] picture with its proper shade or effect."[7]

In early manifestations of gestural acting, actors focused on the creation of heightened moments within their performances that could, like paintings, capture still images of passions. Such freeze-frame moments of stupefaction, as they were called, allowed spectators to focus on the portrait's most expressive details. In short, these actors displayed their era's taste for artifice. As Clairon observes, "I have often smiled at the folly of those who have upbraided me for having recourse to art. Alas! What should I have been without it?"[8]

---

[6] For most of the twentieth century, scholars dismissed melodrama as unworthy of serious attention, but starting in the late 1970s leading scholars such as Eric Bentley (*The Life of the Drama*), Peter Brooks (*The Melodramatic Imagination*), and Ben Singer (*Melodrama and Modernity*) brought new respect to the genre's strengths. Such critical attention allows us to see many works of tragedy and realism as also melodramatic, including the plays of Alexander Nikolayevich Ostrovsky, which are generally seen as ethnographic realism.

[7] Hyppolite Clairon, "Reflections on Dramatic Art," in Toby Cole and Helen Chinoy, eds. *Actors on Acting* (New York: Crown Publishers, 1970), 173.

[8] Ibid., 172.

Among the most famous gestural actors of Chekhov's day was Sarah Bernhardt (1844-1923), the French actress who became an international star through her many tours, including those to Moscow in 1881, 1891, and 1908. Her acting technique can be best understood by looking at one key moment in her 1899 production of Shakespeare's *Hamlet*,[9] in which she performed the title role as an impulsive young man dedicated to truth. She saw Hamlet's encounter with the Ghost as one of resolute bravery. When the ghost appeared upstage, she turned her back on the audience, threw off her hat, and left her arms extended upward into the air, freezing for some time in this beautifully expansive moment of stupefaction. Moreover, she repeated this exultant posture at several other key moments in the play, making this gesture characteristic of her young prince.[10]

At its best, gestural acting was stunningly visual and highly artistic in its impact. No wonder its most talented actors were lavishly acclaimed for their artistry! "Actors are everything in such theater," Konstantin Stanislavsky observed.[11] At its worst, gestural acting in the hands of lesser talents became craft without art; gestures appeared mechanical, as if emotional content had been bled from its form. Stanislavsky called such empty gestures "clichés," silly tricks-of-the-trade that may have been "vital and communicative at some time in the past, but have now lost all connection with 'the life of the human spirit' [...] like a shell without the nut."[12] Contemporary American actors call the use of empty conventional signs "indicating"—that is to say, an actor "indicates" looking without really seeing or drinking without ever tasting. Stanislavsky gives several examples from the conventions of melodrama: "a black dress, powdered face, sorrowful nodding of the head, nose blowing, and wiping of dry eyes" portray grief; "pressing a

---

[9] Bernhardt first staged and starred in *Hamlet* in Paris at *Le Théâtre des Nations* (The Theatre of the Nations), a theater renamed for her as *Théâtre Sarah Bernhardt* also in 1899.

[10] Tony Howard, *Women as Hamlet: Performance and Interpretation in Theatre, Film and Fiction* (New York: Cambridge University Press, 2007), 101-2; image on 107.

[11] K. S. Stanislavskii, unpublished typescript of an early draft of an acting manual with handwritten notes (n.d.), housed at the Bancroft Library, University of California at Berkeley, 21.

[12] Ibid., 11, 49, 21.

telling finger to the lips and a solemn stealthy walk" telegraph secretiveness; "clutching one's chest or tearing at the collar of one's shirt" indicates death.[13]

European melodrama reached Russia at about the same time as vaudeville had in the early nineteenth century. Immediately popular with audiences, social critics like Belinsky (Chapter 2) felt that melodrama's penchant for exaggerated emotionalism and spectacular effects was at war with the literary goals behind realism's artistry and social commentary. Such criticism, however, did little to stem the tide of melodrama's growing audience appeal, making the genre a lucrative vehicle for the stage.

Moreover, its moral underpinnings suited the expectations of the Russian censors, who had long concerned themselves with providing moral examples to the population through literature.[14] Censors tended to approve melodramas for publication and performance, only requesting modifications to ensure that a work's moral precepts outweighed its depictions of villainy and vice. The censor's reaction to Chekhov's depiction of Arkadina's unwed sexual relationship with Trigorin in *The Seagull* typified the government's attitudes toward melodrama: "The problem is not in the cohabitation of the actress and the writer, but in the matter-of-fact way with which the son and brother treat the affair."[15] While Chekhov countered by telling the censor that "the son's tone makes it perfectly clear that he is against his mother's love affair," the author had no choice but to strike out those words and phrases that conceivably could be interpreted otherwise.[16]

Russian authors were soon producing melodramas that spoke to the cataclysmic changes that the reforms of the 1860s had brought to their society. The liberation of the serfs, new freedoms for the press, and the growing educational opportunities for common people had forever overturned the old social rules (Chapter 2). The former serf, Firs, testi-

---

[13] K. S. Stanislavskii, *Sobranie sochinenii* [Collected Works], Vol. 6 (Moscow: Iskusstvo, 1994), 51.

[14] Balmuth, *Censorship in Russia*, 75.

[15] I. Litvinov, cited in A. P. Chekhov, *Polnoe sobranie sochinenii i pisem v tridtsati tomakh* [The Complete Works and Letters in Thirty Volumes], Vol. 13 (Moscow: Nauka, 1978), 361-2.

[16] Chekhov, cited in Ibid.

fies to this wrenching period in *The Cherry Orchard* (Act II), when he recalls his emancipation as a "calamity."

> It was so very good in the old days. They flogged you at least. [...]
> The peasants and the masters, the masters and the peasants, but now everything's mixed up, you can't understand anything. (trans. Carnicke, 269)

While Slavic scholars and readers may be familiar with Ivan Sergeyevich Turgenev's subtle and insightful portraits of Russia's "superfluous men" who had lost their moorings within the changing social norms, more crudely painted portraits turned up in melodramas by Ippolit Vasilyevich Shpazhinsky (1844-1917), Viktor Aleksandrovich Krylov (1838-1906),[17] Boleslav Mikhailovich Markevich (1822-84), and others. Unlike Russian vaudevilles (which retained much of their foreign flavor even when masked with local references) native melodramas addressed national issues more closely. However, like Russian vaudevilles, they were turned out by the dozen; and most were of inferior literary quality.

CHEKHOV'S LOATHING OF MELODRAMA

In contrast to Chekhov's guilty but avid love of vaudeville, he held an exceedingly low opinion of the literary conventions of melodrama and the histrionic gestural acting that the genre inspired. In Act I of *The Seagull*, Treplev's disdain for his mother's acting rests squarely upon her talent for melodrama; her son specifically mentions her appearances in Dumas' *The Lady of the Camellias* (above) and Markevich's *The Fumes of Life* (*Chad zhizni*, 1884), about a woman who has multiple affairs, one of them with a man who robs and abandons her.[18] While the stories

---

[17] Mila B. Shevchenko examines in detail Shpazhinskii's and Krylov's cultural themes in *Melodramatic Scenarios and Modes of Marginality: The Poetics of Anton Chekhov's Early Drama and of Fin-de-Siècle Russian Popular Drama* (Ph.D. Dissertation, University of Michigan, 2008).

[18] For more on *The Fumes of Life*, see Senelick, *Anton Chekhov*, 22-3. In *The Cherry Orchard*, Chekhov implicitly references Markevich's play through Lyubov Andreyevna's Parisian lover, who robs and then abandons her.

in these referenced plays clearly reflect Arkadina's unseemly sexual behavior and Trigorin's later abandonment of Nina, the style of these plays also represents the excess of sentiment that Chekhov personally abhorred. Recall his advice to the writer Lidia Avilova—when he tells her that to draw tears from her readers she has to write more "coldly" (19 March 1892). Recall as well the lack of overt emotional commentary in his own stories (Chapter 2).

Chekhov particularly disliked Markevich's melodramas and publicly damned one of them in a review. *The Abyss* (*Bezdna*, 1883), wrote Chekhov, is "a thin gruel" and "the news [of its publication] as pleasant as yesterday's oatmeal served with vinegar or a chronic cold."[19] Chekhov followed this review with a scathing parody of *The Fumes of Life*, but thought better of publishing it. Instead, he asked his editor, Nikolay Leikin, to tear up the manuscript, explaining that:

> B. Markevich usually cries, whenever he reads something unpleasant about one of his things, cries and complains... You then have to argue with his admirers and friends, whether or not you publish under a pseudonym. (5 or 6 Feb. 1884)

Along with Treplev's criticisms of his mother's art, Chekhov also invites us to watch Arkadina at work as a melodramatic actress in Act III of *The Seagull*. When Trigorin tells her that he wants her to release him so that he can pursue an affair with the younger Nina, Arkadina kneels in supplication before him. "You are the last page of my life!" she intones. "My happiness, my pride, my bliss..." She then "hugs his knees" and threatens madness. "If you throw me over, even for one hour, I will not survive, I will go mad. My remarkable, exceptional man, my lord and master..." (trans. Carnicke, 92).

The grandiose rhetoric of Arkadina's love captures the emotional style of melodramatic writing; her exaggerated gestures place her

---

[19] A. P. Chekhov, *Polnoe sobranie sochinenii i pisem v tridtsati tomakh* [The Complete Works and Letters in Thirty Volumes], Vol. 16 (Moscow: Nauka, 1979), 60. He published this review on 22 Oct. 1883 under a pseudonym in a column entitled "Fragments of Moscow Life" for the journal *Oskolki* [Fragments], edited by N. A. Leikin.

squarely into the gestural approach to acting made famous by stars like Bernhardt.[20]

Chekhov publicly critiqued Bernhardt's performance in Moscow as the title character in Scribe's melodrama, *Adrienne Lecouvreur*,[21] which, like *The Lady of the Camellias*, depicts a self-sacrificing prostitute. In a review from 1881 for *The Spectator* he writes:

> Every sigh Sarah Bernhardt sighs, every tear she sheds, every *ante mortem* convulsion she makes, every bit of her acting is nothing more than an impeccably and intelligently learned lesson. A lesson, reader, and nothing more! As a very clever lady who knows what works and what doesn't, a lady of the most grandiose taste, a lady deeply read in the human heart and whatever you please, she very deftly performs all those stunts that, every so often, at fate's behest, occur in the human soul. [...] In her acting, she goes in pursuit not of the natural, but of the extraordinary. Her goal is to startle, to amaze, to dazzle [...] We watched Sarah Bernhardt and derived indescribable pleasure from her hard work. There were brief passages in her acting which moved us almost to tears. But the tears failed to well up only because all the enchantment is smothered in artifice.[22]

---

20 Cynthia Marsh in "The Stage Representation of Chekhov's Women," in Gottlieb and Allain, eds., *The Cambridge Companion to Chekhov*, 216-27, is especially good at showing how Chekhov's "rethinking of melodramatic content and the melodramatic mode of performance" affects his depiction of female characters (226). Gary S. Morson also builds upon the notion of self-dramatizing characters in his article, "*Uncle Vanya* as Prosaic Metadrama," in Robert Louis Jackson, ed., *Reading Chekhov's Text* (Evanston: Northwestern University Press, 1993). Morson writes, "[Chekhov's] plays center on histrionic people who imitate theatrical performances and model themselves on other melodrama genres. They posture, seek grand Romance, imagine that a tragic fatalism governs their lives and indulge in utopian dreams, while they neglect the ordinary virtues and ignore the daily processes that truly sustain them." (214)

21 Scribe collaborated on this play with Ernest Legouvé; the composer Francesco Cilea transformed it into an opera of the same title in 1902.

22 Anton Chekhov, "More About Sarah Bernhardt," in Senelick, trans. and ed., *Russian Dramatic Theory from Pushkin to the Symbolists*, 86-7. The Russian text can be found in Chekhov, *Polnoe sobranie sochinenii* [The Complete Works], Vol. 16, 12-5.

A contemporary actress preparing for the role of Arkadina and seeking to understand her character's acting might well consider Chekhov's words about Bernhardt.

Chekhov also found irony in the discrepancy between what Bernhardt's glamorous stardom promised the audience and what her acting actually delivered. In a short story entitled "This and That (Letters and Telegrams)," published in 1881 under the pseudonym Antosha Chekhonte, Chekhov creates a fictional collage of reactions from Bernhardt's fans. One gushes admiringly at the fact that "she actually dies standing up." Another vents his disappointment: "It's just rubbish. Nothing special. A waste of money." A third is head over heels from the performance: "I have feasted my eyes on Sarah, and I absolutely insist that you praise her to the skies." A doctor in the audience, however, sees "S. B." only as a body: "Her chest—paralytic and flat. Skeletal and muscular structure—unsatisfactory. Neck—so long and thin that both the *venae jugulares* and even the *arterieae carotides* are clearly visible."[23]

Despite his disdain for melodrama, Chekhov was much influenced by it. The stories that drive his four major plays are decidedly melodramatic: a virtuous woman loses her purity and falls to the seductive charms of a cad (Nina to Trigorin in *The Seagull*; Lyubov Andreyevna to her Parisian scoundrel and Dunyasha to Yasha in *The Cherry Orchard*); a family loses their mortgaged home to someone close to them (the Prozorov sisters to their adulterous, greedy sister-in-law in *Three Sisters*; Lyubov Andreyevna and her brother to their former serf in *The Cherry Orchard*); a wanton woman wreaks havoc through her sexual flirtations or liaisons (Arkadina in *The Seagull*; Yelena in *Uncle Vanya*; and Lyubov Andreyevna in *The Cherry Orchard*); and a central character attempts or threatens suicide when hopes are ravished (Treplev in *The Seagull*; the title character in *Uncle Vanya*; Lyubov Andreyevna and Yepikhodov in *The Cherry Orchard*). There are natural and manmade disasters: storms in *The Seagull* and *Uncle Vanya*; the destruction of the environment in *Uncle Vanya*; a raging fire in Act III of *Three Sisters*; the duel that kills Tuzenbach in *Three Sisters*; the auction of *The Cherry Orchard*. There

---

[23] Cited from the translation by Peter Constantine as "Sarah Bernhardt Comes to Town," in *The Undiscovered Chekhov*, 5-9. The Russian, "I to i se (Pis'ma i telegramy Antoshi Ch.)," can be found in Chekhov, *Polnoe sobranie sochinenii* [The Complete Works], Vol. 1, 106-9.

are even moments that pull at our heartstrings: when the despairing Treplev tears up his manuscript for two full minutes and then exits the stage to shoot himself; when Dr. Dorn whispers to Trigorin that Treplev has killed himself; when Sonya and her Uncle Vanya resign themselves to a loveless life of work; when Irina learns that her fiancé has been killed in a duel; when Vershinin leaves Irina's sister, Masha, in tears; when Lyubov Andreyevna and her brother bid a final goodbye to their lost cherry orchard.

Ultimately, however, Chekhov uses melodrama to undermine melodrama, and by so doing he transforms it into something entirely different. In his hands, the clear moral precepts that divide the world into villains and heroes are swept away. He refuses to cast stones at people whose behavior is in turn vile and then sympathetic; he also refuses to place on pedestals people, who victimize themselves as much as they are victimized by others. Swept away too are melodrama's exciting, action-packed spectacles. Chekhov replaces these with his carefully, often musically patterned flow of seemingly trivial details. In other words, he creates drama from the time people spend waiting for the big events of their lives to take place. Thus, time appears to pass in his plays much as it does in daily life. In this way, time itself becomes one of Chekhov's greatest themes. In *The Cherry Orchard*, when Lopakhin checks his watch to keep track of the arrival and departure of trains, which he does frequently, he draws special attention to this aspect of Chekhov's play.

Finally, through the curative force of laughter, Chekhov turns melodrama's tears of pity into the kind shed when one faces oneself and one's situation without illusions, pretensions, or lies of any kind. Such unvarnished examinations of life not only differentiate his greatest plays from melodrama, but also distinguish his entire approach to art. At times in his life Chekhov succeeded in stripping himself of all illusions. As he tells his closest friend, Suvorin:

> You [...] think me smart. Yes, I am smart, at least in so far as I do not keep my illness secret from myself, do not lie to myself, and do not cover up my own emptiness with other people's rags, like borrowing ideas from the [reforms of the] 1860s, etc. (25 Nov. 1892)

Chekhov was all the more adamant about avoiding lies in his art: "We write life as it is, and anything else is neither here nor there..." he tells

Suvorin. "Whip us, but we won't budge" from this goal (25 Nov. 1892). In 1900, he again stressed:

> One must never lie. Art has this great specification: it simply does not tolerate falsehood. One can lie in love, politics, and medicine: one can mislead the public or even God; but there is absolutely no lying in art.[24]

In all his major plays, the characters who face and discard their fantasies and false hopes may end the play in sad circumstances, but, with their eyes now open to the truth, they also end free from lies and illusionary impediments. This freedom creates an opportunity to see and appreciate the actual beauties and joys of life. Such is true of Nina in *The Seagull*, who understands by play's end that neither fame, nor romance, nor art can guarantee happiness. Such is true of Sonya and Vanya in *Uncle Vanya*, when they are disabused of their infatuations for people with feet of clay like everyone else. So too must the Prozorov daughters in *Three Sisters* give up their girlhood fantasies of Moscow if they are to open the doors to the real possibilities in their adult lives. Anya and Trofimov in *The Cherry Orchard* can move forward unafraid into the future because they have freed themselves from the past.

By tracing the process and means through which Chekhov undermines melodrama in his plays one can come to grips with the full revolutionary impact of his dramatic sensibility.

MELODRAMA TURNED INSIDE OUT IN CHEKHOV'S PLAYS

When I review Chekhov's full-length plays in chronological order I am always struck by the fact that with each new play he seems to use fewer and fewer melodramatic devices. Chekhov once described himself as a "young man [who] presses the slave out of himself drop by drop" (to A. S. Suvorin, 7 Jan. 1889). His experiments in playwriting seem to suggest that he was also a young writer, who pressed the melodramatic

---

[24] Cited and translated by Piero Brunello and Lena Lenček, eds., from an undated archival letter, in *How to Write Like Chekhov: Advice and Inspiration, Straight from his own Letters and Work* (Philadelphia: Da Capo, 2008), 25.

effects out of his plays drop by drop, until there emerged an entirely new form of drama.

Chekhov's first full-length play is untitled and generally known by the name of its central character, *Platonov*.[25] Scholars disagree on when he actually wrote it and whether he even considered it finished. He may have begun it in high school; he may have returned to it in the late 1870s; he certainly wrote much of the existing manuscript while in medical school in 1880. After seeking unsuccessfully to get it staged in 1881, he seems to have entirely abandoned it. The manuscript was found among his papers after his death and was published for the first time in 1923. It is interminably long and unwieldy, as if the young writer were packing into his first effort all his ideas for fear of never having another opportunity to write a play.

Platonov also contains more melodramatic conventions than any other Chekhov work and thus reveals how he took his initial inspiration from the standard nineteenth-century melodramas that surrounded him. A recap of the play's action drives this point home. The disaffected schoolteacher, Platonov, is married to a virtuous and self-sacrificing woman, Sasha. Yet, he pursues and is pursued by three other women over the course of the play: Anna Petrovna, a neighboring widow whose husband left her bankrupt and who loses her estate by play's end; Sofia Yegorovna, the wife of Anna Petrovna's stepson; and Maria Yefimovna Grekova, a young chemistry student who is at once attracted to and re-pelled by Platonov's brooding, anti-social behavior. When Sasha learns of her husband's flirtation with the neighboring widow, she attempts suicide by throwing herself under a train,[26] only to be rescued in the

---

[25] The Russian editors of Chekhov's *Polnoe sobranie sochinenii i pisem v tridtsati tomakh* [The Complete Works and Letters in Thirty Volumes], which is con-sidered the definitive edition, title this play *Bezottsovshchina* [Fatherlessness] on the assumption that it is the earliest of his plays, long thought to be lost. See Vol. 11. For more on the play's history and English translations, see Che-khov, *Twelve Plays*, ed. and trans. Hingley, and Chekhov, *The Complete Plays*, ed. and trans. Senelick. The British playwright Michael Frayn translated, cut, and abridged Chekhov's text for production, giving it a new title, *Wild Honey*. This work was published as "a comedy by Michael Frayn from the play without a name by Anton Chekhov" (London: Methuen, 1984).

[26] Sasha's attempted suicide is clearly reminiscent of the suicide of Lev Tolstoy's heroine in *Anna Karenina* (1877).

nick of time by Osip, arguably the play's most innovative character. He is a local horse thief, who has been hired to assassinate Platonov. Yet, despite the lure of easy money, Osip ultimately realizes that he cannot betray his humanity with murder. In him, Chekhov is already beginning to question the clear and easy morality of the melodrama.

As the play continues, Sasha is about to forgive her husband for his dalliance with the neighboring widow, when she inadvertently learns from Platonov of his much more serious relationship with the married Sofia Yegorovna. This affair strikes Sasha as especially egregious, because it threatens not one but two marriages. She reacts by taking poison, a melodramatic convention that Chekhov would later parody to great effect in his one-act *Tatyana Repina* (Chapter 4). The news of his wife's near-death state induces a fit of guilt in Platonov, who tries to set things right by refusing to run away with Sofia Yegorovna as they had earlier planned. The play ends with the desperately passionate Sofia Yegorovna shooting at but missing Platonov. She then aims directly at his heart and kills him on stage in full view of the audience. While one can find in this play subtle touches of characterization and inner action that will later come to the fore in Chekhov's mature drama, *Platonov's* melodramatic devices overshadow the author's incipient dramatic sensibility.[27]

Chekhov wrote his first successfully staged full-length play, *Ivanov*, for Moscow's privately owned Korsh Theatre in 1887, revising it twice before its second production at the imperial Aleksandrinsky Theatre in St. Petersburg in 1889. The title character is an estate owner, once vitally concerned with social and agriculture reforms, but now devoid of civic purpose. Thus, the play's first director and contemporary critics were quick to place Ivanov into the gallery of Russia's nineteenth-century "superfluous men," who, Hamlet-like, are paralyzed into inaction by the enormity of social and political problems.[28]

---

[27] Shevchenko treats at length the melodramatic aspects of *Platonov* in her dissertation.

[28] For more on the influence of *Hamlet* on Russian literature see Eleanor Rowe, *Hamlet: A Window on Russia* (New York: New York University Press, 1976). For more on Ivanov as a "superfluous man," see John McKellor Reid, "*Ivanov*: The Perils of Typicality," *The Bulletin of the North American Chekhov Society* 16, no. 1 (Fall 2008), 19-44.

Ivanov's overall story is conventional in its melodramatic roots. Not only does he stand in danger of losing his estate to his main creditor, the neighboring Lebedevs, but he has also fallen out of love with his wife, née Sarah Abramson, a Jew who was disowned by her family for marrying outside her faith. As was customary at the time, she converted to Christianity upon her marriage and was baptized with a Russian name, Anna Petrovna. Ill with tuberculosis, she now desperately tries to hold onto her husband's love. Along with viewing Ivanov as a "superfluous man," critics of the first production also saw him as a typical villain, selfishly turning his back on his wife, and consequently hastening her death.

Anna Petrovna's rival for Ivanov's love is Sasha, the Lebedevs' young daughter, who naively believes that the power of her love can revive Ivanov's idealism and zest for life. When Anna Petrovna succumbs to her illness, Ivanov and Sasha become engaged against a backdrop of rumor that the dowry from her wealthy parents will all too conveniently save his property from foreclosure. On his wedding day, Ivanov squarely confronts a much more insidious hypocrisy in their relationship: "Just now, I was dressing for our wedding, looked into the mirror, and saw on my temples... gray hair." Facing the difference in their ages unlocks for him an even deeper insight. Stripping away her romantic illusions about saving him from himself, he asks instead that she call off their wedding. "Sasha, we don't have to do this! It's not too late, we must break off this senseless comedy... [...] I was playing Hamlet and you the noble young maid—and now it's over for us."[29] In short, he admits to himself that her futile desire to save him will only drag her down to his level of despair. When she stubbornly insists that the wedding go forward, he shoots himself in order to ensure her future happiness. In this moment, Chekhov's antipathy toward lies exerts itself, but through one of the most melodramatic of conventions, suicide.

Chekhov was confused by the two most prevalent interpretations of his main character, which linked his play to traditional Russian melodrama. As he told his friend Suvorin, "If my Ivanov has turned

---

[29] Chekhov, *Ivanov*, in *Polnoe sobranie sochinenii* [The Complete Works], Vol. 12, 70. The translation is mine. For full English translations, see *Chekhov: The Major Plays*, trans. Ann Dunnigan, and Chekhov, *The Complete Plays*, ed. and trans. Laurence Senelick.

out to be a scoundrel or a superfluous man in the Turgenev stripe, [...] I probably lost my mind and wrote something completely different than I had intended" (26 Dec. 1888). Chekhov had hoped to go against the grain of convention; and he makes his departures from melodrama more visible in *Ivanov* than in *Platonov*. On the one hand, Chekhov uses strong satire that harkens back to the classic Russian comedies of Alexander Sergeyevich Griboyedov (1795-1829) and Nikolay Vasilyevich Gogol (1809-52). The guests at Sasha's name day party in Act I create a kind of chorus of Russian social and comic types, which then continue to surround and critique the central love triangle throughout the play. On the other hand, Chekhov employs elements from vaudeville. Ivanov's conniving estate manager, Borkin, is decidedly vaudevillian. He is full of imaginative but illegal schemes to save Ivanov's property from foreclosure. At their every meeting, Borkin attempts to persuade Ivanov to forgo his former idealism and save his estate through clever maneuvering. As Chekhov continues to forge his unique dramatic voice, he will use more and more elements from vaudeville to undermine melodrama.

To this blending of melodrama with satire and vaudeville, Chekhov also adds his insight as a doctor, making the symptoms and progress of Ivanov's depression an accurate case study of mental illness.[30] In so doing, Chekhov challenges Russia's usual Hamlet-like image of the "superfluous man" by portraying Ivanov's inaction as a symptom of his undiagnosed mental illness, rather than as a result of his political disillusionment. Moreover, Chekhov portrays Ivanov as a patient who senses that he is ill. When speaking with Dr. Lvov, Anna Petrovna's doctor, Ivanov frankly admits that something, which he cannot name, must be wrong with him. As Chekhov explains to Suvorin, "[Ivanov] does not understand what is happening to him" (26 Dec. 1888). No wonder Sasha's desire to revive him through love, Borkin's fantastic schemes, and other attempts at resurrecting Ivanov's former self within the play all misfire! The cures treat the wrong disease. Even Dr. Lvov is too arrogant

---

[30]   Bradley Lewis, "Listening to Chekhov: Narrative Approaches to Depression," *The Bulletin of the North American Chekhov Society* 15, no. 1 (Fall 2007), 7-25. The first to identify Ivanov as "a socio-medical case of neurasthenia" was John Tulloch (see Richard Peace, "An Introduction to Chekhov's Plays," in Eekman, ed., *Critical Essays on Anton Chekhov*, 131).

and inexperienced to interpret Ivanov's shifting moods as anything other than the willful and villainous cause behind his wife's quick deterioration, thus proving how much more difficult it is to diagnose mental, rather than physical, illness.

Nonetheless, melodrama retains its strength in *Ivanov*. Each act ends with a recognizably melodramatic cliff-hanger: Act I with Anna Petrovna's abrupt decision to follow her husband to Sasha's name day party; Act II with Anna Petrovna arriving just in time to catch Sasha and Ivanov in a kiss; Act III with a sharp confrontation between husband and wife; and Act IV with Ivanov's suicide.

Comedy predominates in Chekhov's next full-length play, *The Wood Demon*[31] (1889-90). By play's end three couples find happiness in each others' arms. Initially, Chekhov had planned to co-write his new play with Suvorin, hoping to learn from the older man's greater experience in stagecraft, but Suvorin soon pulled out of the project. How much influence Chekhov's friend had on the play remains a matter of speculation. Whatever the case, melodrama intrudes upon the comedy in Act III with the suicide of a character named Yegor, who is the uncle of Sonya, one of the play's six lovers. When Yegor learns that his late sister's husband selfishly plans to sell the family's estate in order to escape country life, he shoots himself in despair. This death haunts the play's last act and makes the happy ending seem strained and improbable. Of all Chekhov's staged full-length plays, this one attracted the strongest criticism. He endured three cutting rejections before *The Wood Demon* was accepted in 1890 by the Abramova Theatre in Moscow, and then only because any new play by him would allow the privately owned Abramova to compete more successfully with its rival, the Korsh Theatre, which had earlier produced *Ivanov* and a number of his one-acts. After tactfully resisting the efforts of several different editors to secure publication rights to

---

[31] The Russian title, *Leshii*, refers to a wood goblin from Russian folklore. The *leshii* in this play is Dr. Khrushchov, because of his concern for the preservation of forests. Sonya is in love with him, and only her prejudice against his environmental work keeps her from admitting it. By the end of this play, they are engaged and happy. In turning *The Wood Demon* into *Uncle Vanya*, Chekhov renamed Khrushchov Dr. Astrov and made the obstacles between him and Sonya more intractable. In letters, Suvorin makes it clear that he recognizes himself and his second wife in the characters of Professor Serebryakov and his young and beautiful second wife, Yelena.

The Wood Demon, Chekhov finally and bluntly admitted, "I cannot publish *The Wood Demon*. I hate this play and I am trying to forget about it" (to Λ. I. Urusov, 16 Oct. 1899)

Starting with *The Seagull*, which premiered in 1896 in St. Petersburg, Chekhov begins to bleed more and more melodramatic action and emotional rhetoric from his full-length plays. In the process, he also experiments more and more with the balance of comedy and tragedy. When he employs melodramatic conventions in his last plays, he uses them primarily "to expose the melodramatic," something that, as Vera Gottlieb observes, "is not found in the early plays such as *Platonov*."[32] With writers and actors as key characters in *The Seagull*, Chekhov allows his critiques of melodrama and gestural acting free play. As observed above, he works these critiques neatly into Acts I, II, and III through the characters' interpersonal dynamics and the carefully structured patterns of trivial details that form the play's texture of life. Along with parodies of melodrama per se, as in Arkadina's pleading with Trigorin, Chekhov also plants moments of obvious vaudeville. Among these are the estate manager's fulsome comic praise for the last generation of Russia's long forgotten operatic and theatrical stars, the comic chase of Masha after Treplev and Treplev after Nina through the woods, and Polina's silly melodramatic fit of jealousy, in which she tears up flowers that have been given to her lover, Dr. Dorn.[33] Thus, Chekhov successfully undermines melodrama with direct criticism, parody, and vaudeville.

Even so, Chekhov cannot seem to refrain from a genuinely melodramatic confrontation between Nina and Treplev in Act IV. Their conversation taps all the conventional sentiments of lost love and failed ambitions. It prompts the young man to tear up his manuscript for "two minutes," which is, as Gottlieb rightly points out, "a long time in stage terms, and in real time, melodramatic."[34] Treplev then exits the stage to

---

[32] Gottlieb, *Chekhov and the Vaudeville*, 115.

[33] The Act I chase in *The Seagull* always reminds me of the chase of mismatched lovers that occurs in Shakespeare's *A Midsummer Night's Dream*. As for Polina's jealousy, Chekhov had made it very clear in an early version of his play that her daughter, Masha, had been illegitimately fathered by Dr. Dorn. Chekhov took this fact out at the censor's insistence.

[34] Vera Gottlieb, "Chekhov's Comedy," in Gottlieb and Allain, eds., *The Cambridge Companion to Chekhov*, 232.

commit suicide, a melodramatic gesture that, despite its anti-melodramatic positioning offstage, pulls at spectators' heartstrings. It is as if Chekhov loses control of the new form of drama that he is developing at the very end of his otherwise revolutionary play.

In *Uncle Vanya* (1897), Chekhov finally finds his unique dramatic voice. Within this play, all the elements of his new dramatic paradigm work together successfully. Subtext endows the most trivial of conversations with deep emotional undercurrents ("The Pause" in Chapter 3); interactive moments of apparent inaction can move audiences to tears and laughter in rapid succession; a most exquisite patterning of details builds, by play's end, an entirely musical structure ("Soundscapes and the music of everyday life" in Chapter 3).

Before its staging by the Moscow Art Theatre in 1899, provincial productions of *Uncle Vanya* had already attracted much attention and praise. After seeing one of these productions in 1898, the writer Maksim Gorky recognized the play as a turning point for modern drama. He told Chekhov that it seems a "new species of drama" that stubbornly defies easy description:

> A few days ago, I saw *Uncle Vanya*, saw it and—cried like an old woman, even though I am not a person given to such nervous reactions. I went home feeling deaf and dumb from your play with my brow wrinkled [in puzzlement]. I wrote you a long letter and tore it up. I can't say well and clearly just what your play calls forth in my soul. [...] For me—it is an awesome thing. Your *Uncle Vanya* is an entirely new type of dramatic art...[35]

The seamless interweaving of melodrama and vaudeville distinguishes *Uncle Vanya* from the plays that Chekhov wrote previously. (Illustration 11) In his earlier plays, Chekhov laid vaudeville side by side with melodrama in discrete scenes that retained either comic or melodramatic tones. In these early plays, one tone or the other tends to predominate. His new species of play brings vaudeville and melodrama so closely together that they become virtually inseparable, occupying the same scenes at the same time.

---

[35] Maksim Gorky, cited in Chekhov, *Polnoe sobranie sochinenii* [The Complete Works], Vol. 13, 404, and in Chekhov, *Sobranie sochinenii* [Collected Works], Vol. 9, 484.

11. The drunken Dr. Astrov (Konstantin Stanislavsky) comically prods Telegin (Alexander Artyom) to play his guitar, while Sonya (Maria Lilina) contemplates her drunken, despairing uncle (Alexander Vishnevsky) in *Uncle Vanya*, 1899.

Yet, for all its uniqueness, *Uncle Vanya* is also a revision of *The Wood Demon*. From the first, Chekhov did not think of *Uncle Vanya* as a new project, but as a reworking of his earlier much maligned play, sometimes confusing the two titles in his correspondence. In fact, he responded to Gorky's letter of praise by telling his friend, "I wrote *Uncle Vanya* a very long time ago."[36] Later, in 1901, *Uncle Vanya* was denied the prestigious Griboyedov Prize because the selection committee did not consider it a new play.[37] Chekhov's revisions, however, are so extensive that little from *The Wood Demon* remains intact. He cut mercilessly and restructured throughout, retaining only a few scenes, most of them from Act II. Thirteen characters in the earlier play became a tight ensemble of eight in the revision. Three couples, who end happily in 1890, become by 1897 four separate people who end in exactly the same relationships as they begin: Sonya and Dr. Astrov remain alone and unloved; Yelena and her husband, Professor Serebryakov, affirm their loveless marriage.

---

[36] Cited in Ibid., 485.
[37] Senelick, in Chekhov, *The Complete Plays*, 811.

In short, *Uncle Vanya* has one of Chekhov's most notable zero-endings: "Nobody dies. Nobody is paired off. And the general point is clear: life knows no endings, happy or tragic," so says Bentley.[38]

A comparison of *The Wood Demon* and *Uncle Vanya* takes us, as it were, directly into Chekhov's dramatic laboratory where popular theater of the nineteenth century is transformed into recognizably modern drama. Two scholars have traced this alchemical process in great detail. The American critic Eric Bentley, writes that *The Wood Demon* is "what Hollywood would call a comedy drama: that is a farce with melodrama." It is "a conventional play, trying, so to speak, to be something else. In *Uncle Vanya*, it succeeds."[39] Chekhov's British biographer, Donald Rayfield, similarly observes: "A study of the two shows how a bad play can, over eight years, by radical revision, ruthless cuts, cautious additions, be converted into a great play."[40]

How Chekhov reworks the suicide in *The Wood Demon* best reveals how he newly balances the tragic dimensions of melodrama against vaudeville in his mature plays. Sonya's Uncle Yegor in *The Wood Demon* is pushed to suicide by his painful confrontation with his brother-in-law over the sale of the family's estate in Act III. The choice to place a traditionally culminating event in the penultimate act is already radical playwriting on Chekhov's part. Unlike Ivanov's suicide, which conventionally concludes his play, Yegor's melodramatic death recedes into the past as Act IV proceeds to a happy end. In this unusual sequence, Chekhov draws attention to the fact that life, unlike melodramatic art, continues on after climactic events. In reworking *The Wood Demon*, Chekhov appears to have understood that the sequence of events alone did not fully succeed in making his larger point about the difference between life and art. Yegor's actual death had made it too difficult for audiences to move past tragedy and accept the predominantly comic tone of the last act.

Therefore, in *Uncle Vanya* Chekhov changed more than sequence. If, in *The Seagull*, a parody could work to undermine Arkadina's melo-

---

[38]   Bentley, "Craftsmanship in *Uncle Vanya*," in Eekman, ed., *Critical Essays on Anton Chekhov*, 172.
[39]   Ibid., 170-1.
[40]   Donald Rayfield, *Chekhov's Uncle Vania and The Wood Demon* (London: Bristol Classical Press, 1995), 3.

dramatic acting, why not use parody in *Uncle Vanya* to undercut the most iconic of melodramatic events, murder and suicide? In Act III, Vanya reacts in an entirely different way than did Yegor to the same circumstances. Before thinking of suicide, Vanya attempts to kill his brother-in-law for suggesting that the estate be sold; he shouts at and then shoots at his nemesis, comically missing his target at close range. Only after failing at murder does Vanya turn suicidal in Act IV; but in this attempt, too, Chekhov turns melodrama awry. While Ivanov, Uncle Yegor, and Treplev actually succeed in killing themselves, Vanya allows himself to be talked out of it by Dr. Astrov: "Give me back the morphine, or there'll be talk, surmises, people will think that I gave it to you... It's enough that I'll have to do your autopsy... Do you think I'll find that interesting?" (trans. Carnicke, 159-60).

Looking again at the progression of plays within Chekhov's dramatic laboratory, Vanya's attempted murder also bears comparison with Sofia Yegorovna's behavior in Act IV of *Platonov*, when she shoots at but misses her lover. Both Vanya and she miss on their first shots; but unlike Vanya who misses twice, she steps close to her target, aims directly at Platonov's chest, and kills him with a second shot in the heart. The mature Chekhov turns the unironic climax of *Platonov* into Vanya's comical anticlimax. As Richard D. Risso observes, Chekhov has learned the "ironic use of comedy in moments of intense seriousness" as "a parody of melodramatic effects."[41] Truly, the inherent melodrama of the moment misses along with Vanya's shot.

Moreover, Chekhov's revisions have turned the conventional melodrama and traditional comedy of *The Wood Demon* into the comically tragic *Uncle Vanya*. Laughter and tears are no longer segregated from each other in separate scenes. We empathize with Vanya's angry despair as he melodramatically attempts to murder his enemy, even while we laugh as his shots comically miss their target, not just once but twice. "In [Chekhov's] work," John Gassner observes, "comedy may infiltrate tragedy, and tragedy may infiltrate comedy, producing controversy on the part of those who like to busy themselves with the fine points of literary classification."[42] Leaving aside all labels—including

---

[41] Richard D. Risso, "Chekhov: A View of the Basic Ironic Structures," in Barricelli, ed., *Chekhov's Great Plays*, 184.

[42] John Gassner, "The Duality of Chekhov," in Jackson, ed., *Chekhov*, 179.

"tragicomedy," the label most favored by Bentley—Gassner[43] insightfully deems Chekhov "the master of the double mode, [...] because his
various attitudes blended so naturally."[44] Unlike Yegor, Vanya lives to
face another day, and thus literally carries Chekhov's larger point into
the last act. Stripped clean by comedy of all his melodramatic illusions,
Vanya has undergone the sort of unvarnished examination of life that
Chekhov seeks in his art.

After analyzing revisions to the melodrama in *The Wood Demon*,
Bentley ironically observes that Chekhov's changes in *Uncle Vanya*
seem counterintuitive, if one looks at them superficially. From such a
viewpoint, Chekhov seems to get rid of melodrama's most appealing
aspects—the exciting events and grand emotions. "To the Broadway
script-writer [Chekhov's revisions] would look like a deliberate elimination of the dramatic element."[45] Thus, his plays have seemed to some
critics and spectators alike as "the most undramatic plays in the world,"[46]
"anti-theatrical" in their primary impulse,[47] and boring (Introduction).
They do in fact cut against the grain of typical dramatic expectations!

Chekhov's counterintuitive sensibility, however, is directly responsible for his radically new paradigm of dramatic writing. As he honed
his playwriting, he came to rely less and less on overt melodramatic
techniques to tell his still melodramatic stories. By 1897, *Uncle Vanya*
undermines the melodramatic impulse in *The Wood Demon* through
parody and vaudeville. In 1901 in *Three Sisters* only one melodramatic
confrontation occurs on stage. In Act III when Natasha scolds the family's beloved nurse for sitting in her presence, Olga sympathetically defends the tired old woman. But her defense misfires; the battle is brief
and ineffectual, ending in a stalemate and with Olga feeling old. "I've
aged ten years tonight," she says (trans. Carnicke, 212). When Chekhov
writes his last masterpiece in 1904, melodramatic conventions remain

43 Bentley, *The Life of the Drama*, 319. In this book, Bentley defines Chekhov's primary genre as tragicomedy, specifically the kind that presents "comedy with an
   unhappy ending."
44 Gassner, in Jackson, ed., *Chekhov*, 179.
45 Bentley, "Craftsmanship in *Uncle Vanya*," in Eekman, ed., *Critical Essays on Anton Chekhov*, 171.
46 Mirsky, *A History of Russian Literature*, 380.
47 Cited in Donald Rayfield, *The Cherry Orchard: Catastrophe and Comedy* (New
   York: Twayne Publishers, 1994), 8.

only in the distance, like the faintly heard music that underscores Lyubov Andreyevna's Act II monologue. In *The Cherry Orchard*, the guns on stage remain unfired and there are no murders, no successful suicides, and no action-packed fights. The visible interactions between the characters have become as oblique and indirect as Gayev's imaginary billiard game ("Apparent irrelevancies" in Chapter 3). As one of my students aptly put it, "*The Cherry Orchard* is in many ways the anti-melodrama" and therefore cannot support "the overdramatic in acting."[48]

While Chekhov built new character complexity into the vaudeville by adopting and adapting its tried and true techniques, he turned melodrama inside out by putting its conventional events like duels and fires offstage. Thus, in Chekhov's major plays nothing much seems to happen onstage. As Bentley puts it, "Chekhov placed his camera in an unusual relation to the violent action."[49] This innovation can best be seen by reading Boucicault's *The Octoroon* against *The Cherry Orchard*. Both tell the same basic story: a widow, whose husband left her with nothing but debts, finds that her property will be sold at auction. Boucicault depicts murder, fraud, and a climactic onstage auction. In contrast, Chekhov shows what happens to people between the big incidents in their lives. Every action-packed event in *The Cherry Orchard*, even the auction, happens elsewhere. Onstage the characters only wait for and then react to what has happened offstage. We watch them spend time, worry, make plans, have coffee, reminisce, tease, converse, flirt, give a party, and cope with bad news that forever changes their lives. After learning of the auction, the widow collapses into a state of shock, while the buyer of her estate expresses his exultant, yet guilty joy. Nor does Chekhov end the play with these climactic reactions; instead he follows his characters as they pick up their lives, establish new routines, and move on.

While Boucicault depicts the external causes that throw lives into turmoil, Chekhov paints the familiar experience of living from day to day. By turning melodrama inside out, he has also effectively redefined the notion of dramatic action as the inner, psychological, often subtle movements of the soul. As one of my students observed, "Chekhov's portrayal of the tedium of life allows the audience to get to the subtle-

---

[48]   Madelyn Heyman, Theatre Seminar: The Performing Arts, University of Southern California, Spring 2012.

[49]   Bentley, *The Life of the Drama*, 11.

ties of the characters and become more personally attached to them."[50] Even as sophisticated a director as the internationally renowned Michael Cacoyannis can sometimes miss the fact that Chekhov has willfully shifted attention away from melodrama's big events. However beautifully filmed and well-acted Cacoyannis' *The Cherry Orchard*[51] may be, his decision to depict Lyubov Andreyevna's dissipated life in Paris and Lopakhin's drunken bidding for the estate at the auction turns the play back into the traditional melodrama that Chekhov abhorred.

Chekhov also refuses the moralizing of traditional melodrama. He does not sort his characters into easily identifiable heroes and villains; all of them are in turn admirable and silly, cruel and kind. Medicine has taught him that people and their diseases are rarely easy to classify. While writing *Ivanov* in 1887, Chekhov told his brother Alexander:

> Contemporary playwrights fill their plays with angels, villains, and clowns. Go find such types anywhere in Russia! However hard you look, you won't find them anywhere except in plays. [...] I wanted to do something original: I didn't bring into it one villain, not one angel, although I couldn't resist the clowns. (24 Oct. 1887)

In the words of Mila Shevchenko, Chekhov is a playwright who "employ[s] one of the most conservative dramatic structures," (melodrama,) "subverts and rearranges its constituents" in order that "the readily identifiable moral teleology is frustrated."[52] Peter Brooks would identify this subversion through "the paradox of the sympathetic villain,"[53] who had already made an appearance as Osip, the horse thief, in Chekhov's *Platonov*.

Another quick look at Boucicault's *The Octoroon* makes Chekhov's point about angels and villains clear: widow Peyton's only flaw is that she lacks business experience. As for the buyer of her land, Mr. McClosky has only one admirable trait, his well-trimmed mustaches. They are heroine

---

50 Mark Lay, Freshman Seminar: Checking Out Chekhov, University of Southern California, Fall 2008.
51 *The Cherry Orchard*, directed by M. Cacoyannis, Melinda Film Productions, 1999; available on DVD.
52 Shevchenko, *Melodramatic Scenarios and Modes of Marginality*, 10.
53 Brooks, *The Melodramatic Imagination*, 87.

and villain personified. In *The Cherry Orchard*, widow Ranyevskaya may lack business sense but she understands love as her Russian first name implies (Chapter 4). Her nemesis, Lopakhin may exceed her in business savvy, but he is helpless in regard to affairs of the heart. Moreover, his gracious concern for her is as genuine as his joy in buying her estate (Chapter 2). Neither one is fully heroic nor fully villainous. With the inclusion of a few clowns, like the clerk, Yepikhodov, who keeps tripping over his own feet, Chekhov creates a dramatic genre that is neither fully comic nor fully tragic. In his plays, nonsense co-exists with philosophy and conversations about the weather follow climactic moments that decide characters' fates. In short, Chekhov has also transformed melodrama's grand theme—the triumph of virtue—into another more quotidian one about the inconsistencies of human nature.

DETAILS PLUS VAUDEVILLE
PLUS MELODRAMA EQUALS...

The minute details of daily life, the comic techniques of vaudeville that explore the vagaries of interpersonal dynamics, and melodrama turned inside out are the primary ingredients of a Chekhov play. Each ingredient can be identified and examined separately; each can be used to understand the broad themes that drive Chekhov's imagination; but when they all come together in his mature plays, the mixture resists classification. Gorky had struggled to describe *Uncle Vanya* in a long letter, which he ultimately tore up. The most he could say is that Chekhov had created a new type of play (above). Bentley more baldly asserts that Chekhov "enriched his dramas in ways that belong to no school," and I would add, to no established genre; his plays, "at least in their effect, are peculiar to himself."[54] Thus, both his literary style and genre have become points of contention in the examination of his major plays.

As already explored in this book, Chekhov's style is hard to label. Does he write realism or impressionism (Chapter 2)? Does he lay the groundwork for symbolism (Chapter 3)? Some critics have even seen his use of apparent irrelevancies and non sequitors in conversation (Chapter 3)

---

[54] Bentley, "Craftsmanship in *Uncle Vanya*," in Eekman, ed., *Critical Essays on Anton Chekhov*, 172.

as a precursor to absurdism as in the plays of Samuel Beckett.[55] Each of these styles is easily found in Chekhov's work to some measure; each can be identified and examined separately within his plays. But Chekhov's whole is more than the sum of its parts. After puzzling over the unusual style in *Uncle Vanya*, Gorky came to see in it a direct path from realism to philosophical meditation. In a second letter to Chekhov about the play's early provincial production, Gorky writes:

> The public says that *Uncle Vanya* and *The Seagull* are a new species of dramatic art, in which realism is raised to the inspired and deeply profound level of the symbol. I think that this is very well said. Listening to your play, I thought about life sacrificed to false idols, about the intrusion of beauty into the beggary of people's lives, about many other essential and important things. Other dramas do not lead us as human beings in this way from reality to philosophy—your plays do this.[56]

As an actor in the Moscow Art Theatre company, Maria Petrovna Lilina sensed something similar when she first encountered *The Cherry Orchard*. She told Chekhov that "to act in this play, one must be utterly truthful, but without the crudity of realism."[57]

Chekhov's genre is as problematic as his style. Does he write comedy, vaudeville, tragedy, melodrama or tragicomedy? Is it sufficient to call his plays "drama"? Chekhov himself called his plays many things from "jokes" and "comedies" to "dramatic etudes." *Platonov* is simply a "play in four acts"; *Ivanov* and *Three Sisters* are "dramas," and *Uncle Vanya* consists of "scenes from country life." When Chekhov counterintuitively labeled *The Seagull* (which ends in a suicide) and *The Cherry Orchard* (which ends with the passing of an entire lifestyle) "comedies," he started a firestorm of continuing debate about the genre of his plays.

Consider, for example, how Chekhov had ignited such a debate with his correspondence about *The Cherry Orchard*. He had explained to Nemirovich-Danchenko, the co-founder of the Moscow Art Theatre, that "I am calling it a comedy" (2 Sept. 1903). Chekhov told the actor Lilina

---

55 See, for example, Richard Gilman, *Chekhov's Plays: An Opening into Eternity* (New Haven: Yale University Press, 1995), passim.

56 Gorky, cited in Chekhov, *Sobranie sochinenii* [Collected Works], Vol. 9, 485.

57 M. P. Lilina, cited in Chekhov, *Polnoe sobranie sochinenii* [The Complete Works], Vol. 13, 497.

that, "[the play] has turned out not as a drama, but a comedy, in places even a farce" (15 Sept. 1903). He told his wife Olga that, "the whole play is happy, light minded" (23 Oct. 1903). However, the Moscow Art Theatre company reacted to Chekhov's prompts about *The Cherry Orchard* in much more complex ways than its author had anticipated. As the production's director, Stanislavsky sent a telegram to Chekhov on 22 October 1903 immediately following the company's first read-through, reporting that "Everyone cried during the last act."[58] Stanislavsky followed with a long letter and fuller explanation:

> In my opinion, *The Cherry Orchard* is your best play. I fell in love with it more than even *The Seagull*. This is not a comedy, not a farce, as you have written to tell us, but a tragedy, no matter how much you end it by pointing the way to a better life. The impression is enormous, and it achieves half tones, gentle pastel colors. In it is poetry, lyricism, good theater [...] From the first reading [...] I was seized by it, brought to life by your play. [... On the second read,] I cried like a woman, wanted to hold back but I couldn't. I listened to what you told us, "Surely this is a farce"... But no, for the normal person this is a tragedy.[59]

Stanislavsky's wife, Lilina, verified her husband's words to Chekhov: "When we read your play, many of us cried, even the men; it seems to me that it is full of the love of life." But she then describes her further reaction quite differently from Stanislavsky: "Today while taking a walk, I heard the autumn rustle of the trees, and I recalled *The Seagull* and *The Cherry Orchard*, because I suddenly realized that *The Cherry Orchard* is not a play, but a musical work, a symphony."[60] The company's first Treplev, who would soon become a great avant-garde director, Vsevolod Emilyevich Meyerhold, reacted to *The Cherry Orchard* much as had Lilina; he told Chekhov, "Your play is abstract, like a Tchaikovsky symphony. Before all else, a director must catch the sound of it."[61] Alexander Leonidovich Vishnevsky, the original Dr. Dorn in *The Seagull*, used yet

---

58   K. S. Stanislavskii, *Sobranie sochinenii* [Collected Works], Vol. 7 (Moscow: Iskusstvo, 1995), 505.

59   Ibid., 505-6

60   Lilina in Chekhov, *Polnoe sobranie sochinenii* [The Complete Works], Vol. 13, 497.

61   V. Meierkhol'd in Kuzicheva, ed., *A. P. Chekhov v russkoi teatral'noi kritike* [Chekhov in Russian Theatrical Criticism], 334.

another metaphor to describe *The Cherry Orchard*: "This is not a play, but fine, rich lace."[62]

However much the actors were moved by Chekhov's last play, they struggled to describe it as much as Gorky had struggled with *Uncle Vanya*. Their emotionally stated reactions have been translated into more sober, scholarly prose by John Gassner, who writes: "It has often been noted that Chekhov is a great humorist, yet also a profoundly moving writer. What this amounts to in terms of artistry is that his writing simply possesses a rich texture, that it exists on several levels of sensibility at the same time, and that his often limpid simplicity masks considerable complexity."[63]

At base, Chekhov's use of the word "comedy" to describe *The Seagull* and *The Cherry Orchard* reflects his usual penchant for drawing our eye to discrepancies in life. He calls these plays "comedies" in much the same way that he makes a hypochondriac of the healthy Lomov in *The Proposal* (Chapter 4) or sets the most extended love scene in *The Cherry Orchard* to the tune of political rhetoric ("Grandiloquent speech and philosophizing" in Chapter 3). Chekhov builds dissonance by frustrating our expectations of genre, as much as he does our expectations of character and story. He ends his "comedies" with events that one would expect to call sad, much as he sweeps away a father's traditionally comic objections to his daughter's marriage in *The Proposal* and places the melodramatic excitement of an auction offstage in *The Cherry Orchard*. As Gottlieb observes, Chekhov's comedy most often "lies in the disparity between aspiration and reality, or between desire and fulfillment. In most cases, there is little to stop the characters from doing what they want—except themselves. And this, centrally, is where the keynote of Chekhov's comedy lies."[64]

In the last analysis, I largely agree with Gottlieb when she writes that "the sad comicality of life" was Chekhov's subject, and his "treatment was a strong dose of comedy or sense of proportion—and with that, the hope of a better future."[65] Put another way, Chekhov's unique genre

---

[62] A. L. Vishnevskii in Chekhov, *Polnoe sobranie sochinenii* [The Complete Works], Vol. 13, 497.
[63] Gassner in Jackson, ed., *Chekhov*, 179.
[64] Gottlieb in Gottlieb and Allain, eds., *The Cambridge Companion to Chekhov*, 231.
[65] Ibid., 233.

and distinctive style—whatever you might wish to call them—become the means by which he achieves his primary goal—to strip away the lies and illusions which interfere with living in a clear-sighted and life-affirming way. From this perspective, laughter is curative. Dr. Chekhov wrote, "First, I get my patients laughing, and only then do I begin to treat them" (to N. A. Leikin, 20 May 1884). The writer in him says something quite similar:

> I will be reproved for writing only about mediocre events, for not having any positive heroes [... But] we are leading a provincial life, the streets of our city are not even paved, our villages are poor, and our people are worn out. In our youth, we twitter like a bunch of sparrows on a pile of manure. At forty we are already old and starting to think about death. What sort of heroes are we? [...] I only wanted to tell people honestly: look, look how badly you live, how boring your lives are. The important thing is that people should understand this; if they do understand this, they will certainly invent a different and a far better life. A human being will become better only once we have shown him as he really is.[66]

As Bentley sees it, a play by Chekhov "is a pleasure, because it is a shaking into life," which makes the "scales" fall from our eyes. "Suddenly, [we] could see, could live. Need one labor the point that such an experience does have an appeal?"[67]

To "look" and truly "understand"[68] oneself and one's life without illusions one must gain distance. One must become, like Chekhov, "a spectator, and not one of the dramatis personae."[69] One must look at things as he wrote about them: "from afar, from a crack in the wall."[70] Otherwise, there is no "shaking into life."[71] How better to encourage this kind of perception than through the distancing effect of comedy which

[66] Cited and translated by Piero Brunello and Lena Lenček, eds., from an undated archival letter, in *How to Write Like Chekhov*, 51.
[67] Bentley, *The Life of the Drama*, 345.
[68] Cited and translated by Brunello and Lenček, eds., from an undated archival letter, in *How to Write Like Chekhov*, 51.
[69] Tatiana Lvovna Shchepkina-Kupernik in Turkov, ed., *Anton Chekhov and His Times*, 27.
[70] A. P. Chekhov to Al. P. Chekhov, 13 May 1883, quoted first in Chapter 1.
[71] Bentley, *The Life of the Drama*, 345.

can readily spotlight the ridiculous and illogical discrepancies in human behavior!

To view Chekhov's overall dramatic intention as the blending of comedy and tragedy in a realistic play that induces, in turn, laughter and tears is to miss the whole point of his achievement in playwriting. From this frequently encountered, but rather too simplistic point of view, Chekhov's famous insistence that *The Seagull* and *The Cherry Orchard* are comedies would seem willfully eccentric. So, too, from this point of view, would the vaudeville of Masha chasing after Treplev, as Treplev chases after Nina, and the comic parody of Arkadina's melodramatic acting, as she kneels before Trigorin, seem ultimately less important than Treplev's final conversation with Nina and his suicide. Similarly, the comic flirtations among the servants and Trofimov's pratfall down the stairs would seem mere moments of comic relief in comparison with Lyubov Andreyevna and Gayev bidding farewell to their orchard and Firs awaiting death in a locked house. So too would the unidentified sound from afar in *The Cherry Orchard* seem nothing more than an inconvenient problem for a realistic sound designer to solve. The mature Chekhov play is not comic, tragic, melodramatic, realistic, impressionistic, or symbolist; it is all of these at once. Chekhov's achievement resides not in the blending of genres within a predominantly realistic style of writing, but rather in his creation of an entirely new type of genre and a unique dramatic style, both of which resist traditional classifications.

Chapter 6

Chekhov's Plays
as Blueprints for Performances

Chekhov wrote his stories to live on the page, encountered privately by individual readers; but he wrote his plays to live on the stage, encountered publicly by audiences. Therefore, despite similarities in writing technique, his language functions differently in his fiction and his drama. Strings and sequences of words and their suggestive nuances are the sole means by which a writer of fiction can conjure images within the imaginations of his readers. In the theater, however, the old adage holds: actions often speak louder than words. As the Shakespearean scholar and dramatic theorist, Bernard Beckerman sagely points out, literary analysis rarely accounts sufficiently for the "kinetic," "temporal," and "spatial," aspects implicit in a text intended for performance.[1]

Stage directions and dialogue in a play function as clues to its physical embodiment in production. In turn, the play's physical embodiment conjures up images for the spectators. Performance theorist William B. Worthen puts the same thought in other words:

> I argue that the meanings of modern drama cannot be fully seized without considering how those meanings are produced as theater. For in the theater, drama can speak only through the practices of acting and directing, the construction of the *mise-en-scène*, and the arrangement and disposition of the audience.[2]

---

[1] Bernard Beckerman, *Dynamics of Drama: Theory and Methods of Analysis* (New York: Alfred A. Knopf, Inc., 1970), vii.

[2] William B. Worthen, *Modern Drama and the Rhetoric of Theater* (Los Angeles: University of California Press, 1992), 1. The French term *mise-en-scène* throughout this chapter refers to the blocking and movement patterns of the actors on stage.

In short, as Worthen observes, directors and designers make "use" of plays as "instruments" of stage art.[3]

This chapter takes one small step toward an examination of Chekhov's plays as textual "instruments" for production, to borrow Worthen's word. Given the longevity of Chekhov's plays in production, the topic is of enormous historical range and theoretical complexity, far beyond the scope of this book. Nonetheless, Chekhov's plays cannot be fully appreciated without considering them as blueprints for theatrical artists.

In fact, theatrical history was slow to accept Chekhov. His early fame as a writer of fiction and his liberal transplantation of literary techniques into his plays meant that, during his lifetime, theater professionals and critics tended to treat him as a theatrical interloper. As late as 1901, reviewers still preferred his stories:

> [His plays] cannot be considered drama [...]. True, all the character types, the relationships and the action are detailed with the same masterful talent that is familiar to us in other works by Chekhov. But, [his plays] can no more be called "drama," than the foundation of a house [...] can be called a "house."[4]

His contemporaries often thought of him as a good fiction writer, who created some rather undramatic plays.

Only a handful of artists from Chekhov's era could see how radically revolutionary were his dramatic goals. Among them were writers like Maksim Gorky and Vladimir Nemirovich-Danchenko, the former seeing in Chekhov the death of standard realism and traditional dramatic form (Chapters 2 and 5) and the latter understanding that only a new kind of theatrical staging could make visible Chekhov's deeply dramatic, but highly unconventional plays (Chapter 1).

Trusting Nemirovich-Danchenko's literary expertise, Konstantin Stanislavsky set to work on the 1898 production of *The Seagull* for the Moscow Art Theatre, which eventually secured both his and Chekhov's reputations as theatrical innovators (Chapter 1). Stanislavsky directed

---

[3]   William B. Worthen, *Drama: Between Poetry and Performance* (Chichester: Wiley-Blackwell, 2010), xiv-xvii.

[4]   Review of three dramas by Chenko [*sic*], 27 Mar. 1901, cited in Chekhov, *Polnoe sobranie sochinenii* [The Complete Works], Vol. 13 (Moscow: Nauka, 1978), 381.

and played the role of Trigorin. Subsequently Stanislavsky directed and acted in all Chekhov's major plays: *Uncle Vanya*, playing Dr. Astrov in 1899; *Three Sisters*, appearing as Vershinin in 1901; and *The Cherry Orchard*, originating the role of Gayev in 1904.[5] With Stanislavsky's productions Chekhov unquestionably entered into theatrical history.

Today, theater directors worldwide stage Chekhov's handful of plays with nearly the same frequency as they do Shakespeare's more generous output. Moreover, alongside productions that seek to bring Chekhov's texts to life on their own terms, are those that imaginatively reinterpret him. Russia's cherry orchard has been replanted on an antebellum southern plantation in the U.S. (Joshua Logan's *The Wisteria Trees*) and on a plot of land in South Africa (Janet Suzman's *The Free State*); sometimes a *Seagull* flies over Ireland (Thomas Kilroy's adaptation) or New York's Long Island (Emily Mann's *A Seagull in the Hamptons*). In 2008, one hundred and four years after Chekhov's death, a Broadway revival of *The Seagull* was one of only two productions "to have recouped their New York investments" that year, and this while the New York Stock Market plunged.[6] In the summer of 2012, two competing productions of *Uncle Vanya* played to sold-out houses in New York: one by the Soho Rep using Annie Baker's adaptation (Introduction), the other by Australia's Sydney Theatre, starring Cate Blanchett. Laurence Senelick's hefty tome, *The Chekhov Theatre*, charts a century of productions in Russia, the English-speaking world, Europe, Scandinavia, and Asia. Paging through this book should be enough to assure the most hardened skeptic of Chekhov's global impact as a dramatist.

This history of Chekhovian production throws a spotlight onto the various ways that meaning is produced collaboratively in theatrical performance. On the one hand, directors, designers, and actors interpret

---

5   Stanislavsky returned to *The Seagull* in 1916 with Chekhov's nephew, Michael Chekhov, playing Treplev. Rehearsal transcripts survive, but the production, which was set to open in 1917, was aborted due to the Bolshevik revolution. See I. Vinogradskaia, ed., *Stanislavskii Repetiruet: Zapisi i stenogrammy repetitsii* [Stanislavsky Directs: Rehearsal Transcripts and Stenographies] (Moscow: STD, 1987), 189-206; and Laurence Senelick, "Stanislavsky's Second Thoughts on 'The Seagull'," *New Theatre Quarterly* 20, no. 2 (May 2004), 127-37.

6   *The Los Angeles Times: Quick Takes*, 9 Dec. 2008, http://www.latimes.com/entertainment.

Chekhov's plays as they stage them. On the other hand, audiences bring their personal and cultural assumptions to bear as they watch. In both cases, what is Chekhovian becomes a hybrid of the author's intentions and the artists' and spectators' imaginations. Both kinds of hybridization bring their own sorts of analytical difficulties to the table and thus expose how complicated it is to read a play, not as a completed work of literature, but as an incomplete blueprint, that points to its performative potential.

In the first type of hybridization, a Chekhov play is conditioned by the actors, directors, and designers who interpret it, and who have their own distinctive styles and tastes different from that of the author. The British film scholar Paul McDonald brilliantly exposes how actors impact meaning by painstakingly examining Gus Van Sant's 1998 shot-by-shot reconstruction of Alfred Hitchcock's 1960 film *Psycho*. McDonald demonstrates the ways in which the two visually similar films resonate differently simply because Anne Heche and Vince Vaughn play the roles first created by Janet Leigh and Anthony Perkins. Frame for frame, the camera angles, shots, and editing are the same, but the actors' qualities on screen and within each discrete shot are distinctive. The "differences in acting performance come to the fore" precisely because Hitchcock's visual direction is maintained; and "these divergences [in the acting] affect the meaning of the respective films."[7] So, too, would a reconstruction of Stanislavsky's *The Seagull*, crafted from his detailed promptbook for the 1898 production, tell us little about the qualities of the actors' work in the production which so stunned the Moscow audience at the play's premiere (Chapter 1).[8]

Because directorial choices are often more easily documented than the ephemeral work of actors, it is easier to compare different directors' visions of Chekhov than past interpretations of the same role by

---

[7] Paul McDonald, "Why Study Film Acting? Some Opening Reflections," in Cynthia Baron, Diane Carson, and Frank P. Tomasulo, eds., *More than a Method* (Detroit: Wayne State University Press, 2004), 27.

[8] The prominent German director, Peter Stein, staged *The Cherry Orchard* in 1989 using Stanislavsky's 1904 plans. In choosing to reconstruct the original production, Stein explained that, "It is impossible to understand Chekhov's plays without taking into account his personal relationship with the Moscow Art Theatre." See James N. Loehlin, *The Cherry Orchard: Plays in Production* (New York: Cambridge University Press, 2006), 182.

different actors. For example, consider three productions of *The Cherry Orchard*, each embodying an entirely different directorial approach to Chekhov's dramatic style.

In 1904 Stanislavsky asked the Moscow Art Theatre designer, Viktor Simov, to create a detailed illusion of the reality of life on a Russian estate. In fact, Stanislavsky used his own estate, Lyubimovka, as the model for Simov's sets. Stanislavsky knew that Chekhov had begun writing the play while on a visit there with his wife, who would soon play Ranyevskaya. She wrote to Chekhov during rehearsals to tell him that she found herself sitting on a "sofa that is placed [on the stage] just where it was at Lyubimovka, in the connecting room, just by our dining room."[9] In sympathy with this visual design, the director built into the actors' work a quotidian simplicity of gesture and delivery. The Moscow Art Theatre thus set into motion the still prevalent audience expectation for realism in the production of a Chekhov play.

In contrast, the Romanian born, avant-garde director Andrei Serban stressed the play's non-realism in his 1977 New York Shakespeare Festival production. The actors moved through an expanse of empty space, designed by Santo Loquasto and containing only random pieces of furniture and some long-abandoned toys. This expanse was set against a background of starkly beautiful cherry trees. In terms of the actors' work, Serban encouraged broad, even slapstick comedy among the servants and heartfelt emotion from the landowners, as when the actress Irene Worth as Ranyevskaya tearfully scattered torn bits of her lover's telegrams into the river in Act II and made a full sweep around the stage to bid a heartbreaking goodbye to her lost home.[10] For the New York audience, who had come to expect realism from Chekhov, Serban's poetic envisioning of the play, together with his actors' pratfalls and tears, "challenged and invigorated the unadventurous tradition of American Chekhov," to borrow James N. Loehlin's words.[11]

---

[9] Ol'ga Leonardovna Knipper-Chekhova, *Perepiska* [Correspondence], Vol. 1 (Moscow: Iskusstvo, 1972), 334.

[10] I describe the set as I remember it. For more on this production, see Senelick, *The Chekhov Theatre*, 297-9, and Loehlin, *Chekhov*, 155-62. Meryl Streep played Dunyasha in a broadly comic manner; Irene Worth as Ranyevskaya focused on the pathos of the widow's situation; Raul Julia played Lopakhin as hopelessly in love with Ranyevskaya, making sense of his non-proposal to Varya.

[11] Loehlin, *Chekhov*, 155.

Finally, the 1990 production in Moscow, directed by Leonid Trush-kin and designed by Alexander Lisyansky, highlighted Chekhov's affin-ity with the absurdist view of life. Prompted by Gayev's Act I speech in praise of a century old cupboard, Trushkin and Lisyansky set the play in-side an enormous cupboard with a multitude of doors, each one opening to reveal a different scene unfold; the actors, like marionettes, emerged mechanically from behind the doors.[12] The production played against the memory of Russian audiences long familiar with images from Stan-islavsky's productions and ready for something new. Moreover, as the Soviet Union was collapsing, the absurdist style of the Chekhov produc-tion seemed to reflect the absurdism of contemporary Russian experi-ence more surely than realism could.

Each of these productions selected details from Chekhov's text and built creatively upon them. Thus, despite their clear differences in style, each was a valid reading of performative values inherent in the play. Moreover, each also spoke to a different kind of audience, thus raising the next theoretical question about the study of plays on stage.

In the second type of hybridization of a play, audience expectations and cultural backgrounds can and do affect the meaning of individual productions. As Beckerman puts it, "the audience's predisposition, or sensibility [...] serves as a ground for the play as a whole. [...] Depending upon its history, an audience is predisposed to react in certain ways."[13] As years go by, public reference points change and consequently so do the impacts and meanings of a staged text. When a play is produced by different artists over a long span of time and in many different countries, as are Chekhov's plays, audiences will surely interpret his references in ways that the playwright could never have imagined. As the three briefly described productions above suggest, directors do take their audience's expectations into account.

But sometimes the same production can change its meaning sim-ply because it faces a new audience, as often happens when theatrical companies tour. In this case, the work of the same artists can elicit very different audience reactions. Consider, for example, the Russian audi-ences in 1904 and the American spectators in 1923, who both viewed essentially the same Moscow Art Theatre production of *The Cherry*

---

[12] I describe what I remember. For more, see Senelick, *The Chekhov Theatre*, 354.
[13] Beckerman, *Dynamics of Drama*, 138.

Orchard. In the first case, Chekhov as writer and Stanislavsky as director could count on a shared culture and on the extensive literary memories of their countrymen (Chapter 2). Additionally, the 1904 reviews show that few Russians saw Chekhov's play as predictive of revolution, despite the fact that the first failed attempt would occur in 1905. Admirers focused on the production's realism and drew attention to familiar cultural and literary resonances. One reviewer, for example, noted that even the drunken passerby who begs for money by reciting poetry "appears to the spectators for only a moment with unsure steps, with the verses of Nadson and Nekrasov on his lips—but his face flashed before us a complete drama, a whole life, wasted, bitter, pitiful."[14] Detractors berated Chekhov, not for his politics, but for depicting Russia's landowners as "passive, weak-willed, unable to overcome their circumstances and surrendering to an enterprising peasant turned merchant."[15]

In 1923 and 1924, when the Moscow Art Theatre toured the United States with their 1904 production, American audiences found the Russian language and culture exotic and alien. Stanislavsky's realism now served as a keyhole into an unfamiliar life-style. Furthermore, the U.S. government's refusal to recognize the new Soviet State as legitimate made Chekhov's play appear to Americans as a lyrical testament to what had been destroyed by the communist revolution of 1917. Stanislavsky seemed to invite the spectator to become "an actual visitor in a Russian household, [...] watching the family go about its business." One admirer exclaimed, "This is Russia, this is the real thing!"[16] Detractors of the Soviet Union wept in sympathy with the landowners, whom they viewed as unwitting victims of history. As a self-proclaimed "100 Per Cent American" marveled, the "Bolsheviky" [*sic*] actors "that can't talk a word of English," could still make "a hard-boiled egg like me cry like a kid."[17]

---

[14] Yuly Aikhenvald, cited and translated by Senelick, *The Chekhov Theatre*, 76. The poets are Semyon Yakovlevich Nadson (1862-87) and Nikolay Alekseyevich Nekrasov (1821-78).

[15] Homunculus in Chekhov, *Polnoe sobranie sochinenii* [The Complete Works], Vol. 13, 507.

[16] Edmund Wilson and Arthur Ruhl, cited in Carnicke, "Stanislavsky's Production of *The Cherry Orchard* in the US," in Clayton, ed., *Chekhov Then and Now*, 25.

[17] John Weaver in Ibid., 19.

This spotlight on the ways in which theatrical meaning is produced collaboratively by author, theater artists, and audiences also makes sense of Chekhov's ambivalent reactions to the productions of his plays during his lifetime. Consider, for example, how surprised he had been by interpretations of *Ivanov*. As he told his friend, Suvorin:

> If my Ivanov has turned out to be a scoundrel or a superfluous man in the Turgenev stripe, [...] I probably lost my mind and wrote something completely different than I had intended. (26 Dec. 1888; Chapter 5)

The Korsh Theatre's director and audience had seen in Chekhov's work a cultural reference that he had tried to refute. Many of Chekhov's later arguments with the Moscow Art Theatre also stem from the fact that others saw in his work aspects that were not visible to him. Compare, for example, how closely Chekhov's criticism of the Moscow Art Theatre's production of *The Cherry Orchard* compares to his reaction to the Korsh Theatre's *Ivanov*:

> Nemirovich-Danchenko and [Stanislavsky] see something entirely different in my play than what I wrote, and I am prepared to swear that neither one has read my play carefully. (to O. L. Knipper, 10 April 1904)

In short, every production in Chekhov's long stage history is necessarily different from whatever it was that he initially imagined as he wrote in the solitude of his study, both because artists other than he and spectators of many types placed their own interpretative stamps on his plays. The meanings in his plays, when performed, are always contingent upon the artistic and cultural contexts of their productions.

Despite this contingency of meaning, Chekhov has written carefully crafted blueprints, that fully convey to actors, directors, and designers his unique vision for theatrical production. As the earlier chapters in my book demonstrate, his plays provide firm foundations for performance which can be uncovered through close reading. Thus, there is value in looking more precisely at the linkage between text and performance in a specific Chekhov production. Moreover, the most obvious choice for a case study—the 1898 Moscow Art Theatre production of *The Seagull*—is also the best.

Stanislavsky and his partner, Nemirovich-Danchenko, fully committed themselves to the honest exploration of Chekhov's texts. Despite the author's protests to the contrary, they had read and considered his texts closely. Nothing proves this more than the production plans that Stanislavsky wrote for them. In fact, serving the play was chief among the goals that the co-founders of the Moscow Art Theatre had set for their newly founded company. As Stanislavsky writes:

> The task of our theater is to create the inner life of the play and its roles through the physical embodiment of the core and thoughts that impelled the poet or composer to write the work. Every worker in the theater, starting with the usher, the coat-check attendant, and the cashier, who greet the spectators as they arrive, to the administrators and office manager, and finally to the actors whose work people fill the theater to see—all of these serve and are without exception subject to the main goal of our art.[18]

In other words, the Moscow Art Theatre assumes that the play provides the central driving force behind production; that it is the play which guides all members of a theatrical team; that the text sets forth a core of meaning and style, which theater professionals and artists make visible in the material reality of their production. In short, the Moscow Art Theatre believed in treating authors respectfully by bringing every play's unique properties to the audience.[19] From this perspective, the direc-

---

[18] K. S. Stanislavskii, "Etika i distsiplina" [Ethics and Discipline], *Sobranie sochinenii* [Collected Works], Vol. 3 (Moscow: Iskusstvo, 1990), 294-5. Putting the needs of the play first prompts Stanislavsky's often quoted maxim: Love the art in yourself, not yourself in art.

[19] Theatrical history demonstrates that these assumptions have not been universally shared. Italy's *commedia dell'arte* depended upon scenarios of plays which were fleshed out in performance by actors' improvisations. Today, devising texts through actors' improvisations follows the assumption that performances, not plays, generate productions. The British designer and director, Gordon Craig (1872-1966), believed that the director was the primary artist in theater, not the playwright. For his production of *Hamlet* at the Moscow Art Theatre (1911) he turned Shakespeare's play into a monodrama that takes place inside Hamlet's mind, with all the supporting characters positioned as reflections of the protagonist's psyche. In such radical interpretations, directors use the texts of

tors, designers, and actors alike felt ethically obligated to analyze the ways in which Chekhov's plays were innovative and to seek the means to make his innovations visible.

While Stanislavsky's directing choices sometimes famously disappointed Chekhov, they also sometimes delighted him. One often sees Chekhov's discontent quoted, such as his complaint (above) about the company's production of *The Cherry Orchard*. One rarely sees his gratitude in print. Yet, at a very early rehearsal of *The Seagull*, Chekhov "immediately understood how [Stanislavsky's] *mise-en-scène* strengthens the impression of the play."[20] After the production opened, he told a friend that, "the Moscow production is astonishing [...]. The imperial Maly Theatre would blush in shame to see it, and in terms of *mise-en-scène* and design it is far more innovative than the [latest German work] of the Meiningen Theatre" (to P. F. Iordanov, 15 May 1899). While Stanislavsky sometimes disagreed with his partner Nemirovich-Danchenko over specific interpretations of Chekhov's plays and roles, the arguments were, as Stanislavsky observes, "beneficial in that they taught us to deepen our understanding of art."[21] Thus, with whatever flaws one might find in them, the Moscow Art Theatre productions reveal as much about Chekhov, as they do about the company's aesthetics. Stanislavsky wrote:

> [Our Chekhov productions] succeeded in bringing to the stage something of what Chekhov has given us, when others [before us] had failed, and when the actors in our company were still inexperienced. But we succeeded because we discovered a new approach to Chekhov. He is unique. And this uniqueness led us to our own major contribution to theatrical art.[22]

Many aspects of that contribution were crystallized in 1898 in *The Seagull*.

---

plays not as they find them, but as pre-texts for production. Following in Craig's footsteps, avant-garde directors liberally and sometimes literally re-write plays by re-conceiving them in production.

[20] Nemirovich-Danchenko, *Tvorcheskoe nasledie* [Creative Legacy], Vol. 1, letter to K. S. Stanislavsky, 12 Sept. 1898, 236.
[21] Stanislavskii, *Sobranie sochinenii* [Collected Works], Vol. 1, 294.
[22] Ibid., 389.

STANISLAVSKY'S SCORE FOR *THE SEAGULL*

Stanislavsky has frankly admitted his initial puzzlement over the seemingly prosaic and uneventful surface action in Chekhov's drama:

> The plays of Chekhov do not reveal at first their poetic significance. Reading them one says to oneself: 'It's good, but... nothing special, nothing amazing. Everything is as it should be. It's familiar... truthful... nothing new...' In fact, the first acquaintance with his works is often disappointing. It seems like there is little to say about it.[23]

However, over time Stanislavsky learned the power of Chekhov's counterintuitive playwriting; and disappointment turned into admiration:

> I had occasion to act some of Chekhov's characters several hundred times, and I do not remember a single performance in which I did not discover some new feeling in my soul, and new depths and subtleties in the works themselves which had escaped me earlier.[24]

Directing and acting had forced Stanislavsky into paying the kind of attention to detail that is necessary for a full appreciation of Chekhov's craft.

In reading Stanislavsky's autobiography, one can see how accurately he came to understand Chekhov's dramaturgy. First, consider subtext. In describing a typical Chekhovian scene, Stanislavsky conjures up the image of "a man and woman [who] exchange almost meaningless words that do not express what they feel. (Chekhov's people often behave that way.)"[25] Stanislavsky correctly suggests that one must intuit subtext through the mundane interactions that take place between people who do not speak their minds. Next, recall Chekhov's elimination of overt melodramatic action in favor of more subtle types of action. Stanislavsky writes: "[Chekhov's] plays are very active, but not in an external sense, rather in their internal developments. The very inaction of the people he

---

[23] Ibid., 289.
[24] Ibid., 290.
[25] Ibid., 292.

creates conceals their complex inner action."[26] Third, despite the Moscow Art Theatre's early dedication to realism on stage, Stanislavsky clearly sees Chekhov as more stylistically complex. "In some places, he is an *impressionist*, in other places—a *symbolist*, and when necessary a *realist*, sometimes even a *naturalist*."[27] Such a mixture heightens the audience's senses: Chekhov "makes more subtle and deepens our understanding of the life of things, sounds, lights on stage, all of which in the theater as in life, exert a great deal of influence on our souls."[28] Lastly, despite Stanislavsky's reputation for having emphasized the tragic in Chekhov's plays, the director clearly understood the importance of comedy to the author:

> Chekhov like no one else, knows how to choose and convey the variety of human moods through sharply different kinds of scenes from daily life, interspersing them with the brilliance of his cleansing sense of humor.[29]

In short, Chekhov grew on Stanislavsky, much as Chekhov grows in the hearts of so many of us, who have occasion to work with his texts (Introduction).

Stanislavsky's iconic 1898 production of *The Seagull*[30] opened in the shadow of the equally legendary fiasco that took place on 17 October 1896, when the play premiered at the imperial Aleksandrinsky Theatre as a benefit for the comic actress Levkeyeva (Chapter 1). The premiere's director was the well-known Yevtikhy Pavlovich Karpov (1857-1926), who had previously staged one of Chekhov's least favorite melodramas, *The Fumes of Life* (Chapter 5). Karpov read *The Seagull* as primarily Nina's story, which is one of the most melodramatic layers in the play. With

---

26 Ibid., 290.
27 Ibid., 291. The italics are Stanislavsky's.
28 Ibid., 292.
29 Ibid., 291.
30 My study greatly benefits from the publication of Stanislavsky's detailed promptbooks and the photographs that document them. My analysis of *The Seagull* uses K. S. Stanislavskii, *Chaika* [The Seagull] in *Rezhisserskie ekzempliary K. S. Stanislavskogo* [Directorial Plans], Vol. 2 (Moscow: Iskusstvo, 1981), 51-166. Photographs are available in Vera Gottlieb, ed. and trans., *Anton Chekhov at the Moscow Art Theatre: Illustrations of the Original Productions* (New York: Routledge, 2005).

Chekhov's advice (as documented by their correspondence) Karpov cast the actors, who promptly memorized their roles as expected; Karpov then rehearsed them according to the usual schedule: a first reading, five general and two dress rehearsals. Despite inappropriate laughs from Levkeyeva's fans on opening night, Karpov, the critics, and even Chekhov generally felt that the play was well-acted. Despite having fled the theater on opening night, Chekhov told Karpov that the actors were "not bad. Only they act too much. I'd like them to act less. They have to do everything simply, like people do in ordinary life." The expert director, who naturally expected actors to act, answered, "How can you do things like that on stage, I don't know."[31] As a writer, Chekhov certainly did not know either.

Given recent theatrical experiments with realism in Germany and France, Stanislavsky had an idea of how one might fulfill Chekhov's desire to do things on stage as in life. Stanislavsky had admired how Duke Georg of Saxe-Meiningen at Germany's court theater was using the stage's perspective to produce realistic crowd scenes and how he was creating historically accurate productions by researching all aspects of set and costume. Under Meiningen's influence, the Moscow Art Theatre had already produced Aleksey Konstantinovich Tolstoy's *Tsar Fyodor Ioannovich* (1868, a tale of medieval Russia) in the realistic style.

But Stanislavsky was also intrigued by the latest ideas of the French director André Antoine. At *Le Théâtre Libre* (The Free Theatre, founded in Paris in 1887) Antoine had advanced the idea that actors should behave as if they were in a real room with one of the four walls removed to allow the audience to watch. To denote the imaginary wall through which spectators eavesdrop on the life of the play he coined the term "fourth wall," still used liberally by theatrical professionals. Antoine's ideas in conjunction with those of Meiningen prompted Stanislavsky to imagine how one might bring ordinary life onto the stage as Chekhov wanted. In *The Seagull*, Stanislavsky placed actors with their backs to the audience while they watched Treplev's play-within-the play, thus

---

[31] A. P. Chekhov and E. P. Karpov, cited in K. Rudnitskii, "Rezhisserskaia partitura K. S. Stanislavskogo i *Chaika* na stsene MKhT v 1898 gody" [The Directorial Score by K. S. Stanislavsky and *The Seagull* on the Moscow Art Theatre Stage in 1898], in Stanislavskii, *Rezhisserskie ekzempliary* [Directorial Plans], Vol. 2, 50.

productively borrowing from Antoine.[32] Moreover, the notion of eaves-dropping onto a play's action through an invisible fourth wall mirrors Chekhov's desire to write as if he were objectively eavesdropping on life (Chapter 1). As he explained to his eldest brother Alexander, "If I write, then it will surely be from afar, from a crack in the wall" (13 May 1883). In the realistic theater forged by Antoine, spectators emulate this angle of vision.

After two days of discussions about *The Seagull* with Nemirovich-Danchenko, Stanislavsky retreated to the countryside near the southern town of Kharkov in the summer of 1898 to devise his production plan. No doubt, his partner's interpretation of the play had armed him well for the task, but grappling with the play on his own proved no easy matter. When he began, he said that, "this was a difficult task, because, to my shame, I did not understand the play."[33] However, as he worked his way slowly and painstakingly through it, everything changed for him. "To my surprise, the work seemed easy: I saw, I felt the play."[34] He sent his plan—act by act—back to Moscow, where Nemirovich-Danchenko began rehearsing in earnest.

Stanislavsky's promptbook for *The Seagull* makes apparent more than his attraction to European realism; it also testifies to his intuitively clear-sighted understanding of Chekhov's dramaturgy. Yet, relatively few scholars have used Stanislavsky's written plan to examine how he actually read Chekhov and, through that reading, reconceived directing and acting not only for Chekhov's plays, but also for plays more generally.[35]

---

[32] For more on these two influences, see Carnicke, *Stanislavsky in Focus*, Chapter 1.

[33] K. S. Stanislavskii, *Sobranie sochinenii* [The Complete Works], Vol. 5:2 (Moscow: Isskustvo, 1994), 85.

[34] Stanislavskii, *Sobranie sochinenii* [The Complete Works], Vol. 1, 267.

[35] Among those who have done so are Rudnitskii, in Stanislavskii, *Rezhisserskie ekzempliary* [Directorial Plans], who looks at Stanislavsky's directorial innovations; the Serbian scholar Jovan Hristić, "'Thinking with Chekhov': the Evidence of Stanislavsky's Notebooks," *New Theatre Quarterly* 11, no. 42 (May 1995), 175-83; and Bella Merlin in *Konstantin Stanislavsky* (New York: Routledge, 2003), Chapter 3, who looks at the ways that the plan predicts aspects of Stanislavsky's later System. In this chapter, I am especially indebted to Rudnitskii and Hristić for their insightful examinations of the links between play and production.

Stanislavsky's promptbook for *The Seagull* represents the first bold step in a new theatrical approach that was largely prompted by Chekhov's unique playwriting. However, in this plan and in subsequent production plans for Chekhov's plays Stanislavsky relied upon his earliest method of directing—the total envisioning of the play before going into rehearsals with the actors. Thus he describes in his promptbooks "the sets, costumes, make-up, manners, gaits, mechanical devices, personal habits of the characters depicted in it, etc., etc."[36] Later, after Chekhov's death, Stanislavsky would extend his theatrical experiments into the realm of acting, thereby developing his world famous System, which in turn would ultimately lead him to develop an entirely new approach to rehearsing and directing called Active Analysis. This innovation creates a production through the collaborative work of director and actors in the rehearsal room.[37]

In short, while the seeds of Stanislavsky's future acting System can be found in his directorial plans for Chekhov's plays, the plans themselves assume a director who controls all aspects of production, from sets to the blocking and performances of the actors. By the time Stanislavsky was developing Active Analysis, he had come to see his earlier directorial process, by which he staged Chekhov's plays, as outmoded. Thus, in 1925, when the scholar Sergey Dmitriyevich Balukhaty sought permission to publish the 1898 production plan for *The Seagull*, Stanislavsky said no: "Keep in mind that the *mise-en-scène* for *The Seagull* was prepared in the old method, now no longer used, of imposing upon the actor my own feelings, and not according to the new method that teaches actors to prepare the materials themselves in order that they find on their own what's necessary for the *mise-en-scène*."[38] Logically, however, because Stanislavsky's early method had been to write down in advance all the

---

[36] Stanislavskii, *Sobranie sochinenii* [The Complete Works], Vol. 1, 267.

[37] For more on the development of the System and Active Analysis, see Carnicke, *Stanislavsky in Focus*.

[38] Letter to Balukhatyi, 14 Feb. 1925, in K. S. Stanislavskii, *Sobranie sochinenii* [The Collected Works], Vol. 9 (Moscow: 1999), 177. Balukhatyi published the plan in 1938, the year of Stanislavsky's death; Balukhatyi's edition has been translated into English: S. D. Balukhatyi [sic], ed., *The Seagull Produced by Stanislavsky*, trans. David Magarshack (London: Methuen, 1952). Since then, Stanislavsky's directorial plans for Chekhov's plays, including the one for *The Seagull*, have been published in the multi-volume Russian edition from 1981, cited above.

various aspects of a production, his promptbooks provide direct access to his readings of Chekhov's plays.

Stanislavsky focused on three key aspects in Chekhov's four major plays that scholars have also come to see as especially significant to his innovative playwriting: first, the inherently musical structure of the plays; second, the ensemble nature of the casts; and third, the juxtaposition of different aesthetic styles. In my examination of Stanislavsky's plan for *The Seagull*, I will analyze how Stanislavsky turns each of these aspects into his directorial principles.

First, Stanislavsky called his plan a "score" (in Russian *partitura*), a musical term that had never before been used in connection with a spoken play. He even makes his notebook look like a score by using numbers to notate where his directorial notes link to specific lines of text, much as musical scores mark measures of music. Indeed, the plan is a "score" because Stanislavsky sees both the play and its performance as musically structured. He embodies this musicality in the actors' vocal work, the production's sound design, and the physical rhythms of the actors' movements and actions. The leading Russian theatrical scholar, Konstantin Rudnitsky gives special weight to Stanislavsky's rhythmic treatment of acting in *The Seagull*: "This was the first time in the history of the theater that the development of dramatic action was construed on the musical principle of *counterpoint*."[39]

All these musically based techniques can be found in a brief moment in Act I, shortly after Treplev aborts Nina's performance of his play, when the estate manager, Shamrayev, recalls a long-ago operatic performance, presumably acted with full histrionic flair, by a Belgian tenor who toured Russia in the early nineteenth century. I quote below from both Chekhov's text (which originally appeared on the left page of the note book) and Stanislavsky's numbered comments (originally on the right), interleaving these in a continuous flow for ease in reading:

No. 79. Shamrayev suddenly laughs for no apparent reason (too loudly and not tunefully), and then he starts to tell his story to Medvedenko and Dorn, who are seated next to him at the table.

Shamrayev: I remember, once in Moscow, at the opera, the famous Silva sang a low C. And, as if on purpose, one of the basses from

---

39   Rudnitskii in Stanislavskii, *Rezhisserskie ekzempliary* [Directorial Plans], 21.

our church choir happened to be sitting in the balcony. You can imagine our surprise, when suddenly from the balcony we hear, "Bravo, Silva," one full octave lower... Like this: (*In a low bass voice*) "Bravo, Silva..." The whole theater froze.

Pause.

No. 80. No one has laughed, so Shamrayev himself laughs even more strongly than before; then he abruptly stops and once more repeats "Bravo, Silva" before falling silent as unexpectedly as he had earlier begun laughing. There is a pause of 15 seconds. No one moves, the only sound that can be heard is the distant singing of peasants, the croaking of frogs, and the cry of a corncrake.

Dorn: An angel of silence has flown by.

No. 81. Again a pause, 10 seconds. Nina gets up sharply. (trans. Carnicke, 68; Stanislavskii, 77)[40]

In this passage, the changes of tone and loudness in Shamrayev's laughter and his repetition of "Bravo, Silva" in a bass voice work as vocal counterpoints to the silent immobility of the others in the group, until Dorn breaks the quiet moment with his line.

Within the quiet pauses, one finds Stanislavsky's often criticized imposition of sound effects on Chekhov's texts. Most theater folk know that this aspect of Stanislavsky's direction annoyed Chekhov, not only in *The Seagull*, but in all the Moscow Art Theatre productions of his plays. As late as 1903, after a rehearsal for *The Cherry Orchard*, Chekhov threatened to write the following opening line for his next play: "How wonderful, how quiet! Not a bird, a dog, a cuckoo, an owl, a nightingale, no clocks, no jingling bells, not even one cricket to be heard."[41] However, given the company's inexperienced actors, Stanislavsky actively used these effects to stimulate their imaginations. He understood that sound could help induce the actors' belief in the world of the play, and thus sound was a large part of his earliest method of directing. The sounds

---

[40] A corncrake is a type of bird; Dorn's line is a common saying when a conversation falls silent. Throughout this chapter I quote the Chekhov texts from my translations as published in *Chekhov: 4 Plays and 3 Jokes*, 53-113; and Stanislavsky's score from K. S. Stanislavskii, *Chaika* [The Seagull] in Stanislavskii, *Rezhisserskie ekzempliary* [Directorial Plans], Vol. 2, 51-166. I give the page numbers for both of these sources in parentheses following the quotations.

[41] Stanislavskii, *Sobranie sochinenii* [Collected Works], Vol. 1, 345.

detailed in No. 80 effectively ground the actors by giving them something on which to focus as they sit without moving or speaking. Later Stanislavsky would train the same kind of concentration of attention as a basic acting skill by adapting exercises from yoga.[42]

However, Stanislavsky also understood how sound enhances audience perception, as an argument between him and his partner best illustrates. Ironically, Nemirovich-Danchenko would later agree with Chekhov about Stanislavsky's too liberal use of sound effects. Yet, records from the rehearsals on *The Seagull* prove that Nemirovich-Dancheko was at that time adding his own touches of sound to the mix. For example, in No. 80 (above) he added "nine very, very, *very* soft bell chimes"[43] in order to mark the lateness of the hour. He strongly objected, however, to Stanislavsky's inclusion of croaking frogs to underscore Treplev's play-within-the-play and insisted instead upon "complete, mysterious silence." Stanislavsky argued that frogs provided that silence. Without them, Stanislavsky said, one would too easily focus on the ambient sounds of the audience coughing, turning pages, and settling in their seats; such irrelevant sounds disrupt the illusion of silence.[44] Stanislavsky's response reminds us that he was a canny director, interested in inspiring not only the actors, but also the audience with the appropriate mood.

Nina's sharp movement in the passage quoted above not only ends the silent moment prompted by Shamrayev, but also shows how Stanislavsky used physical action as part of his rhythmic approach to the play. Nina's abruptness of motion is set against the stillness of the others, just as Shamrayev's abrupt laughter had earlier served as counterpoint to silence.

In addition to these discrete musical and rhythmic techniques, one can see as well Stanislavsky's precise control as director when he notes the duration of the pauses. In other scenes, he also times different kinds of physical events. Thus, Treplev kisses Nina for a bashful five seconds

---

[42] See Carnicke, *Stanislavsky in Focus*, Chapter 9.

[43] Cited by Rudnitskii in Stanislavskii, *Rezhisserskie ekzempliary* [Directorial Plans], 18, from the archival records. The italics are Nemirovich-Danchenko's.

[44] Cited in O. A. Radishcheva, *Stanislavskii i Nemirovich-Danchenko: Istoriia teatral'nykh otnoshenii: 1897-1908* [Stanislavsky and Nemirovich-Danchenko: A History of a Theatrical Relationship] (Moscow: Artist, Rezhisser, Teatr, 1997), 79-80.

in Act I, but Trigorin kisses her more aggressively for ten seconds in Act
III. The precision of rhythms in the score suggests that Stanislavsky sees
himself as an orchestral conductor and the actors as the orchestra's individual instruments. Perhaps Stanislavsky took his cue from Chekhov,
whose stage direction in Act IV requires Treplev to spend two minutes
destroying his manuscript before exiting to his suicide.

While in clear sympathy with Chekhov's writing, Stanislavsky's con-
ducting of time on stage unfortunately resulted in a performance which
lagged, a complaint echoed by both journalists and author. Knipper
remembers Chekhov taking out his pocket watch during a rehearsal of
Act IV, coming onto the stage and pleading with the actors, "I beg you to
end the play with the third act; I won't allow you to play the fourth."[45]

At the very end of Act I, another instance of Stanislavsky's concern
with the musicality of Chekhov's play is also worth examining.

> *Masha*: I'm suffering. No one, no one knows how I'm suffering!
> (*Places her head on [Dr. Dorn's] chest, softly.*) I love Konstantin.
>
> *Dorn*: How skittish you all are! How skittish! And how much love
> you have... Oh, it must be that enchanted lake! (*Tenderly.*)
>
> No. 113. Dorn sits down on the bench.
>
> [*Dorn:*] But what can I do, my child? What? What?
>
> No. 114. Masha lowers herself to her knees and hides her head on
> Dorn's knee. A pause of 15 seconds. Dorn strokes Masha's head.
> A tempestuous waltz is heard getting louder and louder, a bell
> sounds, singing of the peasants, frogs, corncrakes, the beating
> of a watchman's stick, and other sounds of the night. Curtain.
> (trans. Carnicke, 71; Stanislavskii, 85)

As the Serbian scholar Jovan Hristić has rightly pointed out, the passionate waltz (presumably played by Arkadina who has already returned
to the house), "reveals two worlds which are regarding each other like
two opposing mirrors, two worlds which simultaneously exist yet take
no account of each other, one nonetheless making its own terrible commentary on the other."[46] In other words, in this moment of the pro-

45 Cited in Chekhov, *Polnoe sobranie sochinenii* [The Complete Works], Vol. 13,
    385-6.
46 Hristić, "'Thinking with Chekhov,'" 182.

duction Stanislavsky expands Chekhov's text in exactly the same way that the author uses unrelated details to comment upon actions within a scene ("Apparent non sequiturs in conversations and behavior" in Chapter 3). Furthermore, when one realizes that Masha will later waltz to Treplev's offstage melancholy piano in Act IV, one fully understands how apt a choice Stanislavsky has made for the play. He has read, understood, and then actively collaborated with Chekhov's text on the author's own terms by providing one more apparently trivial, but actually crucial detail.

In sum, this first musical principle in Stanislavsky's directing—signaled at the outset by his use of the word "score" and realized in numerous ways throughout the plan—is in clear harmony with Chekhov's own musical structuring of his plays.

Second, in direct contrast to Karpov's 1896 belief that *The Seagull* tells one central story, Stanislavsky and Nemirovich-Danchenko reconceived Chekhov's play as one that brings out "the hidden dramas and tragedies in *every* character in the play."[47] Hence, the second principle in Stanislavsky's directing is the creation of an ensemble of actors, all equally important to the creation of the performance. As he so often said: there are no small parts, only small actors. From this conceptual point of view, Stanislavsky paid equal attention to all the roles in the play, not just those one might consider central; and he uncovers in all of them what is hidden in the characters' thoughts and desires.[48] In the careful detailing of the characters' physical actions Stanislavsky suggests the content of their inner lives, much as Chekhov himself uses details of behavior as symptoms of the psyche (Chapter 2). Furthermore, like Chekhov, Stanislavsky also emphasizes how these details emerge through interpersonal interactions (Chapter 4).

The Moscow Art Theatre's dedication to ensemble acting stands in stark contrast to the star performances upon which nineteenth-century theater depended. While Karpov had relied primarily upon his star actress Levkeyeva to anchor his 1896 production of *The Seagull*, Stanislav-

---

47 Cited by Rudnitskii in Stanislavskii, *Rezhisserskie ekzempliary* [Directorial Plans], 21. The italics are Nemirovich-Danchenko's.

48 Ironically, the only role that did not receive as full a treatment is Dr. Dorn, perhaps because Stanislavsky had originally intended to play it himself. See Merlin, *Konstantin Stanislavsky*, 93-4.

sky's cast shared a common vision of the play, communicated to them through his score. This shared vision allowed them to work in concert with each other, thus becoming a true ensemble. No wonder Rudnitsky describes Stanislavsky's production plan for *The Seagull* as "a great experiment in polyphonic organization of the whole structure of dramatic action"![49] Naturally, individual actors had varying levels of success in performance. At one end of the scale, Maria Petrovna Lilina as Masha and Olga Leonardovna Knipper as Arkadina received the highest praise, even though Knipper was deemed far too young for her role. Stanislavsky was generally applauded but criticized for having played Trigorin as too weak-willed. At the other end of the scale, Maria Lyudomirovna Roksanova as Nina was universally panned, so much so that after nine performances Chekhov requested that she be removed from the role.[50] Yet, the 1898 production as a whole succeeded, despite the uneven performances, precisely because of the strength of its ensemble.

The level of ensemble acting achieved in *The Seagull* was entirely new and became a hallmark of the Moscow Art Theatre throughout the world. By the time Stanislavsky staged *The Cherry Orchard*, he had become particularly adept at creating what one Russian critic called "a rhythmic sense of life."[51] He did so by insuring that individual scenes knitted together so seamlessly that the play's action seemed continuous, in contrast to star performances with moments of virtuosity, which elicited applause that interrupted the continuous flow of action during performance.[52] In Stanislavsky's directing one could not always say where one scene ended and the next began. This effect directly resulted from the actors' close collaboration with each other. Vera Pashennaya (an actress at the Maly Theatre, engaged to play Varya during the 1923 American tour) wrote that the Moscow Art Theatre actors differed from those in her home theater because they play a "symphony," in which each instrument gets lost in the whole.[53] During the tour, a reviewer

---

[49] Rudnitskii in Stanislavskii, *Rezhisserskie ekzempliary* [Directorial Plans], 21.

[50] Ibid., 40.

[51] N. D. Volkov, "K. S. Stanislavskii," in *Ezhegodnik Moskovskogo Khudozhestvennogo Teatra: 1943* [The Moscow Art Theatre Yearbook: 1943] (Moscow: Muzei MKhAT, 1945), 38.

[52] Such interruptive applause still occurs regularly in opera performances.

[53] Vera Pashennaia, *Iskusstvo aktricy* [The Art of an Actress] (Moscow: Iskusstvo, 1954), 104-5.

of *Three Sisters* noticed how even the most well-known of the actors, like Stanislavsky and Knipper, blended into the whole without drawing attention to themselves as stars:

> A peculiar thing about the Russian actors is that the most impor-
> tant of them can come into a room or leave it without theatrical
> emphasis. You suddenly discover that they are present or that
> they are absent.[54]

This professional humility, which is as rare in the twenty-first century as it was in Chekhov's day, again testifies to the Moscow Art Theatre's central intention to stage plays rather than showcase actors' or directors' performances.

One example from Act IV will suffice to show both the care with which Stanislavsky detailed actors' performances and how he treats silent interactions between characters. Masha—now married to the local schoolteacher—and her mother are in Treplev's study making up a bed for Sorin, who is gravely ill. Because Masha still pines for Treplev, Polina Andreyevna has just asked him "to be a little nicer" to her daughter; he exits without answering. Soon, he begins to play "a melancholy waltz two rooms away":

> No. 19. Pause: 10 seconds—they make the bed. The sounds of
> the piano are heard—very distantly. Both women slowly break
> off their work, freeze in their poses and stand still for another 10
> seconds—only then does Polina Andreyevna speak.
>
> *Polina Andreyevna*: Kostya is playing. He's sick at heart.
>
> *Masha*: (*Without making any noise, she dances a few steps of the
> waltz.*)
>
> No. 20. Masha sighs, takes some snuff. She closes the lid on the
> tobacco box with bitterness.
>
> [*Masha*:] The most important thing, mama, is for me not to see
> him. As soon as they give [my husband] the transfer, believe me,
> after one month I'll forget everything. It's all nonsense.
>
> No. 21. She sighs again, waltzes over to the window, stops there,
> looks out into the darkness and, so that her mother will not notice,

---

54 Percy Hammond, review of *Three Sisters*, in Emeljanow, ed., *Chekhov*, 238.

takes out a handkerchief to wipe away two or three tears. Pause (the music continues). Polina Andreyevna has stopped making the bed, and looks at her daughter thoughtfully. (Evidently, she is thinking of her own affair with Dorn.) (trans. Carnicke, 98; Stanislavskii, 139)

In this moment, the physical symptom of Masha's love is her waltzing alone to Treplev's music. Her bitter, unhappy frustration with her lot in life is also manifest in her snorting snuff and then emotionally snapping shut the lid of the snuffbox. Her physical actions do not merely create an illusion of realism, but reveal her hidden drama. Stanislavsky has already prepared the ground for her subtext by underscoring her previous crying with the strains of Arkadina's playing of a passionate waltz. When Masha now hides her tears from her mother, we better understand how her decisive line about coming to grips with Treplev's unrequited love is a lie both to herself and to her mother. Simultaneously, Stanislavsky makes clear Polina Andreyevna's subtext. She wants at least as much love for her daughter as she has had from Dorn.

In this scene, Stanislavsky creates the subtlest of interactions between the two women in the moments of silence between them by asking the actors to pay close attention to each other. Masha looks out the window in order to turn her back on her mother and hide her tears; her mother stands still to look at her daughter's back because she knows all too well what Masha feels. They neither look at each other, nor speak, and yet their awareness of each other is palpable. One Russian spectator recalled this moment in the production as astonishing theater:

If you had seen it, you would never forget it: those speechless waltz turns which Masha makes almost like an automaton with deep sadness, a terrible, almost terrifying, feeling in her soul. [...] At no other time in the play was her crippled life so painfully clear as in those speechless seconds.[55]

Finally, Stanislavsky's grasp of Chekhov's innovative use of style and genre is best revealed in the director's handling of the Act III scene in which Trigorin begs Arkadina to allow him to pursue an affair with

---

[55] N. E. Efros, cited by Rudnitskii in Stanislavskii, *Rezhisserskie ekzempliary* [Directorial Plans], 36.

the young and hopeful actress, Nina. Chekhov actively draws upon the conventions of melodrama to allow Arkadina's professional talents as a gestural actor to emerge; she uses every trick of her trade to hold on to his love (Chapter 5). So too does Stanislavsky in his score describe Arkadina as behaving as if she were performing "a real tragedy, better yet a melodrama" (Stanislavskii, 125).

But how can a director ensure that spectators will see Arkadina as consciously acting in this scene when all that they see in the entire play is an actress embodying the character through acting? Stanislavsky's dilemma is further complicated by the fact that his audience takes gestural acting as the standard for all roles, and thus expects to see the same melodramatic techniques used throughout the evening.

To make Arkadina's acting visible as such, Stanislavsky has to make sure that the audience can see a distinct difference in how she behaves in other scenes throughout the play. The use of Antoine's realism certainly helps him break away from contemporary histrionic acting within the production as a whole, but Stanislavsky further guarantees that the audience see the actress at work in Act III by setting the starkly melodramatic scene between her and Trigorin against an extreme version of realism in the tumultuous argument between her and her son which immediately precedes her performance for Trigorin. This earlier scene begins with Arkadina mothering Treplev, who has recently attempted suicide; but her mothering soon devolves into a heated exchange of insults. Stanislavsky makes his intent to create a clash of acting styles impossible to miss. Just as he notes that Arkadina plays melodrama with Trigorin, he gives the opposite direction to her and Treplev: "N.B. In order to give the play more life, and make it more understandable to the public, I very much recommend that you not be afraid of the keenest realism in this scene" (Stanislavskii, 121).[56] Moreover, Stanislavsky achieves this clash of styles by his different use of physical objects within the two contiguous scenes.

In the score, realism in acting depends upon the use of everyday objects. More than any other scene within the production, the interaction between Treplev and Arkadina is embedded in an environment of things, which requires of the actors specific physical actions that take time and

---

[56] N. B. stands for the Latin "Nota Bene" for "note well." The underlining is Stanislavsky's.

concentration to execute properly. Chief among these is Arkadina's bandaging of Treplev's wounded head. Stanislavsky embroiders Chekhov's more general stage direction with highly detailed instructions that effectively foreground the physical activity over the psychological action. As Treplev recalls the ballerinas who lived nearby when he was a child, Arkadina methodically tends to his wound:

> No. 67. There is business in this whole scene, in specific: Arkadina fills two glasses with water, pours the water into a saucer, then adds the medicine, measuring it into a table spoon and pouring it from the spoon into the saucer—she mixes the water and the medicine in the saucer. She takes a rag, tears it, folds it for the bandage, dampens it with the prepared liquid. (Stanislavskii, 119)

The careful bandaging continues in the same detailed way as the argument between them begins in earnest. As they trade insults: "No. 72. Treplev throws the bandage to the side" (Stanislavskii, 121). Thus, he effectively rejects his mother by rejecting the object with which she mothers him and rendering useless all the work that she has just done to prepare the bandage. This rejection sends their argument spiraling out of control.

Arkadina betrays her impatience and anger by her use of other things within the room. She drums on the table, walks around the table, and drinks water. As the argument subsides, Stanislavsky writes:

> No. 79. After a pause Arkadina goes over to the table and drinks some water—her hands are trembling. She wipes her face with a napkin, paces back and forth in the room (upstage of the table), again swallows some water, and calming herself, approaches Treplev and strokes his head. (Stanislavskii, 123)

In contrast to this world of things, Stanislavsky allows the actors no objects other than a chair in the next scene between Arkadina and Trigorin. Now he foregrounds gestures and postures that derive from nineteenth-century traditions of acting. (Illustration 12) This shift in acting style occurs as soon as Arkadina realizes that Trigorin's new infatuation threatens their long-time relationship.

12. Arkadina (Olga Knipper) uses a conventional melodramatic gesture of despair to plead with her lover, Trigorin (Konstantin Stanislavsky) in *The Seagull*, 1898.

No. 93. Arkadina turns toward him, looking him straight in the eye. She understands everything. A Pause. She shakes her head no. Trigorin loses his nerve, no longer bold when he says in a begging tone of voice "Let's stay," and, having lost his nerve, he sits on the chair.

Arkadina: My darling, I know what's keeping you here. But take control of yourself. You're a little intoxicated. You need to sober up. (trans. Carnicke, 92; Stanislavskii, 123)

As the language in the scene builds in melodramatic intensity, Arkadina's gestures, and even Trigorin's, become progressively more histrionic. She trembles, sobs, lowers herself before her lover, grasps him tightly; he holds his head in his hands, rushes toward her, and then refuses to look at her. I invite you to observe the equal escalation of rhetorical language and emotional gesture in the extended section I quote below, which occurs just after Trigorin has asked Arkadina to "sacrifice" herself by breaking off their affair so that he can go to Nina.

No. 103. Arkadina sits on an ottoman and cries.

Trigorin: (*Holding his head in his hands.*)

No. 104. Trigorin grabs his head with both hands in despair.

[*Trigorin*:] She doesn't understand! She doesn't want to understand!

No. 105. Arkadina continues crying, sobbing. Trigorin rushes to her in order to prevail upon her, but he doesn't make it in time because Arkadina has thrown herself at him, embraces him, kisses his hands, gets down on her knees, playing a real tragedy, better yet a melodrama.

Arkadina: Am I really so old and ugly, that you can talk to me about other women without feeling embarrassed? (*Hugs him and cries.*) Oh you've lost your senses! My excellent, marvelous... You are the last page of my life! (*Kneels.*) My happiness, my pride, my bliss... (*Hugs his knees.*) If you throw me over, even for one hour, I will not survive, I will go mad. My remarkable, exceptional man, my lord and master...

No. 106. Trying to free himself from her, but Arkadina clutches him even more strongly.

Trigorin: Someone may come in. (*Helps her up.*)

No. 107. She now speaks in the kind of tone and with the kind of pathos that one finds in melodrama.

Arkadina: <u>Let them. I'm not ashamed of my love for you.</u>[57] (*Kisses his hand.*) My treasure, you may be in despair, you may want this madness, but I don't want it for you, I won't let you... (*Laughs.*)

No. 108. Trigorin falls weakly into the chair, Arkadina all the more energetically holds him—Trigorin sits like a mummy no longer trying to defend himself.

[*Arkadina*:] You are mine... You are mine... This is my forehead, my eyes, and this beautiful silky hair is mine... You are all mine. You are talented, smart, better than any other living writer, Russia's best hope... You have sincerity, simplicity, freshness, good humor... In a single line you convey what's most important about a person or a landscape, you create living characters. It's impossible to read you without going into ecstasies! You think I'm exaggerating? That I'm flattering you?

No. 109. Arkadina throws herself on her knees before him and turns his face toward hers so that he will look at her.

[*Arkadina*:] Well, look me in the eyes... Come on, look... Do I look like a flatterer? You see, I'm the only one who really knows your worth. I'm telling you the truth, darling, sweetheart...

No. 110. She searches Trigorin's eyes. Arkadina stands up, her back completely to the audience. Trigorin sits on the chair, his face toward the audience.

[*Arkadina*:] Will you come with me? Yes? Will you throw me over?...

Trigorin: I have no will of my own... I have never had a will of my own... I'm flaccid, soft, submissive—do women really find this attractive? Take me with you, carry me away, but don't ever let me out of your sight...

No. 111. Arkadina throws herself on his neck, a prolonged kiss, then stands. (trans. Carnicke, 92-3; Stanislavskii, 125-7)

When Arkadina stands up with her back to the auditorium, her posture makes it clear that she performs only for Trigorin. Stanislavsky's blocking thus draws equal attention to the fact that Arkadina is acting in the

---

[57] The underlining is Stanislavsky's.

style which has made her famous, but also that she does so in her real life to get what she wants from her lover. At this moment in Stanislavsky's score, gestural acting collides with Antoine's realism, just as melodrama meets vaudeville in Chekhov. Through this meaningful blocking, Stanislavsky not only interprets Chekhov accurately, but collaborates with him as well by clarifying what is already inherent in the play through the *mise-en-scène*.

Once victorious, Arkadina drops her gestural acting and returns to the kind of behavior with objects that betokens real life within Stanislavsky's production plan.

> *Trigorin*: No, let's go together.
>
> No. 115. As if nothing has happened, Arkadina turns and goes around the table to her purse, takes a bottle of smelling salts and smells it, then some perfume and puts it on. A pause of 10, 15 seconds. Trigorin sits in a sour mood, looking off to the side, then lazily takes out his notebook and writes (there is nothing else for him to do!!).
>
> *Arkadina*: As you like. Together then, together... (trans. Carnicke, 93; Stanislavskii, 127)

By having established a baseline for the ordinary behavior of real life through the actors' use of objects, Stanislavsky makes visible by contrast the gestural acting at which Arkadina excels. By dropping that excellence so abruptly and returning to the baseline, Stanislavsky also makes visible how easily Arkadina can turn her acting on and off. Her ability to stop acting when she gets what she wants exposes her as more than a talented actress; she is also a talented manipulator.

Chekhov's craft shines through in Stanislavsky's direction. Chekhov's friend, Tatiana Lvovna Shchepkina-Kupernik, saw the 1898 production and reports that Knipper conveyed "[Arkadina's] humiliation, her flattery, the selflessness with which she drops to her knees before [Trigorin.] When he agrees to leave—[she heaves] a deep, heavy sigh as if she only just escaped a terrible danger." There follows "a short pause [in which] she trembles all over, *probably like Arkadina trembles on stage* in the climactic moment of a dramatic role, and suddenly *changes her mask*." Knipper now speaks "with a calm voice, full of self-possession, knowing that she has triumphed."[58] Clearly the theatrical effect that Stanislavsky saw in Chekhov's text was realized by Knipper on the stage of the Moscow Art Theatre that night.

THE SCORE OF *THE SEAGULL* AS REALISED ON STAGE, 1898

In contrast with the handful of rehearsals held at other theaters of the day, the Moscow Art Theatre held twenty-four rehearsals for *The Seagull*, fifteen of which were conducted by Nemirovich-Danchenko and nine by Stanislavsky. These were followed by yet another three dress rehearsals. Also in contrast to the standard practice of pulling sets from stock and requiring actors to provide their own costumes, the Moscow Art Theatre had hired Viktor Andreyevich Simov (1858-1935) to design a coherent visual look for the production. Simov had met and befriended Chekhov's elder brother, Nikolay, while both were studying art. While the preparatory work for *The Seagull* had far exceeded the norm, the directors and cast still felt unprepared at the opening on 17 December 1898. Making them even more nervous was the fact that the financial fate of the young theater hung in the balance and the auditorium was only half full. At the end of the first act, they feared that they had failed because the curtain closed with "dead silence in the auditorium." As Stanislavsky stood backstage, he noticed that "one actress had fainted; and I too could barely stand on my feet from despair. Then suddenly, after a long pause, there was a roar, a big noise, furious applause from the public."[59] Rather than fail, *The Seagull* had made theater history for both the young company and the author.

But the production on stage was not exactly as Stanislavsky had envisioned the play. Nemirovich-Danchenko praised the score as "a striking

---

[58] T. L. Shchepkina-Kupernik, cited by Rudnitskii in Stanislavskii, *Rezhisserskie ekzempliary* [Directorial Plans], 33. The italics are hers.

[59] Stanislavskii, *Sobranie sochinenii* [Collected Works], Vol. 1, 296. See Chapter 1 for Nemirovich-Danchenko's description of this same moment. The full cast for this premiere was: Arkadina—O. L. Knipper; Treplev—Vs. E. Meyerhold; Sorin—V. V. Luzhsky; Nina—M. L. Roksanova; Masha—M. P. Lilina; Shamrayev—A. P. Artyom; Polina Andreyevna—E. M. Rayevskaya; Trigorin—K. S. Stanislavsky; Medvedenko—I. A. Tikhomirov.

example of Stanislavsky's creative intuition"[60] and made few changes to it. Yet, those he did recommend and those made by Simov as designer resulted in a production that had taken much of the edge off Stanislavsky's bold vision for Chekhov's play. In some places, Nemirovich-Danchenko and Simov softened or amended Stanislavsky's plan. In others, they overturned him completely. Some of these changes reflected the entire team's desire to avoid the kind of scandal that had occurred at the 1896 premiere of the play. Other changes were made for pragmatic reasons; the company's inexperienced actors and contemporary stage technology could not always fulfill Stanislavsky's directions.

The clearest road into understanding how changes in Stanislavsky's score for *The Seagull* affected the Moscow Art Theatre's production is through an examination of its visual design. Unlike dialogue, which most actors memorize exactly, stage directions are often treated cavalierly when a play is produced. The author's descriptions of sets are the easiest part of the blueprint to ignore. Some authors are unaware of production realities and thus write novelistic stage directions that are impossible to realize. But even when the playwright is also a savvy theatrical professional or, like Chekhov, an author who provides straightforward descriptions, directors and designers still give themselves wide latitude in visualizing the stage on which their productions will take place. Recall, for example, the three productions of *The Cherry Orchard* directed by Stanislavsky, Serban, and Trushkin (discussed above). One created realistic environments, one a theatricalized and largely empty space, and one replaced all Chekhov's descriptions with a huge cupboard with doors. The sets for these productions reflected Chekhov's stage directions variously, looked nothing like each other, and thus demonstrate this latitude. In my examination of *The Seagull* on stage I draw your eye specifically to the sets for Acts I and III.[61]

From the outset, the production team had agreed that their stage would break with nineteenth-century tradition. Rather than furnishing

---

[60] Cited by Rudnitskii in Stanislavskii, *Rezhisserskie ekzempliary* [Directorial Plans], 11.

[61] In my examination of the Moscow Art Theatre sets I am especially indebted to Rudnitskii in Stanislavskii, *Rezhisserskie ekzempliary* [Directorial Plans], 17-33; and Viktor Berezkin, *Khudozhnik v teatre Chekhova* [The Designer in Chekhov's Theatre] (Moscow: Izobrazitel'noe iskusstvo, 1987), 12-30, for their analyses of Simov's design.

a main playing area as was usual, smaller areas over the whole stage could be used by groups of actors simultaneously. All three believed that this layout would best support Chekhov's talent for creating the illusion of continuous life. This spatial decision is especially obvious in the outdoor set, devised for Act I and also used for Act II: there are multiple pathways, several open areas, and various structures that cover the entire stage space.

Chekhov describes the set for Act I in this way:

> A section of the park on Sorin's estate. A wide pathway leading from the auditorium into the depths of the park toward a lake, which is completely obstructed from view by a stage. The stage has been put together hastily in preparation for an amateur play. To the left and right of the stage are bushes. There are several chairs and a table. (trans. Carnicke, 54)

Chekhov places Act II elsewhere on the estate, behind the "house with a large terrace" and "to the left [of] the lake," where there is "a croquet lawn" and "flowerbeds" (trans. Carnicke, 71). In the score, Stanislavsky drew diagrams for both sets, but the Moscow Art Theatre used Sorin's park for the first two acts, no doubt to save money for their financially strapped theater.

Stanislavsky diagrams the park somewhat differently than Chekhov describes it. One wide pathway has become a number of walks that snake through the shrubs and trees. Stanislavsky divides the space into three planes for action. Near the front of the stage are swings and park benches to provide seating for the characters when they watch Treplev's play-within-the-play. He notes that this area should be dimly lit by a lantern, while the stage on which Nina performs is more brightly lit by the moon. This lighting effect would turn the onstage audience into barely visible silhouettes against which Nina's performance would shine. He also intended this variegated lighting to create the beauty and atmosphere of the park at night, reflecting Chekhov's love of nature. In the middle and to the left of the stage a corner of Sorin's house becomes a visible reminder of the life that unfolds on this estate. Alongside the house, covering the middle plane of the stage is a rather neglected expanse of park. Far upstage is a painted backdrop that depicts the landscape of the lake, in front of which stands Treplev's stage, a crude affair made from a platform with a frame for the curtain. Stanislavsky's diagram shows the platform dead center, but not large enough for its curtain to obstruct a view of the lake, as Chekhov tantalizingly suggests that it does ("Stage Settings and the Emotional Progression of a Play," Chapter 3).

To Stanislavsky's plan Nemirovich-Danchenko added a gazebo (nowhere mentioned by Chekhov). He placed it to the left of the stage in order to better accommodate the scenes from Act II that will be played in this same park. Moreover, conversations between the play's lovers could be framed more romantically in the gazebo. He removed Stanislavsky's swings and added a long bench, so that more actors could sit during Nina's performance. This decision meant that actors could no longer use the relaxed and repetitive motion of swinging to create the lazy atmosphere of the park. Nemirovich-Danchenko also wanted to add a view of Nina's house in the distance across the lake and a set-within-the-set for Treplev's stage—a large rock from which Nina would rise like a statue to perform. (Illustration 13)

Unfortunately, the new company was renting the Ermitazh Theatre for their first season and the physical stage was too small to include the

13. The 1898 set for Acts I and II of *The Seagull*. At the left stands the gazebo; at the center is the set-within-the set on which Nina performs Treplev's play-within-the play in Act I; and downstage is the long bench on which Treplev's family and friends sit to watch the performance. This photograph from 1905 depicts the moment in Act II when Trigorin (Konstantin Stanislavsky) notices the dead seagull which Treplev has shot and presented to Nina (Maria Lilina).

whole of Stanislavsky's vision and Nemirovich-Danchenko's additions. Simov therefore transformed Stanislavsky's three planes for action into two. This immediately made the lighting that Stanislavsky had envisioned impossible; the onstage spectators were simply too close to Nina's performance for the two stage areas to be lit differently. Since all actors were equally visible, those sitting downstage with their backs to the public drew as much audience attention as Nina's upstage performance.

Additionally, Simov had to make compromises on the number of structures that could fit into the dimensions of the stage. To include Nemirovich-Danchenko's gazebo, Simov moved Sorin's house first to the far left, and then offstage with only a glow from the windows suggesting its presence. Simov finally cut Sorin's house from the design entirely. The distant view of Nina's home on the backdrop was also cut. The painted landscape was already not fully successful in creating a realistic illusion of the lake and sky. Painting more details on the canvas backdrop would only draw further attention to an already weak aspect of the production. Simov included Nemirovich-Danchenko's rock as the set for Treplev's stage, but he removed the wooden proscenium frame on which Stanislavsky had planned to hang a curtain. Simov tried suspending a curtain from two trees, but in the end he simply eliminated it, leaving the lake in full view.

The design succeeded in creating multiple playing spaces but clearly lacked the obstructed view of the lake that Chekhov describes and the atmosphere that Stanislavsky had envisioned. Photographs show the gazebo and the rock on Treplev's stage as the most visible landmarks; and these focal points seem to contradict Treplev's line, which stresses simplicity: "There's a theater for you! A curtain, the first set of wings, the second, and then an empty space. No set." Once the curtain opens, there is "a direct view of the lake and the horizon" (trans. Carnicke, 56).

Simov agreed that the finalized set was not fully satisfactory. In his unpublished memoir, housed at the Moscow Art Theatre, he writes: "I will say frankly that the garden on stage turned out perfectly well in and of itself, but it did not suit the basic tone of the play."[62] His assessment goes to the heart of this chapter—Chekhov's plays in production do not so much express his works as present a collaborative hybridization of them to the public.

---

[62] Simov, cited by Rudnitskii in Stanislavskii, *Rezhisserskie ekzempliary* [Directorial Plans], 18.

Changes made to Stanislavsky's plan for the room in which Act III takes place even more vividly illustrate how the material production of a play can affect its emotional tenor. The production team's initial decision to create multiple playing areas for Acts I and II supported the company's experimentation with European realism, but Stanislavsky's score for Act III takes Antoine's work with the invisible fourth wall in a new direction. Stanislavsky uses the visual aspects of the production as part of his musical structuring of the play by envisioning the sets as "accompaniment to the action."[63] Unlike Antoine, who sought to expose how environments condition social behavior, Stanislavsky wanted onstage environments to reveal the personalities of those who live in them, much as their physical behaviors suggest their inner emotional lives. Nowhere is Stanislavsky's intention clearer than in the third act set he describes in his plan for *The Seagull*.

Chekhov's Act III takes place in Sorin's dining room where a series of high-stakes one-on-one encounters and arguments occur, all of which end anticlimactically. The two scenes discussed in detail above participate in this innovative dramatic structure. Treplev and Arkadina hurl cutting insults at one another; and such an argument in a traditional play would forever change the relationship between them. In *The Seagull*, however, the argument begins, escalates, and ends like a passing thunderstorm, having little to no impact upon Treplev's relationship with his mother. In the next scene the melodramatic moment between Arkadina and Trigorin reverts even more quickly and easily back to the usual pattern of interaction between the couple.

Stanislavsky embodies these anticlimaxes by having the characters eat their lunches in the dining room between the emotional disruptions that take place there. This mundane activity serves as counterpoint to the stormy arguments that erupt within the Act. For example, just before Arkadina's argument with Sorin and her vehement refusal to give an allowance to her son, Stanislavsky provides the following notes:

> No. 31. Arkadina eats, drinks wine. Sorin has his hat on the back of his head [because he is] ready to go out [to town]; he sits down, drinks a little wine, picks his teeth or smokes and waves the smoke away from Arkadina.

---

[63] Stanislavsky, cited in ibid., 15.

Arkadina: (*After a pause.*)

No. 32. During the pause Arkadina makes thumping sounds with the dishes. Sorin sighs sadly.

[*Arkadina:*] Well, live if you must, but do it here, and don't get bored, and don't catch cold. Look after my son. Watch out for him. Straighten him out. (*Pause.*)

No. 33. The same business.

[*Arkadina:*] I'm going away, and so I won't be able to find out why Konstantin tried to shoot himself. I think that the main reason is jealousy, and the sooner I take Trigorin away from here, the better.

No. 34. The same business: Sorin picks his teeth, cleans a match with his finger nail, and Arkadina eats. (trans. Carnicke, 87; Stanislavskii, 113)

Stanislavsky draws attention to Chekhov's ironic use of anticlimax by the addition of other mundane behaviors—smoking, picking one's teeth, playing with a match, etc.—which are then juxtaposed to the high emotions during the arguments. Because this reflection of Chekhov's structure relies largely upon acting, and because Knipper as Arkadina followed Stanislavsky's directions so precisely in her performance, this aspect of his plan was realized well on stage.

Stanislavsky's diagram for the room, however, was completely overturned in production. Chekhov describes the set for Act III in the following words: "The dining room in Sorin's house. Doors to the right and left. A sideboard. A cabinet with medicines in it. A table in the middle of the room. A suitcase and boxes; obviously a departure is planned" (trans. Carnicke, 84). While nothing in Stanislavsky's score violates this blueprint, he exaggerates its elements in a radically new way that anticipates expressionism, a school of art that uses physical environments to express the inner emotional states of characters. In his score, Stanislavsky sets the dining room at an extreme angle to the audience, so that the spectators who eavesdrop on the fights and tantrums will see the action from a skewed position. In doing so he mirrors the characters' frustrations and emotional upsets in the off-centered room that frames them. This angle of vision is intended to create a tense, uneasy atmosphere for the duration of the act. Such expressionistic use of a set provides an excellent example of what Stanislavsky means when he metaphorically says that he wishes his sets to serve as "accompaniment to the action."[64]

In addition, Stanislavsky brings more luggage into the room than Chekhov calls for in his stage directions. Trunks and bags are everywhere, making clear Arkadina's and Trigorin's imminent departure. The sheer amount of baggage gives the impression of a household that has been in turmoil over the extensive preparations for the trip. When Trigorin begs Arkadina to stay at the estate, the heaps of luggage would seem to suggest that he has little hope of changing her mind.

Stanislavsky's expressionist plan for Act III was turned into a comfortably realistic set for the production. Simov placed the room square to the audience with the dining table parallel with the edge of the stage. He included only a few small pieces of luggage as directed by Chekhov. The effect was one of calm familiarity. As one viewer told Chekhov, "The dining room in Act III of *The Seagull* is set so well that when the curtain goes up, you immediately feel as if you are sitting in it."[65] In fact, this sensation was Simov's intention—to make the rooms in both Acts III and IV seem inviting. In full accord with Antoine's invisible fourth wall, Simov's design for the dining room showed primarily the economic and social class of its occupants. His resulting set was in stark contrast to Stanislavsky's vision. Moreover, photographs of Simov's set seem utterly standard to contemporary eyes, as against Stanislavsky's diagram for Act III, which retains its innovative edge.

The visual history of the 1898 production of *The Seagull* can serve as a simple reminder that the pragmatics of stage production and the collaborative nature of theater work are always factors that can significantly affect what seems inherent in a play. Additionally, the specific changes made to Stanislavsky's plan for Act III reveal how the material reality of production communicates to audiences as loudly as the words written by the author for the actors to speak. Reading Chekhov's play in tandem with Stanislavsky's score, I find myself wanting to see the imaginative production that he had seen in his head.

---

64 Ibid.
65 Aleksandr Ivanovich Kuprin, cited in ibid., 30.

Conclusion

A Matter of Perspective

The journey into Chekhov's plays begins with his stories for many reasons. Studying his narrative techniques lays a firm foundation for understanding his dramatic artistry as one that crafts meaning and elicits emotion through the rich and complex patterning of small, apparently trivial details (Chapters 2 and 3). From this patterning he creates the illusion of unspoken thoughts that prompt dialogue (subtext); he pays close attention to the small physical signs that suggest what goes on inside the hearts and minds of his characters (inner action); and he arouses ambivalent responses of laughter-through-tears by revealing discrepancies in human behavior. These central techniques drive all Chekhov's works, but in his plays they especially challenge the entrenched dramatic conventions of exposition (about story, character, and emotion), overt onstage action, and the established modes of comedy and tragedy (Chapters 4 and 5).

Chekhov's stories provoke productive questions about his artistic style and its problematic relationship to Russia's standards of nineteenth-century realism (Chapter 2). When these questions are placed alongside his admiration for early twentieth-century symbolist drama (Chapter 3), his unique approach to dramatic style also comes into sharp focus. Mundane and poetic details combine seamlessly with musical and symbolic effects to form the fabric of a Chekhovian work, inviting playwrights, stage directors, actors, and designers alike to rethink their own stylistic assumptions.

Next, experiencing something of the French comic vaudeville (which Chekhov loved) and the moralistic melodrama (which he loathed) further exposes his new vision of drama. His borrowings, adaptations, and rejections of conventions from these nineteenth-century forms of popular theater are the experiments that allowed him to develop his voice as a dramatist. In rethinking the traditions of French comic vaudeville he restructured stage action as the silly, subtle, and even heartrending dynamics of human interaction (Chapter 4). By using melodramatic techniques to undermine melodrama, he banishes overt action and spectacle from the stage, while simultaneously bringing comedy and tragedy so close together that there can be no separating them (Chapter 5). His resulting approach to action and genre shakes up theatrical assumptions as surely as does his blending together of various artistic styles.

Finally, by taking a look at how his plays move into the material reality of theatrical production, one realizes how his innovations have influenced more than the conventions of playwriting. At the outset, his unusual plays proved to be the necessary vehicles for the Moscow Art Theatre to overturn the star system and create, instead, a collaborative ensemble of actors, who engage deeply as artists with each other and with the plays they bring to life. Thereafter, Chekhov has continued to prompt directors to rethink the staging of plays and actors to reconsider their approaches to acting. No wonder his writings have become inspirational to theater professionals worldwide!

As the first chapter in this book suggests, the relationship between an artist's life and his work is complex, often unfathomable. Yet, I cannot help but think that Chekhov's illness played some role in his unique perspective on art. He had begun to suffer the symptoms of tuberculosis while he was in medical school. As a trained doctor, he would have understood the poor prognosis promised by his hospitalization in 1897 (just one year before the Moscow Art Theatre's production of *The Seagull*). He lived for nearly a decade, knowing that he was dying. This period coincided with the decade of his most sustained efforts in playwriting. In short, he wrote from the perspective of one who is dying.

He completed *The Cherry Orchard* during 1903, the last year of his life. He was very ill and thus the work was painfully slow, interrupted by bouts of coughing, diarrhea, an inability to eat, and depression. Whereas writing had once flowed easily from him, now he could write only a line or two a day. "There is still weakness and coughing," he told his wife Olga. Yet, "I write every day; although only a little, still I write" (2 Oct. 1903). At times, he confessed to her that he felt despair. "I am beginning to lose heart. It seems to me that I have outlived my time as a writer, and that every sentence I write seems to serve no purpose, and no need whatever" (20 Sept. 1903). Despite his condition, he forged ahead, promising her that his "last act will be merry, and indeed the whole play will be light and merry" (21 Sept. 1903). Finally in October he sent the play to the Moscow Art Theatre, telling his wife that he was pleased with the result. He worried only that, "I did not write in one sitting, but over a long, very long time, and so it will probably seem somehow drawn out." He added, "Darling, how hard it was for me to write the play!" (12 Oct. 1903).

With death so present during the years that he wrote his greatest plays, many otherwise monumental problems—be they fears of proposing, jealousies, or the loss of property—pale in importance; life's priorities become clear. It has long seemed to me that this kind of clarity lies at the heart of Chekhov's major plays. By facing the reality of death, Chekhov could write plays that are neither fully comic nor tragic, with characters who are neither heroes nor villains and who speak nonsense and philosophy with equal fluency.

The seeds of Chekhov's perspective on life and his mature approach to drama can be found in one of his earliest and briefest dramatic dialogues. *On the Moon* was written in 1883, when a fire all but destroyed

14. Two astronomers *On the Moon*, observing earth, 1885, as drawn by V. Porfiryev.

the Ukrainian city of Berdichev. Chekhov was at that time in medical school and already suffering from tuberculosis; he was also caring for his elder brother Nikolay, who would die of tuberculosis in 1889. A mere half-page of text, On the Moon was first published in 1885. It appeared with an accompanying cartoon that depicts two clowns sitting on a crescent moon as if on a swing and peering at the earth through handheld telescopes.[1] (Illustration 14) Because of its rarity, I translate the entire dialogue below:

> First Lunar Astronomer: Hey colleague, look—there, at that bright light on earth, near the city of Berdichev! It must be a huge fire... The whole city is probably in flames.
>
> Second Lunar Astronomer: Oh, please! It's just the illumination from a happy amusement of some kind going on somewhere!
>
> First Lunar Astronomer: Why do you think that?
>
> Second Lunar Astronomer: I assume that if such a terrible fire were taking place, people would be running about, making a fuss, would start collecting signatures to help the unfortunate people who have been burned, set up charitable committees, pass around a collection box on behalf of those who no longer have roofs over their heads... And there's none of that going on. Everything on earth is quiet, calm, and everyone has gone to sleep, a deep and peaceful sleep. So, obviously, everything is fine.

First, Chekhov's preferred point of view—as a distanced observer who watches life's action unfold "from a crack in the wall"[2]—is embodied by the astronomers who look at life on earth from the surface of the

---

[1] Na lune was published in the journal Oskolki [Fragments], edited by N. A. Leikin; the cartoon is by V. I. Porfir'ev; the Russian text and cartoon can be found in Chekhov, Polnoe sobranie sochinenii [The Complete Works], Vol. 3, 457. When Chekhov published On the Moon, he changed Berdichev to the southern Russian city of Grodno because a fire had more recently raged there. In my translation, I have restored the reference to Berdichev because Chekhov later used the sound of "Berdichev" to create an atmosphere of quiet intimacy in Three Sisters, when Dr. Chebutykin and Irina repeat the city's name several times ("Soundscapes and the music of everyday life" in Chapter 3).

[2] Letter from A. P. Chekhov to Al. P. Chekhov, 13 May 1883, first cited in Chapter 1.

moon. By observing from afar, Chekhov had achieved the objectivity of description for which he is well known. By placing the astronomers on the lunar surface in this early work, he draws attention to their extreme removal from the action, and hence, to their perspective, thus making the very nature of comic distance one of his subjects.

Second, the astronomers' conflicting interpretations of what they see mirror Chekhov's penchant for bringing tragic and comic events together in the same dramatic moment. In *On the Moon*, a staple of melodrama converges with vaudevillian humor (a dangerous fire and clowns) in order to expose discrepancies in human behavior with a laugh. Thus, this short piece already points toward the collision of traditional genres in Chekhov's mature plays.

Third, Chekhov's keen comic appreciation of life's discrepancies drives the whole conception of the piece. The solid logic with which the second astronomer dismisses the possibility of a fire on earth underlines the illogical fact that people often do nothing when faced with crises and social need. They sleep while fires burn or, as in *The Cherry Orchard*, dance as their land is auctioned. Thus, Chekhov uses comedy to suggest that "what is" need not remain so, once one can see clearly enough to laugh. Comedy points the way to a better life. As Dr. Chekhov once told Nikolay Leikin, the editor of this very dialogue, laughter begins the cure (20 May 1884). In short, like his later, greater plays, this little joke in one act is, to quote Eric Bentley, "a shaking into life."[3]

Finally, the only characters in *On the Moon* are clowns, as the accompanying cartoon makes absolutely clear. As Chekhov once told his brother Alexander, "I wanted to do something original [in my writing]: I didn't bring into it one villain, not one angel (although I couldn't resist the clowns)" (24 Oct. 1887). Chekhov's characters are always good and bad, heroic and villainous, silly and serious and always seeking a better life. But only those who come to see life clearly as it is, who face and discard their illusions and lies, can find what they seek (Chapter 5).

In other words, *On the Moon* provides a final snapshot of our journey through Chekhov's plays and his overarching artistic perspective on the divine comedy of life.

---

[3] Bentley, *The Life of the Drama*, 345.

ANNOTATED BIBLIOGRAPHY

CITATIONS TO CHEKHOV'S WORKS

The Letters:
All cited passages are from A. P. Chekhov, *Polnoe sobranie sochinenii i pisem v tridtsati tomakh* [The Complete Works and Letters in Thirty Volumes], Moscow: Nauka, 1974-84. Each letter is identified by the person to whom Chekhov wrote and the date with this information given in the text and/or in parentheses. All translations from Chekhov's letters are mine unless otherwise indicated.

The Plays:
All cited passages are from Anton Chekhov, *Chekhov: 4 Plays and 3 Jokes*, trans. Sharon Marie Carnicke, Cambridge: Hackett Publishing Company, Inc., 2009; page references are given in parentheses within the text. For plays not included in this collection, I cite the source in a footnote. All translations from the plays are mine unless indicated otherwise.

Russian Language Sources:
All translations from Russian are mine unless otherwise indicated in a footnote.

CHEKHOV'S STORIES, LETTERS,
AND PLAYS IN SELECTED ENGLISH EDITIONS

Benedetti, Jean, trans. and ed. *Dear Writer, Dear Actress: The Love Letters of Anton Chekhov and Olga Knipper*. Hopewell, NJ: Ecco Press, 1997.

_____. *The Moscow Art Theatre Letters*. New York: Routledge, 1991. [Includes letters by and to Chekhov, Knipper, Nemirovich-Danchenko, Stanislavsky, and other members of the Moscow Art Theatre company.]

Chekhov, Anton. *A Tragic Man Despite Himself: The Complete Short Plays*. Translated by George Malko. Los Angeles: Green Integer. 2005. [Includes some short dialogues that do not appear in other editions, including *On the Moon*.]

_____. *The Complete Plays*. Translated and edited by Laurence Senelick. New York: W. W. Norton, 2006. [Includes Chekhov's long and short plays and their multiple revisions.]

_____. *Chekhov: 4 Plays and 3 Jokes*. Translated by Sharon Marie Carnicke. Cambridge: Hackett Publishing Company, Inc., 2009. [Includes all four major plays and three one-acts in faithful, actor-friendly translations which have been widely produced.]

_____. *Chekhov: Four Plays*. Translated by Carol Rocomora. Lyme: Smith and Kraus, 1996.

_____. *Chekhov: The Major Plays*. Translated by Ann Dunnigan. New York: Signet, 1964. [American English translations, including *Ivanov*.]

_____. *Chekhov: The Major Plays*. Translated by Jean Claude Van Itallie. New York: Applause, 1995. [Adaptations made from earlier translations in English and French.]

_____. *Chekhov: Plays*. Translated by Michael Frayn. London, Methuen, 1991. [British English translations, including a handful of Chekhov's one-acts.]

_____. *Four Great Plays by Anton Chekhov*. Translated by Constance Garnett. New York: Bantam Books, 1958. [Early translations into English that use Victorian English.]

_____. *Five Major Plays*. Translated by Ronald Hingley. New York: Bantam Books, 1977. [Very accurate, but somewhat stilted British English translations.]

_____. *The Plays of Anton Chekhov*. Translated by Paul Schmidt. New York: Harper Perennial, 1999. [American English translations with contemporary slang and Americanized names.]

_____. *The Selected Letters of Anton Chekhov*. New York: Farrar, Straus, 1955.

_____. *Stories*. Translated by Richard Pevear and Larissa Volokhonsky. New York: Bantam Books, 2000. [Lively and accurate translations of Chekhov's major stories.]

_____. *Twelve Plays*. Translated by Ronald Hingley. New York: Oxford University Press, 1992. [Includes many short plays and *Platonov*.]

Constantine, Peter, trans. and ed. *The Undiscovered Chekhov: Forty Three New Stories*. New York: Seven Stories Press, 1998. [Includes a good selection of Chekhov's earliest comic stories.]

Frayn, Michael and Anton Pavlovich Chekhov. *Wild Honey*. London: Methuen, 1984. [This play is Frayn's adaptation of Chekhov's unfinished play, generally known as *Platonov*.]

Garnett, Constance, trans. and ed. *Letters of Anton Chekhov to Olga Knipper*. New York: Blom, 1968.

Karlinsky, Simon and Michael Henry Heim, trans. and eds. *Anton Chekhov's Life and Thought: Selected Letters*. Berkeley: University of California at Berkeley, 1975.

Mamet, David. *The Cherry Orchard by Anton Chekhov*. New York: Grove Press, 1985. [An adaptation made from a literal translation that reflects Mamet's style of playwriting.]

Plays by Anton Chekhov. No translator given. New York: Concord Books, 1935.

Yarmolinsky, Avrahm, ed. *Letters of Anton Chekhov*. New York: The Viking Press, 1973.

SOURCES IN RUSSIAN

Balukhatyi, S. D. *Voprosy poetiki* [Questions of Poetics]. Leningrad: Izdatel'stvo Leningradskogo Universiteta, 1990.

Berezkin, Victor. *Khudozhnik v teatre Chekhova* [The Designer in Chekhov's Theatre]. Moscow: Izobraziteľ'noe iskusstvo, 1987. [Includes illustrations of major Russian productions of Chekhov's plays in the twentieth century.]

Bunin, I. A. *O Chekhove* [About Chekhov] New York: Chekhov Publishing House, 1955.

_____. *Polnoe sobranie sochinenii* [Complete Collected Works]. Vol. 6. Petersburg: A. Marks, 1915.

Chekhov, A. P. *Polnoe sobranie sochinenii i pisem v tridtsati tomakh* [The Complete Works and Letters in Thirty Volumes], Moscow: Nauka, 1974-84. [The standard scholarly edition of Chekhov's works.]

_____. *Sobranie sochinenii* [Collected Works]. 12 vols. Moscow: Izdatel'stvo khudozhestvennoi literatury, 1954-57.

Chekhova, Mariia P. *Iz dalekogo proshlogo* [From the Distant Past]. Moscow: Gosudarstvennoe izdatel'stvo khudozhestvennoi literatury, 1960.

Ezhegodnik Moskovskogo Khudozhestvennogo Teatra: 1943 [The Moscow Art Theatre Yearbook: 1943]. Moscow: Muzei MKhAT, 1945.

Knipper-Chekhova, Ol'ga Leonardovna. *Perepiska* [Correspondence]. Vol. 1. Moscow: Iskusstvo, 1972.

Kuzicheva, A. P., ed. *A. P. Chekhov v russkoi teatral'noi kritike* [Chekhov in Russian Theatrical Criticism]. Moscow: Chekhovskii poligraficheskii kombinat, 1999. [A generous anthology of Russian criticism on Chekhov's drama.]

Melkova, A. S., ed. *L. N. Tolstoi i A. P. Chekhov: Rasskazyvaiut sovremenniki, arkhivy, muzei* [Tolstoy and Chekhov: What Their Contemporaries, Archives, Museums Say About Them]. Moscow: Nasledie, 1998.

Nemirovich-Danchenko, Vl. I. *Tvorcheskoe nasledie: Pis'ma* [Creative Legacy: Letters]. Vol. 1. Moscow: Moskovskii khudozhestvennyi teatr, 2003.

Papernyi, Z. *"Vopreki vsem pravilam...": P'esy i vodevili Chekhova* ["Contrary to the Rules...": The Plays and Vaudevilles of Chekhov]. Moscow: Iskusstvo, 1982.

Pashennaia, Vera. *Iskusstvo aktrisy* [The Art of an Actress]. Moscow: Iskusstvo, 1954.

Radishcheva, O. A. *Stanislavskii i Nemirovich-Danchenko: Istoriia teatral'nykh otnoshenii, 1897-1908* [Stanislavsky and Nemirovich-Danchenko: The History of a Theatrical Relationship]. Moscow: Artist, Rezhisser, Teatr, 1997.

Stanislavskii, K. S. *Rezhisserskie ekzempliary K. S. Stanislavskogo* [Directorial Plans]. Vol. 2. Moscow: Iskusstvo, 1981. [Includes an important introductory essay on the Moscow Art Theatre Production of *The Seagull* by Konstantin Rudnitsky.]

_____. *Sobranie sochinenii* [Collected Works]. 9 vols. Moscow: Iskusstvo, 1988-99. [Vol. 1 is Stanislavsky's autobiography, *My Life in Art*.]

_____. Unpublished typescript of an early draft of an acting manual with handwritten notes (n.d.), housed at the Bancroft Library, University of California at Berkeley.

Vinogradskaia, I., ed. *Stanislavskii Repetiruet: Zapisi i stenogrammy repetitsii* [Stanislavsky Directs: Rehearsal Transcripts and Stenographies]. Moscow: STD, 1987.

SOURCES IN ENGLISH

Allen, David. *Performing Chekhov*. New York: Routledge, 2000.

Balmuth, Daniel. *Censorship in Russia, 1865-1905*. Washington, D.C.: University Press of America, 1979.

Balukhatyi [sic], S. D., ed. *The Seagull Produced by Stanislavsky*. Translated by David Magarshack. London: Methuen, 1952. [The only Stanislavsky production plan published in English.]

Baron, Cynthia, Diane Carson, and Frank P. Tomasulo, eds. *More than a Method*. Detroit: Wayne State University Press, 2004.

Barricelli, Jean-Pierre, ed. *Chekhov's Great Plays: A Critical Anthology*. New York: New York University, 1981. [Includes essays by major scholars.]

Barton, John. *Playing Shakespeare*. London: Methuen, 1986.

Beckerman, Bernard. "Dramatic Analysis and Literary Interpretation: *The Cherry Orchard* as Exemplum," *New Literary History: A Journal of Thought and Interpretation* 2, no. 3 (Spring 1971): 391-406.

_____. *Dynamics of Drama: Theory and Methods of Analysis*. New York: Alfred A. Knopf, Inc., 1970.

Belknap, Robert. Personal email to author, 5 May 2008, 11:12 a.m.

Bentley, Eric. *The Life of the Drama*. New York: Atheneum, 1975.

Borodin, George. *This Thing Called Ballet*. London: Macdonald and Co, Ltd., 1945.

Brook, Peter. *The Empty Space*. New York: Avon Books, 1968.

Brooks, Peter. *The Melodramatic Imagination: Balzac, Henry James, Melodrama, and the Mode of Excess*. New Haven: Yale University Press, 1976.

Brunello, Piero and Lena Lenček, eds. *How to Write Like Chekhov: Advice and Inspiration, Straight from his own Letters and Work*. Philadelphia: Da Capo, 2008.

Carnicke, Sharon Marie. *Stanislavsky in Focus: An Acting Master for the Twenty-First Century*. Second Edition. New York: Routledge, 2009. [A detailed study of the differences between Stanislavsky's System and the American Method.]

Chekhov, Mikhail. *Anton Chekhov: A Brother's Memoir*. Translated by Eugene Alper. New York: Palgrave MacMillan, 2010.

Clayton, J. Douglas, ed. *Chekhov Then and Now: The Reception of Chekhov in World Culture*. New York: Peter Lang, 1997.

Cole, Toby and Helen Chinoy, eds. *Actors on Acting*. New York: Crown Publishers, 1970.

Collins, James. "Ephebes and Precursors in Chekhov's *The Seagull*," *Slavic Review* 44, no. 3 (Fall 1985): 423-37.

Crittenden, Cole M. "Playing with Time: Chekhov's Drama and Modernism," *The Bulletin of the North American Chekhov Society* 17, no. 1 (Winter 2010): 1-18.

Diderot, Denis. *Denis Diderot, The Paradox of the Actor*, and William Archer, *Masks or Faces?* New York: Hill and Wang, 1957. [A single volume with two classic texts on acting, introduced by Lee Strasberg.]

Eekman, Thomas A., ed. *Critical Essays on Anton Chekhov*. Boston: G. K. Hall & Co., 1989.

Ehrenburg, Ilya. *Chekhov, Stendhal, and Other Essays*. London: MacGibbon & Kee, 1962.

Emeljanow, Victor, ed. *Chekhov: The Critical Heritage*. Boston: Routledge and Kegan Paul, 1981. [Includes a wide variety of theatre reviews of Chekhov's plays in production.]

Finke, Michael C. *Seeing Chekhov: Life and Art*. Ithaca: Cornell University Press, 2005.

_____ and Julie de Sherbinin, eds. *Chekhov the Immigrant: Translating a Cultural Icon*. Bloomington: Slavica, 2007.

Gerould, Daniel. "Russian Formalist Theories of Melodrama," *Journal of American Culture* 1, no. 1 (Spring 1978): 152-68.

Gilman, Richard. *Chekhov's Plays: An Opening into Eternity*. New Haven: Yale University Press, 1995.

Gottlieb, Vera, ed. and trans. *Anton Chekhov at the Moscow Art Theatre: Illustrations of the Original Productions*. New York: Routledge, 2005.

_____, *Chekhov and the Vaudeville: A Study of Chekhov's One-Act Plays*. Cambridge: Cambridge University Press, 1982.

_____ and Paul Allain, eds. *The Cambridge Companion to Chekhov*. Cambridge: Cambridge University Press, 2000. [An anthology of critical articles.]

Hackett, Jean, ed. *The Actor's Chekhov*. Portland: Smith and Kraus, 1992. [Interviews about performing Chekhov's plays with director Nikos Psacharopoulos and actors of the Williamstown Theatre Festival.]

Howard, Tony. *Women as Hamlet: Performance and Interpretation in Theatre, Film and Fiction*. New York: Cambridge University Press, 2007.

Hristić, Jovan. "'Thinking with Chekhov': the Evidence of Stanislavsky's Notebooks," *New Theatre Quarterly* 11, no. 42 (May 1995): 175-83.

Jackson, Robert Louis, ed. *Chekhov: A Collection of Critical Essays*. Englewood Cliffs, NJ: Prentice-Hall, Inc., 1967. [Includes essays by major scholars from Russia.]

_____, ed. *Reading Chekhov's Text*. Evanston: Northwestern University Press, 1993. [Includes essays by leading contemporary scholars.]

Lewis, Bradley. "Listening to Chekhov: Narrative Approaches to Depression," *The Bulletin of the North American Chekhov Society* 15, no. 1 (Fall, 2007): 7-25.

Loehlin, James N. *Chekhov: The Cherry Orchard*. Plays in Production. Cambridge: Cambridge University Press, 2006.

Los Angeles Times: Quick Takes. 9 December 2008. http://www.latimes.com/entertainment (accessed 11 December 2008).

Maegd-Soëp, Carolina de. *Chekhov and Women: Women in the Life and Work of Chekhov*. Bloomington: Slavica, 1987.

Magarshack, David. *Chekhov the Dramatist*. London: John Lehmann, 1952.

Matlaw, Ralph E., ed. *Anton Chekhov's Short Stories: Texts of the Stories, Backgrounds, Criticism*. New York: W. W. Norton and Company, 1979. [Includes stories and critical essays.]

Merlin, Bella. *Konstantin Stanislavsky*. New York: Routledge, 2003. [Includes a study of Stanislavsky's production of *The Seagull*.]

McVay, Gordon. *Chekhov's Three Sisters*. London: Bristol Classical Press, 1995.

Mirsky, D. S. *A History of Russian Literature from its Beginnings to 1900*. New York: Vintage Books, 1958.

Nemirovitch-Dantchenko [sic], Vladimir. *My Life in the Russian Theatre*. Boston: Little, Brown, and Co., 1937.

Pendle, Karin. *Eugène Scribe and French Opera of the Nineteenth Century*. Ann Arbor: UMI Research Press, 1979.

Pervukhina, Natalia. *Anton Chekhov: The Sense and the Nonsense*. New York: Legas, 1993. [An excellent study of Chekhov's use of humor and absurdity.]

Pitcher, Harvey. *Chekhov's Leading Lady: A Portrait of the Actress Olga Knipper*, New York: Franklin Watts, 1980.

_____. *Responding to Chekhov: The Journey of a Lifetime*. Cromer: Swallow House Books, 2010.

Popkin, Cathy. *The Pragmatics of Insignificance: Chekhov, Zoshchenko, Gogol*. Palo Alto: Stanford University Press, 1993.

Rayfield, Donald. *Anton Chekhov: A Life*. New York: Henry Holt and Company, 1997.

_____. *Chekhov's Uncle Vania and The Wood Demon*. London: Bristol Classical Press, 1995.

_____. *The Cherry Orchard: Catastrophe and Comedy*. New York: Twayne Publishers, 1994.

_____. *Understanding Chekhov: A Critical Study of Chekhov's Prose and Drama*. Madison: University of Wisconsin Press, 1999.

Reid, John McKellor. "*Ivanov*: The Perils of Typicality," *The Bulletin of the North American Chekhov Society* 16, no. 1 (Fall 2008): 19-44.

Rosen, Nathan. "Chekhov's Religion in 'The Student'," *The Bulletin of the North American Chekhov Society* 14, no. 1 (Fall 2006): 1-9.

Rowe, Eleanor. *Hamlet: A Window on Russia*. New York: New York University Press, 1976.

Russian Fairy Tales, trans. Norbert Guterman. New York: Pantheon Books, 1973. [Includes stories that were recorded from oral traditions by the folklorist, Alexander Afanasyev.]

Rzhevsky, Nicolas. *The Modern Russian Theater: A Literary and Cultural History*, London: M. E. Sharpe, 2009.

Sekirin, Peter, ed. and trans. *Memories of Chekhov: Accounts of the Writer from his Family, Friends and Contemporaries*. Jefferson: McFarland and Co., Inc., 2011.

Senelick, Laurence. *Anton Chekhov*. New York: Grove Press, 1985.

_____. *The Chekhov Theatre*. Cambridge: Cambridge University Press, 1997.

_____. "Offenbach and Chekhov; or, *La Belle Yelena*," *Theatre Journal* 42, no. 4 (December 1990): 455-67.

_____, trans. and ed. *Russian Dramatic Theory from Pushkin to the Symbolists: An Anthology*. Austin: University of Texas Press, 1981.

_____. "Stanislavsky's Second Thoughts on *The Seagull*," *New Theatre Quarterly* 20, no. 2 (May 2004): 127-37.

Shevchenko, Mila B. "Melodramatic Scenarios and Modes of Marginality: The Poetics of Anton Chekhov's Early Drama and of Fin-de-Siècle Russian Popular Drama." Ph.D. diss., University of Michigan, Ann Arbor, 2008.

Simmons, Ernest J. *Chekhov: A Biography*. Chicago: The University of Chicago Press, 1962.

Singer, Ben. *Melodrama and Modernity: Early Sensational Cinema and Its Contexts*. New York: Columbia University Press, 2001.

Slonim, Marc. *Russian Theatre: From the Empire to the Soviets*. New York: The World Publishing Company, 1961.

"Stagewrite Productions Archive," *National Theatre Education*, http://www.nt-online.org (accessed 20 August 2002).

Stanton, Stephen S., ed. *Camille and Other Plays*. New York: Hill and Wang, Inc., 1957.

_____. *English Drama and the French Well-Made Play, 1815-1915*. Ann Arbor: University Microfilms, 1955.

Styan, J. L. *Chekhov in Performance: A Commentary on the Major Plays*. New York: Cambridge University Press, 1971.

Turan, Kenneth. "Translating a Masterpiece," *Los Angeles Times: Calendar Live*, 5 April 2002, http://www.calendarlive.com/movies/Reviews (accessed 29 April 2009).

Turkov, Andrei, ed. *Anton Chekhov and His Times*. Translated by Cynthia Carlile and Sharon McKee. Fayetteville: University of Arkansas Press, 1995. [Contains an excellent collection of reminiscences about Chekhov, as well as a good selection of his letters.]

Valency, Maurice. *The Breaking Sting: The Plays of Anton Chekhov*. New York: Schocken Books, 1983.

Whyman, Rose. *Anton Chekhov*. New York: Routledge, 2011. [An introduction to Chekhov's era and his works.]

Williames, Lee J. *Anton Chekhov, The Iconoclast*. Scranton: University of Scranton Press, 1989.

Worthen, William B. *Drama: Between Poetry and Performance*. Chichester: Wiley-Blackwell, 2010.

_____. *Modern Drama and the Rhetoric of Theater*. Los Angeles: University of California Press, 1992.

INDEX OF NAMES, TERMS, AND CHEKHOV'S WORKS

INDEX OF CHARACTER NAMES
FROM CHEKHOV'S MAJOR PLAYS

The Cherry Orchard

CPSIA information can be obtained at www.ICGtesting.com
Printed in the USA
BVOW06s1912060815

412093BV00005B/8/P